Reclaiming Nostalgia

Under the Sign of Nature

EXPLORATIONS IN ECOCRITICISM

Reclaiming Nostalgia

Longing for Nature
in American Literature

JENNIFER K. LADINO

University of Virginia Press
CHARLOTTESVILLE AND LONDON

University of Virginia Press

Printed in the United States of America on acid-free paper

First published 2012

9 8 7 6 5 4 3 2 1

LIBRARY OF CONGRESS CATALOGING-IN-PUBLICATION DATA

Ladino, Jennifer K.
  Reclaiming nostalgia : longing for nature in American literature / Jennifer K. Ladino.
    p.   cm. — (Under the sign of nature: explorations in ecocriticism)
  Includes bibliographical references and index.
  ISBN 978-0-8139-3334-4 (cloth : acid-free paper)
  ISBN 978-0-8139-3335-1 (pbk. : acid-free paper)
  ISBN 978-0-8139-3336-8 (e-book)
  1. American literature—History and criticism. 2. Nature in literature. 3. Nostalgia in
literature. 4. Homesickness in literature. I. Title.
PS163.L33   2012
810.9'36—dc23

2012026242

THE
AMERICAN
LITERATURES
INITIATIVE

A book in the American Literatures Initiative (ALI), a collaborative
publishing project of NYU Press, Fordham University Press, Rutgers
University Press, Temple University Press, and the University of Virginia
Press. The Initiative is supported by The Andrew W. Mellon Foundation.
For more information, please visit www.americanliteratures.org.

for Evan Page and Elliott Miles

Contents

Preface

At some point in her career, every park ranger hears the question: "Do you get to wear the 'Smokey the Bear Hat'?" It is striking how many family members, friends, acquaintances, and strangers want to know. For many, the familiar Stetson hat is a symbol of a bygone era, of simpler times, of friendly authority figures, maybe of the cartoon rangers who supervised Yogi the Bear in "Jellystone." There is something about this hat that evokes nostalgia. But nostalgia for what, exactly? And why is it such a powerful symbol?

During the course of thirteen summers as a seasonal ranger in Grand Teton National Park—in the midst of hiking the park's trails and climbing its mountains, directing visitors to the nearest restroom, suggesting activities for tourists, and most recently, writing news releases about park happenings—I began to wonder about these and other related questions. Why is so much of the touring public fascinated by park rangers?[1] Why are national parks, famously dubbed "the best idea America ever had," such popular tourist destinations—both for U.S. citizens and for visitors from other countries (Stegner, "Capsule History" 128)? Exactly what kind of nature do tourists hope to find there? Are park visitors nostalgic for nature? If so, what implications does that nostalgia have for different groups of people and for the more-than-human world?

Let me confess that I myself am nostalgic for nature, especially now that my professional adventures (and obligations) have turned those seasons in the Tetons into fond memories. Occasionally in spring I'll catch a whiff of foliage that—quick as a madeleine—takes me back to the early-season rushing of Cottonwood Creek, the evocative aromas and sounds that surround the government-issue 1930s-era log cabin at the base of the jagged Teton Range, where I returned each summer to reunite with other "career seasonal" rangers and permanent park employees who share my desire to promote the ethical stewardship of American nature. Even during those idyllic summers when I donned the green and gray uniform (yes, I did wear the "Smokey the Bear Hat," but only outdoors), I felt a strange longing for the nature I was supposed to help preserve. Perhaps it had to do with the transient lifestyle of seasonal employees and our ever-present awareness that summer would end and that we may or may not make it back next year. But I suspect it was more than that. My longing implied that the park's nature had somehow already been lost.

Although the mountains that tower over Jackson Hole are quite real, even comforting in their apparent stability, there are also ways in which the nature in this and other national parks *has* been lost. Some losses are tangible, like the shrinking glaciers that belie the mountains' suggestion of nature's permanence. Others are more difficult to pinpoint, such as the growing suspicion that visitors increasingly experience the parks from inside vehicles. Camping is less popular. Many of today's park visitors want to remain plugged in—iPod buds in their ears, cell phones in their hands, and Internet access in their temperature-controlled hotel rooms—more than they want to enjoy time outdoors.

Many of the visitors I met did seem to share my nostalgia, though I doubt we longed for exactly the same "nature." Sometimes I got the feeling that these visitors were actually nostalgic for *me*—or at least for my ranger identity. During the three seasons of the year when I was not living and working in the park, most people reacted with curiosity, questions, and, often, admiration when I would tell them about my summer job. They would encourage me to stick with it, as if my own satisfaction could somehow be theirs too. During the summers, park visitors treated me like a scientist, a police officer, even a medical doctor (none of which I am) simply because I sported the recognizable National Park Service (NPS) uniform. Tourists I talked with in visitor centers frequently expressed regret—"I wish I'd done something like this when I was your age"—and offered encouragement. "Good for you," they would say wistfully. "You should do this sort of thing while you still can." Sometimes tourists would ask to have their picture taken with me, especially when I was wearing the familiar hat. I posed with many a family in front of the Teton Range, and the grins on our faces seemed as big as the peaks.

Of course, nostalgia experienced by an individual is rarely, if ever, *just* personal. Like all emotions, it responds to and gestures toward broader contexts. For instance, the sentimental infatuation with the NPS uniform suggests several things about national parks and nature management. Despite the hat's misnomer (Smokey the Bear was initially part of a National Forest Service campaign, not an NPS icon), the reverence many Americans feel toward this romantic symbol indicates an intuitive understanding that tradition is an important part of nature management. This intuition picks up on, even as it subscribes to, a nostalgic location of nature itself, along with the organizations that manage it, in the past. In fact, there seems to be something about nature tourism itself that is fundamentally nostalgic. Like museums, which contain and represent cultural relics from the past, national parks demarcate and display nature as itself a sort of relic. Perhaps the strange sense of loss many tourists experience makes sense, then. The nature of national parks has been defined, institutionalized, preserved, and re-presented for public consumption in ways that both promote and capitalize on nostalgia. The parks are often experienced and remembered through picturesque postcards, drive-by photographs, and symbolic uniforms—markers of the nostalgia that will likely ensue when the visits come to an end.

The touristic interest in superficialities like uniforms glosses over a complex institutional history. The seeds for the NPS's formation were planted early in the nineteenth century, and Yellowstone became the first official national park in 1872.[2] Although Yellowstone was routinely invoked as a model for later parks' preservation, the NPS had no real precedents for its resource management and only resorts like Niagara Falls on which to model its facilities. Despite its gradual accession into public favor, the NPS's institutional birth in 1916 required some narrative legitimation. At the material level, the new agency needed to secure funding to keep itself, and the parks, running. But at the ideological level, it also needed to secure the imaginations of potential tourists and entice them to visit "their" parks. "Tradition" itself had to be created before it could become a definitive part of the agency. One strategy for doing this was the invention of origin stories that would feed into what Robert Gottlieb characterizes as a widespread "'back to nature' appeal [that] was part nostalgia and part therapy, an arcadian myth in an increasingly urbanized and industrial society" (31). As a ranger, I symbolized and reinforced the "appeal" of getting "back to nature."

As nature management has become more complex in the new millennium, generating this "appeal" requires new tactics. Edward Abbey lamented the rise of industrial tourism forty-five years ago, but today's parks greet a new kind of visitor: the technological tourist. Park rangers are reaching out to an increasingly tech-savvy (and tech-dependent) public via cell phone tours, electronic field trips, Facebook status updates, and video rivers.[3] These new kinds of tourism raise questions about nature's purity and the persistent nostalgia for "authentic" natural experiences, as well as about the degree to which evolving ways of accessing "nature" consti-tute loss. Does taking an e–field trip or becoming a Web ranger foster the same kind of human-nature connection as going for an in-person hike or attending a ranger-led campfire program? How does seeing Grand Teton's video river in the visitor center (or on the Internet) change the way tourists interact with the actual Snake River, just beyond the center's walls? If these new experiences are qualitatively different, then is something "pure" being tainted? Do these technological tourists, whose encounters are mediated and often preceded by third-nature representations, experience first nature as even more of a relic? Do their encounters generate more nostalgia? Or has the next generation of tourists already reached the point of no return that Aldo Leopold feared more than sixty years ago—the point at which they no longer feel nostalgia for "real" nature at all?

As much as change can seem like loss, it also marks the start of some-thing new. What that something new might be—that is, what kinds of beginnings nostalgia for nature makes possible—is one subject of this study. While the project grew, in part, out of my work with the NPS, where my seasons as a ranger first raised questions for me about the rela-tionships between nostalgia and nature, my "seasons" in the academy have motivated and empowered me to start answering those questions. Many academics speak with sincerity about their personal experiences with nostalgia even as they assume that it could never promote progres-sive politics. Intellectuals tend to share the wariness of Don DeLillo's wry professor, Murray Jay Siskind, who declares, "I don't trust anyone's nostalgia but my own" (White Noise 258).

It is not difficult to find conservative, reactionary examples of nostal-gia. But as David Lowenthal points out, not all uses of nostalgia come from the political right. Lowenthal notes Marxist writers who invoke nostalgic narratives of proletariat unity and struggle. Similarly, Lynne Huffer explains that "nostalgia also functions within oppressed groups struggling for liberation," citing the ways that African American stud-ies has pointed to a longing for "mother Africa" as a means of resisting white racist culture (16). And as my National Park Service experience first suggested to me, nostalgia can aid in environmental movements by invoking an organic or unspoiled natural world in order to enlist sympathetic proponents of preservation. Indeed, the more I learned about the history of nostalgia, and the more I read literature with an eye toward nostalgia's function in it, the more I came to accept as fact what had started as only a hunch: that nostalgia often transcends its stigmatized role, and in surprising ways.

As the colloquialism "back to nature" implies, American nature narratives are often infused with nostalgia—for the western frontier, for unspoiled landscapes, for a preindustrial golden age, or for pastoral communities with close connections to their environments. But despite the exciting growth of ecocriticism and increasing attention to nostalgia in both academic and popular culture, there is very little scholarship—and no book-length study—that considers nostalgia and nature together. The general skepticism toward nostalgia has foreclosed a crucial question: Can it function progressively? *Reclaiming Nostalgia* answers this question in the affirmative. My project tracks the nostalgia-nature nexus from the end of the nineteenth century into the twenty-first in order to begin marking American literature in which nostalgia works as a productive force—an individual emotional experience, a source of collective consciousness, or a narrative catalyst that imagines ways to facilitate social or environmental justice.

The popularity of television shows like *Survivor* and *Lost*, along with cultural phenomena like Disney's Frontier Land, Cormac McCarthy's neo-westerns, and international ecotourism, indicate that a nostalgic infatuation with nature remains a powerful force in popular culture. At the same time, concerns about natural disasters, species extinction, and "nature-deficit disorder" point to the growing urgency with which nature is dominating academic, political, scientific, and economic conversations around the world. In this climate of widespread concern about environmental issues, any potentially useful political strategy demands full consideration—even nostalgia. Founding ecocritic Scott Slovic is onto something when he suggests that "as we face the environmental predicaments of a new millennium, a millennium surely to be marked by ever-deepening crisis and despair and emotional numbness, the primary challenge for literary artists and for interpreters of literature may be to understand the evolving discourse of warning and nostalgia, or love and loss" ("Be Prepared" 59). My book takes this suggestion seriously as it begins to trace nostalgia's evolving relevance not just for "environmental predicaments" but for social ones as well. I hope readers will be surprised by what follows.

Acknowledgments

I am grateful to the following organizations for supporting this project: the Walter Chapin Simpson Center for the Humanities at the University of Washington, Creighton University, the Fulbright Scholar Program, the University of Bergen, the University of Idaho, and the University of Virginia Press.

I would also like to thank Kate Cummings, for being, by all accounts, the most dedicated graduate student mentor one could ask for; Caroline Simpson, Carolyn Allen, and Linda Nash, for offering constructive insights about my dissertation; Kathleen Woodward, Miriam Bartha, Brian Reed, David Shields, and the other Simpson Center fellows, for providing provocative suggestions on chapter 4; Bridget Keegan, for being a motivating friend, mentor, editor, and running partner; John Tallmadge, for offering generous and thoughtful readings of my manuscript; the anonymous second reader, for doing the same; Michael Branch, for encouraging me through long-distance mentoring; Cathie Brettschneider, Ellen Satrom, and the University of Virginia Press editorial staff, for seeing the project through to publication; and Doug Heckman, for giving me the love and support that allowed me to finish this.

Thanks, too, to the many other colleagues, students, and academic acquaintances who have contributed in large and small ways to this project, especially Kathy Aiken, Gary Williams, David Sigler, Donna Haraway, Sarah Franklin, John Su, Lawrence Buell, Lance Newman, Amy Vidali, Jill Gatlin, Ron Steffens, Greg Zacharias, Nina Ha, Krystal Kirwan, T. J. Mullaney, and Erin Herrmann. Finally, thanks to all the cafés that have hosted me and my laptop, especially Java Bean and Top Pot in Seattle, Blue Line in Omaha, and One World Café in Moscow.

Portions of the introduction and chapter 1 were published as "Longing for Wonderland: Nostalgia for Nature in Post-Frontier America," *Iowa Journal of Cultural Studies* (Fall 2004). Selections of chapter 5 appear in "'Local Yearnings': Re-Placing Nostalgia in Don DeLillo's *Underworld*," *Journal of Ecocriticism* (January 2010).

Reclaiming Nostalgia

Introduction

On September 19, 1870, a small group of tired, hungry men held a legendary conversation around a campfire at Madison Junction, the confluence of the Firehole and Gibbon rivers in what is now Yellowstone National Park. The Washburn-Langford-Doane Expedition, consisting of nine amateur explorers, three packers, two African American cooks, and five soldier-escorts, had set out on horseback from Helena, Montana, on August 17 "to investigate tales of scenic wonders in the area" (Sellars 8). Along the way they created maps and designated names for some of the most famous hot sulphur springs, boiling mud cauldrons, and explosive geysers in the Yellowstone region.

Since winter comes early to the Greater Yellowstone Ecosystem, their trip was not always comfortable. They were pelted with rain, hail, and snow on September 13, and they awoke the next day to two feet of wet, heavy snow. A torrential rainstorm greeted them on the 18th. Only one man—Nathaniel Langford, whose published diary of the expedition is widely known among park historians and naturalists—had a pair of waterproof boots. Some were sick from drinking the sulphuric water. They traveled in fear of being attacked by Indians, and a dearth of competent marksmen in the expedition required them to rely on "vigilance" to survive (Langford 7). One member of the party was lost for thirty-seven days (he was later found by a team of "experienced" mountaineer-trappers), and others harbored "dread apprehensions" of getting "inextricably involved in the wooden labyrinth" that engulfed them (Langford 100–101, 22). While they were certainly awestruck by the area's unique features and sublime beauty—Langford even quotes Keats and Byron in his diary—by September 19 most of the party's members were also dirty, exhausted, homesick, thin from subsisting on dwindling provisions (mostly dried lake trout in those final days), and guilty about their still-missing companion.

This might not sound like a glamorous scene to contemporary ears—and it probably wasn't, perhaps least so for the two African American cooks, who remain voiceless in the historical record—but the campfire story has nevertheless become a familiar part of national park folklore, the best-known account of the idea for Yellowstone and all other national parks. When Richard West Sellars recounts the tale in his influential history of the National Park Service (NPS), *Preserving Nature in the National Parks*, he explains how most versions of the story omit or downplay the hardships that my description accentuates. More popular renditions go something like this:

> As they relaxed and mused around their wilderness campfire, the explorers recalled the spectacular sights they had seen. Then, after considering the possible uses of the area and the profits they might make from tourism, they rejected the idea of private exploitation. Instead, in a moment of high altruism, the explorers agreed that Yellowstone's awe-inspiring geysers, waterfalls, and canyons should be preserved as a public park. This proposal was soon relayed to high political circles, and within a year and a half Congress established Yellowstone Park. (Sellars 8)

In this version of the tale, our explorer-protagonists seem quite comfortable, able to "relax" and "muse" around a campfire while recalling the "spectacular" nature they'd seen—much as today's park tourists might do at a manicured campground. They were visionary heroes, far-sighted altruists whose love of this place was intense enough to inspire the American public and compel government bureaucrats to preserve this and other national treasures. Sellars goes on to provide a more nuanced historical account that complicates the campfire story and informs my analysis here; however, the mythical version is the one most people know. Even Wallace Stegner feeds into this version in "A Capsule History of Conservation," where he describes Yellowstone as the result of the "spontaneous overflow of public enthusiasm" initiated by these "Montana tourists," who were "struck by the wonders" of the area (126).

This romantic origin myth is a gem. It offers a succinct, vivid story that is easily remembered and passed on; it creates compelling, heroic

FIGURE 1. 1957 reenactment of the campfire conversation held by members of the Washburn-Langford-Doane Party's Expedition of 1870 at the junction of the Firehole and Gibbon rivers (Madison Junction), the legendary origin of the National Park Idea. (Courtesy of the Department of Interior, National Park Service Historic Photograph Collection, Harpers Ferry Center; photographer, John A. Tyers)

characters in an inspirational setting; and it casts the NPS in favorable terms that are music to the ears of a public eager to consume the resources the agency manages. As Sellars puts it, this creation story gives the NPS a "virgin birth," free of any complicating socioeconomic and political factors (8). But as Michel Foucault and Edward Said warn, origin stories like this one can be deceiving for a variety of reasons. Typically, they assume narrative coherence (or an "essence"), continuity (a linear progression of events, instigated by the one in question), and an almost "divine" passivity; the event develops an aura of sacredness that can be put to various uses. Sacred origins leave out the complexity of factors and the dynamics of power that characterize historical events. As one of nostalgia's most common narrative incarnations, origin stories simplify and restore an idealized past toward which audiences can turn for explanation and reassurance. The campfire chat implies a coherent, unifying vision shared by the parks' founding fathers—the vision of preservation rather than development. Nature seems to accept its role as the spectacle that condones the men's plan. One can almost see Old Faithful spouting its patriotic affirmation.

Like most nostalgic tapestries, though, this one's threads start to unravel upon careful scrutiny. In fact, the story perpetuates some troubling figurations: the inherent separation of humans from the natural world; the construction of nature as an aesthetic spectacle; and the exclusion of non-white people from the nation's "public playgrounds." In regard to this last point, it is notable that, despite the fact that the Crow, Shoshone, Sheep Eater, and Bannock Indians all relied on Yellowstone's resources, there are no Indians in the mythical version of the story. As Langford's diary indicates, the expedition did encounter plenty of evidence of Indian life: Crow hunters inside what are now the park's boundaries; abandoned Indian camps; used Indian trails; a teepee; a game run; and piles of lodgepole pines stacked for later use. In accordance with nationally circulating ideologies about Indians as perpetually "disappearing," the explorers "dismissed these signs as ancient remnants of vanished Indians" (Spence 42). Along with such denials of Indian use, new myths emerged to justify Indian expulsion. For instance, these early explorers believed regional tribes feared Yellowstone's geysers—presumably (and nonsensically) as manifestations of a Christian hell—and so steered clear of the area now preserved.

Another tenuous thread of this nostalgic origin story is the idea that the parks' founding fathers "rejected the idea of private exploitation." Their expedition was partially funded by the Northern Pacific Railroad Company, a corporation that subsidized artist Thomas Moran and lobbied successfully for the formation of the parks. Unlike the fabled explorers in the campfire myth, the railroad could hardly claim "high altruism"; its primary motive was the development of a monopolistic trade corridor across southern Montana Territory (Sellars 10). From the perspective of the railroad, government-managed nature would prevent private land claims, haphazard development, and competing commercial uses. As Robert Sterling Yard's various editions of *The National Parks Portfolio* illustrate, the railroad industry and parks both wanted to promote tourism (and sustain their own organizations) by advertising the parks' accessibility and their link to a national heritage rooted in the natural world. Funded in part by the United States Railroad Administration, Yard's park literature often cross-referenced railroad propaganda, using some of the same photos and verbatim written blurbs to describe the parks. Far from being untouched by financial interests, park management was shaped by corporate influence long before the NPS was formed.

We can see, then, what Foucault means when he suggests that "what is found at the historical beginning of things is not the inviolable identity of their origin; it is the dissension of other things. It is disparity" ("Nietzsche" 142). For the National Park Service, "disparity" is written into its very mission in the form of what is sometimes called its "dual mandate," as defined by its founding legislation, the Organic Act. The act instructs the NPS "to conserve the scenery and the natural and historic objects and the wild life therein and to provide for the enjoyment of the same in such manner and by such means as will leave them unimpaired for the enjoyment of future generations" (qtd. in Sellars 38).[1] Sellars argues that the contradictory language of the act reveals what park policy has historically shown: there was never any explicit intention toward preservation. The institution's main concerns were protecting scenery, encouraging tourism, and efficiently managing the parks—concerns better addressed by landscape architects than by biologists and other scientists (29). Yet the influence of tradition within the NPS, exemplified by the circulation of origin stories like the Madison Junction campfire conversation, tends to safeguard the agency's decisions from criticism. Can all these people wearing the "Smokey the Bear Hat"—people who clearly love their jobs and the environments they work to protect—possibly fail to put nature first?[2] In this context, nostalgia may comfort tourists and park officials alike, but it obscures the sticky politics involved in managing nature.

* * *

Nostalgia's faults have been well rehearsed. As David Lowenthal succinctly explains, nostalgia stands accused of being "ersatz, vulgar, demeaning, misguided, inauthentic, sacrilegious, retrograde, reactionary, criminal, fraudulent, sinister, and morbid" (27). In some cases, it is guilty as charged. Nostalgia's scapegoat status stems from a range of admittedly problematic traits: its easy cooptation by capitalism, which critics like Fredric Jameson say generates a postmodern cultural paralysis in which old styles are recycled and marketed without critical effect (or affect); its ubiquity in the media and the arts, which signifies a lack of creativity, alienation from the present, and complicity in consumer culture; its tendency to romanticize the past through imagining an origin that is too simplistic; and its reactionary bent—the use of nostalgia by right-wing forces to gloss over past wrongs and glorify tradition as justification for the present.

Because of these associations, the term nostalgic is often used interchangeably with words like conservative, regressive, ahistorical, or uncritical to disparage or dismiss writers, politicians, scholarship, and cultural texts. Scholars have attended to nostalgia's social dimensions most frequently through exposing its ideological ramifications. Susan Stewart, who is often cited for her characterization of nostalgia as a "social disease," explains that nostalgia "is always ideological: the past it seeks has never existed except as narrative, and hence, always absent, that past continually threatens to reproduce itself as a felt lack. Hostile to history and its invisible origins, and yet longing for an impossibly pure context of lived experience at a place of origin, nostalgia wears a distinctly utopian face, a face that turns toward a future-past, a past which has only ideological reality" (23).

Stewart's point is well taken. But the past has a material, geographical reality as well as an ideological, narrative one. Considering how nostalgic longing takes nature as an object complicates the notion that the past is "only" ideologically real. There are material components that must be accounted for, even if those components have been radically altered over time. In order to grasp the ideological dimensions of nostalgia, we must attend to its environmental dimensions as well.

Although critics, doctors, writers, and social scientists have largely considered nostalgia as a temporal longing, as Stewart does when she theorizes its "future-past," nostalgia's spatiality has been latent from its first diagnosis. In fact, nostalgia was originally conceived of as a bodily, and so a material, condition. It was also linked to particular geographies. First diagnosed in 1678 by Swiss doctor Johannes Hofer, nostalgia was considered "an affliction of the imagination" (Ritivoi 16) caused by "the desire for return to one's native land" (Hofer, qtd. in Boym 9). In 1720 another Swiss doctor named Theodore Zwinger identified nostalgia's symptoms in soldiers, students, prison inmates, exiles, or "anyone for whom homecoming was not an available option" (Ritivoi 20). Furthermore, the nostalgic was someone for whom "longing for their native *land* became their single-minded obsession" (Boym 10, my emphasis). Despite the obvious importance of physical environment to these early diagnoses, nostalgia's temporal dimensions were paramount. Patients were conceived of, primarily, as "cut off from their past" rather than separated from a familiar environment (Ritivoi 20). Of course, physicians could not locate the disease in the body or come up with a unified taxonomy of causes. Accordingly, nostalgia was de-medicalized around the turn of the twentieth century, at which point it lost its bodily connotations and became even more linked with time, rather than space.[3]

I suspect it is "free-floating nostalgia" that most distresses scholars, since an abstract, romanticized relationship to the past is unlikely to yield critical thinking about the present or progressive thinking about the future (Wall 110). But what if we stopped privileging temporality and began to *map* nostalgia, to follow its winding courses and plot its particular trajectories? I believe re-placing nostalgia[4] in this way renders the object of longing more tangible and opens up new possibilities for how nostalgia might function. My project reclaims nostalgia by foregrounding its nature—that is, by re-centering the environmental dimensions that were key to its first diagnosis—and by carving out a new discursive "place" for nostalgia within scholarly discourse.

Specifically, I seek to participate in and extend conversations about nostalgia "as a more ambivalent, more engaged, critical frame" by highlighting its spatial characteristics and exploring its nuances (Scanlan 4). As both an emotion and an ideological narrative—a narrative Linda Hutcheon deems capable of the "twin evocation of both affect and agency"—nostalgia exceeds its typecast roles ("Irony" 199). It is high time to breathe new life into nostalgia, to revitalize and rearticulate its diverse possibilities, and to put it to work in the service of more progressive politics. In the chapters that follow, I hope to show how examining nostalgia's spatial dimensions becomes especially important when questions of environmental and social justice are at stake.

Literature emerges as an indispensable ally in this effort. While much contemporary theory subscribes to the standard criticisms of nostalgia, a surprising amount of American fiction envisions nostalgia as a disruptive, productive, even progressive force. Perhaps because it is typically less confined by expectations of coherence or didacticism than traditional scholarship, literature contributes its own "theories" of nostalgia, many of which are unique and transformative. Literary texts implicitly define nostalgia as both a narrative device—a way for authors to manipulate language, drive plot, develop characters, and influence readers—and an emotion, which is felt by readers and characters (and sometimes, the authors themselves), shared by groups, perpetuated by institutions, and instilled by both texts and lived experience. Accordingly, my project treats nostalgia as a longing to return home that can be felt, wielded, manipulated, and retold in a variety of ways. My formulation of counter-nostalgia, which I define below, suggests nostalgia should not be dismissed as inherently conservative or reactionary. Rather, in some contexts, it can be a mechanism for social change, a model for ethical relationships, and a motivating force for social and environmental justice.

Nostalgia that takes nature as its object of longing has been prevalent throughout U.S. history. But despite the frequency with which nostalgic discourse governs conversations about nature, there is very little scholarly work that links nostalgia and nature. William Cronon and Raymond Williams are salient exceptions. Cronon, in particular, has been instrumental in exposing how mainstream environmentalism has been nostalgic in troublesome ways. In his seminal essay "The Trouble with Wilderness; or, Getting Back to the Wrong Nature," Cronon points to Bill McKibben's *The End of Nature* as a notable example of this prevalent environmentalist nostalgia. (I revisit Cronon's critique in chapter 5.) Williams's *The Country and the City* reveals the tendency of the pastoral tradition to be ahistorical and demythologizes the idea that there was ever an Edenic origin. Via a sort of historical "escalator" that traces nostalgic narratives further and further back in time (10–12), Williams exposes how instances of pastoral nostalgia are "reaction[s] to the fact of change" and directs our attention to nostalgia's particular sociohistorical contexts (35).

Both thinkers offer what I call anti-nostalgic arguments about nature: they use an expository, didactic genre to condemn nostalgia for being a totalizing,[5] romantic, and oversimplified narrative approach to a complex socioeconomic past. Similar critiques have challenged nostalgia throughout the twentieth and twenty-first centuries—usually for good reason. However, by focusing only on its detrimental effects, anti-nostalgic criticism tends to foreclose the possibility that nostalgia might, as Scott Slovic puts it, "work in opposite directions" and in more complex ways than we might expect ("Authenticity" 270). One of the first in the field of ecocriticism to think beyond anti-nostalgic assumptions and gesture toward nostalgia's positive potential, Slovic encourages us to appreciate "the potent emotional tug of nostalgia as one of the most vigorous and useful strategies in the literature of social reform" ("Be Prepared" 56). This call to action challenges entrenched scholarly assumptions that nostalgia is a natural enemy of reformist politics.[6]

Like Slovic, I am invested in exposing the multidirectional capacities of nostalgia, and I also approach this task from an ecocritical perspective. However, I prefer the phrase green cultural studies to eco-criticism, since the former more directly references the interdisciplinar-ity, the willingness to engage a range of cultural texts, and the attention to power dynamics that have been fundamental priorities for both cultural studies scholars and most ecocritics.[7] My working definition of cultural studies follows the one given by Lawrence Grossberg et al. in their landmark anthology *Cultural Studies*, where they describe the field as a sort of "bricolage" that probes the "everyday terrain" of people and cultures, enlists "whatever fields are necessary" to answer the questions at stake in a given project, and seeks to intervene in, not just "chronicle," cultural trends (2, 11, 2, 5). Combining a cultural studies methodology with more traditional ecocritical strategies, green cultural studies is an approach committed to confronting networks of power while explor-ing the socio-environmental dimensions of various kinds of texts. It is the task of green cultural studies, Jhan Hochman asserts, to add nature to the "nexus of concerns" already addressed by cultural studies (race, class, gender, sexuality, age, disability, etc.) in order to make sense of how ever-more complex representations of nature have effects on their audiences and, through us, the material world (2).[8] The term ecocriticism seems to be here to stay. But with the expansion of ecocriticism into the interdisciplinary areas of animal studies, film studies, and postcolonial studies, among others, it seems safe to say that, whether or not they label it as such, many contemporary ecocritics are doing green cultural stud-ies work.

In keeping with these trends, my book's project diverges from more traditional ecocritics; mine is not explicitly an eco-activist endeavor or a deep ecological lesson in "earthcare" (Buell, *Future* 21). It may even be more anthropocentric than ecocentric, more cultural studies than green. If "nature proper" is seldom a primary object of my analysis, it is partly because I remain more invested in how nostalgia points toward social justice issues and partly because there is no "nature proper." Most scholars—whether they prefer "nature-culture" (Latour), "worldnature" (Hochman), or some other phrase—now understand nature as inescap-ably tied to human culture. Since this is the case, my analysis often slips from nature to humanity (and back), just as I jumped, in the preface, from the rugged mountains and rushing creeks of Grand Teton National Park to the NPS uniform and what it signifies. Chapter 1 starts with changing conceptions of wilderness but moves to discussions of the savage-civilized binary as it affects human cultures. Other chapters take us from pastoral landscapes to the American counterculture, or to precolonial indigenous communities, or to a neo-agrarian ideal that works against global agribusiness. Often, my analysis shows how a nostalgic relationship to a particular landscape can propel a character, an author, or a reader into an insightful critique of present-day concerns, such as poor working conditions, racist ideologies, toxic environments, or the downsides of a postnatural consumer culture. Because "nature" can refer to objects or ideals as diverse as an unpopulated wilderness area, an organic crop, or an indigenous community, I find it inevitable to turn to human politics and environmental justice and consider such things as race, class, postcoloniality, and global capitalism alongside the more-than-human world.

Some chapters—chapter 5, in particular—take shifting understandings of nonhuman nature as a central focus because the texts demand it. In general, though, the emphasis of this study is on following the multiple directions of nostalgia where they lead, beginning with the natural sites, and nature narratives, invoked in a given text. I make every effort to be explicit about whether wilderness, frontier, pastoral, or postnature narratives are at stake in each text—even when the text itself confuses them—without losing sight of my main goal, which is to re-place and reclaim nostalgia so as to draw attention to issues of power and justice. Instead of reifying nostalgia as always fostering problematic environmental or social narratives, my book works at the intersection of green cultural studies and American studies to reveal how nostalgia might lead to more informed, more nuanced, and more ethical conceptions of the human and the more-than-human.

In the United States, nature has often been invoked as "proof" of American exceptionalism. Indeed, nature and nation are joined etymologically as well as ideologically, since they share a common root: *nasci*, "to be born." Especially after the closing of the western frontier in 1890, many American nature narratives are tinged with nostalgia—for that very frontier, for untouched wilderness, for a preindustrial agrarian society, for pastoral communities in which humans and nature coexist in peace, or simply for a time when "nature" was easier to define. Following Kate Soper and others, my project treats nature as both a material reality—that which exists autonomously from human control—and a social construction, produced by humans within specific contexts for particular purposes. My use of nature invokes this "realist position" and assumes that discursive, socially constructed "nature" and material, or "first," Nature are always imbricated in complex ways (Soper, *What Is Nature?* 8). Often figured as the quintessential home, and frequently posited as the Eden from which humanity has tragically fallen, nature demands attention as a slippery object of nostalgic longing throughout U.S. history.

Scholars have made headway in charting the American nature myths of the frontier and the pastoral—myths that are often nostalgic—and my study is indebted to this scholarship. Richard Slotkin's influential work on the frontier, along with scholarship by "New Western" historians such as Richard White and Patricia Limerick, has problematized the version of the frontier popularized by Frederick Jackson Turner and Theodore Roosevelt. My study certainly does not attempt to redeem a myth that has earned its bad reputation—indeed, I would be surprised to see anyone vouch for a concept that historians have dubbed the "the f-word"—though I do point out when authors seize frontier rhetoric for their own ends (Limerick, "Adventures" 72). More broadly, I find that the frontier and the pastoral are often connected in American literature as consecutive phases of the Turnerian "civilizing" process. Since frontiering is understood to yield a pastoral environment—which, for Turner, precedes an urban one—it is no surprise that many backward-looking texts reference both pioneers and their second-nature pastoral environments.

Though the frontier myth is arguably beyond recuperation, scholars have found positive potential in the seemingly more benign pastoral. Leo Marx, with his formulation of a "complex pastoral," was the first to do so in an American context; his opposition of a complex to a "sentimental" pastoral begins to demonstrate how the pastoral sometimes serves "politically oppositional ends" (Marx, *Machine* 5; Buell, *Future* 145). Following his lead, Lawrence Buell and Terry Gifford have explored the complexity of pastoral narratives in reinvigorating studies of their own. Greg Garrard, too, has called for scholars to reevaluate the pastoral's capacity to "engender a genuine counter-hegemonic ideology"—a challenge that was taken up with great interest at the 2011 ASLE Conference ("Radical Pastoral?" 464).[9] These laudable efforts nonetheless warrant a word of caution from Buell, who reminds us that "we would be quixotic to expect to sift 'progressive' pastoral from 'regressive' using some political program as a litmus text. . . . For pastoral as ideological *form* tends to remain more or less constant even as ideological content changes" (*Environmental Imagination* 51–52, original emphasis).

With sensitivity to this difficulty, I nevertheless intend to defend nostalgia from the common charge that it is inherently "regressive" by showing that nostalgic narratives can, in some cases, be "sifted" according to their progressive functions. To prevent this rescue mission from being too "quixotic," it is necessary to gain a clear picture of the windmills I am up against—that is, to understand how nostalgia works for worse as well as for better. According to Svetlana Boym, "nostalgic manifestations are side effects of the teleology of progress"; even as it mourns some of progress's casualties, nostalgia implicitly reaffirms the assumptions that underlie progress narratives (19). With the centrality of spatial expansion to American history, nostalgia has sometimes worked to underscore the nation's faith in its Manifest Destiny and, so, to legitimate U.S. imperialism. On a large scale, nostalgic longing can take the shape of what Renato Rosaldo has termed "imperialist nostalgia," one incarnation of which occurs when first-world countries long for environments they have played a leading role in destroying.[10] Shari Huhndorf makes the similar point that nostalgia can "reaffirm the racialized, progressivist ethos of industrial capitalism" (14). Indeed, nostalgia at its worst can elide oppressive or violent histories, silence the people whom those histories have victimized, and construct an idealized, coherent version of the nation that is itself bulletproof.

Frequently, nostalgia at the national level can promote a sense of a shared past as "a place of sacrifice and glory" by creating a kind of "collective belonging that . . . transcend[s] individual memories" (Boym 15). Jennifer Delisle argues that it is precisely this slippage from the personal to the national, this "drive to create cohesive imagined communities, where the nation is privileged over the individual lives of its citizens, that makes nostalgia dangerous" (31). Delisle suggests, then, that we distinguish between "the *experiential nostalgia* of individuals, and the *cultural nostalgia* created by national memory, myth, and simulation"—terms she fashions as two ends of a continuum (17, original emphasis). It is hard for me to see, though, how the experiential and the cultural do not inevitably collapse. Her assertion that "personal and therapeutic uses" of nostalgia should be distinguished from "nationalistic, consumptive, aggressive temptations" only works if we understand "the personal" as distinct from other scales of belonging (31). I find it more useful to treat *all* nostalgia as cultural—not in the sense that it is necessarily collective, but in the sense that even personal nostalgia can't help but participate in cultural tropes.

Delisle is right to note how "dangerous" national myths can be, but there are other scales at which nostalgic tropes circulate. It is crucial to theorize the ways in which nostalgic longing refuses to privilege the nation and instead imagines belongings at other scales—sometimes smaller, more localized, at other times larger, even transnational. Reclaiming nostalgia involves a renewed attention to the ways in which the United States' "racialized, progressivist ethos" has relied on—but can also be countered by—nostalgic nature narratives. This book foregrounds alternate narrative births that oppose dominant conceptions of the American nation, fraught as it is with imperialist tendencies. As a broad, affective narrative with the potential to unite disparate groups of people, nostalgia acts as midwife to various kinds of newborn stories.

With this variety of stories in mind, I do not intend to glorify nostalgia as essentially positive or to set up an inviolable binary between "conservative" and "progressive" nostalgia. Like all nostalgic narratives (and like all narratives about the past) nostalgia for nature serves a range of political agendas. It can justify both localized and national violence, as in Thomas Dixon's *The Clansman*, or envision inclusive social justice movements on a global scale, as in Leslie Marmon Silko's *Almanac of the Dead*. Sometimes, nostalgia can be both progressive and problematic at the same time, as was the case when the environmentalist campaign "Keep America Beautiful" attempted to generate nostalgia for a disappearing natural world by affiliating that world with American Indians. Since it functions at so many registers and operates at a range of scales, and because it means different things in different historical moments, it can be hard to get a handle on just what nostalgia is. That there is no formula for exactly how nostalgia becomes progressive—no checklist of six traits like the one Gifford generates for his post-pastoral framework—is, I think, a testament to its complexity.[11] Nostalgia is not a single origin myth or a recurring narrative structure, even if the world it invokes is sometimes a conventional pastoral one. It does not have a constant ideological form, even though it functions with/in other narratives that do.

My project begins, then, with a new theoretical framework—underwritten by a new vocabulary—to enable more nuanced discussion of such diverse narratives and effects. The work of Boym, Andreea Deciu Ritivoi, and John Su provides useful starting points for thinking about nostalgia in more nuanced ways.[12] In *The Future of Nostalgia*, Boym proposes a model based on two kinds of nostalgia: restorative and reflective. She formulates her terms by dividing the word nostalgia into its two parts—nostos, the "return home," and algia, the "longing." Restorative nostalgia, linked with nostos, poses as truth, embraces tradition, and seeks a reconstruction of the lost "home," imagined as a return to a coherent origin. She links this sort of nostalgia with national memory and identity. Boym locates transformative potential in longing, which she associates with reflective nostalgia. "Ironic, inconclusive and fragmentary," reflective nostalgia does not attempt to reconstruct a coherent "home" but opts to "explore ways of inhabiting many places at once" (50). This kind of nostalgia embraces ambivalence with the intention of fostering creative dialogue through collective, local memory rather than national metanarratives of linear progress. Ritivoi's *Yesterday's Self: Nostalgia and the Immigrant Identity* shares Boym's goal of recovering productive uses for nostalgia and offers important insight toward that end. Rather than being inherently conservative, she argues, nostalgia can "signal the breech [between past and present] and inaugurate a search for the remedy" (39). This "breech" can be a productive site from which to construct alternate narratives and look toward positive social change.

In the same vein, Su's ambitious study of nostalgia in Anglophone literature, *Ethics and Nostalgia in the Contemporary Novel*, suggests that looking backward is a precondition for imagining a better future. Loss and nostalgic yearning can, and do, shape "ethical visions" in numerous literary texts, and many authors "consciously exploit nostalgia's tendency to interweave imagination, longing, and memory" in ways that can challenge social injustices (Su, *Ethics* 3). Su attends to the "lost or imagined homelands" the authors in his study long for and the ways that these homelands are "deeply flawed or never even existed"; yet he rightly explains how these authors still embrace and exploit nostalgia to explore "relationships and communities that *could have been*" (12, original emphasis). Even if it can only indirectly help move us in more ethical future directions, nostalgia "enables a more precise sense of how previous systems of social relations failed to address genuine human needs" (175). Su's study does attend to nostalgia's particular objects, including nature, but his primary investment lies in recuperating nostalgia from its position as memory's embarrassing right-wing relative by exploring its relationship to ethics. Unlike Su's study, which reads a range of Anglophone texts, my own is grounded in particularly American narratives, and my inquiry focuses on how nostalgia for nature functions at the national scale as well as within individuals and more intimate collectives.

Building on the theories of nostalgia that Boym, Ritivoi, and Su articulate, I introduce "counter-nostalgia" as an operative term in a genealogy[13] of nostalgia that theorizes new ways of imagining both the "return" and the "home" (or origin) for which nostalgic narratives long. Much nostalgia is characterized by totalizing metanarratives of return that posit coherent origins as points on a progressive timeline leading to the present day. Its purpose is to justify the present, and to stabilize history. Counter-nostalgia, however, does something quite different. Nostalgia becomes "counter-" when it is strategically deployed to challenge a progressivist ethos. Counter-nostalgia is nostalgia with a critical edge. Counter-nostalgia depends upon a tactical reappropriation of more dominant strands of nostalgia through creative, often literary, means; for that reason, its functions are historically contextual. It can be reflective, in Boym's sense: ambivalent, localized, contingent, and ironic. It often depicts "home" as fragmented, complicated, and layered. But it can also be restorative, insofar as it mimics totalizing or coherent narratives in order to challenge or reinvent them for its own ends. When the counter-nostalgic text envisions a home that is a pure origin—a cohesive site or event constructed by simplifying and romanticizing a complex past—it has devised that origin in a performative, strategic manner. Such is the case, for instance, with Claude McKay's *Home to Harlem*, which invokes nostalgia for Haiti, for Africa, and even for the pastoral American South in order to draw attention to the violence of colonialism and slavery and, at the same time, to excavate and celebrate a distinctive African American history.

Because of their nuances and complexities, I distinguish counter-nostalgic from *anti*-nostalgic texts, like Cronon's and Williams's, which work within an expository, theoretical genre of writing that seeks closure in the form of argument. In such texts, nostalgia is the object of critique. In counter-nostalgic literature, nostalgia is the vehicle through which critique happens. The authors in this study deploy nostalgia. They wield it. They toy with dominant nostalgic narratives in order to subvert them. They manipulate their readers by eliciting nostalgia. Counter-nostalgic texts work within the blurry realm of readers' emotions rather than the rule-bound world of argument, asking us to help construct the "arguments" at stake and grapple with questions about the worlds we inhabit. For instance, when Don DeLillo's Murray speculates that "it is possible to be homesick for a place even when you are there," concerned readers can't help but wonder if he is right (*White Noise* 257).

Like Murray's homesickness, all nostalgia is a form of longing. While Boym emphasizes longing as a transformative emotional state, I focus on the "return home" and the ways in which specific literary homes are imagined as sites from which the politics of the present may be renegotiated. What distinguishes counter-nostalgia, then, is its attitude toward the object of this longing—the home—and the ways in which it envisions a return to this space and time. Anyone who has felt nostalgic for a family quarrel on Christmas, an overdeveloped suburban landscape, or a "cozy" studio apartment that felt more like a prison cell at the time, will recognize that the homes we long for are often fraught. As I will continue to suggest, longing can be a personal emotion as well as a larger, collective, even national sentiment. While much nostalgia, especially at this national level, encourages its adherents to return to a celebrated origin to find both comfort and justification for the present, counter-nostalgia revisits a dynamic past in a way that challenges dominant histories and reflects critically on the present.

As Foucault explains, a historical event "is not a decision, a treaty, a reign, or a battle, but the reversal of a relationship of forces, the usurpation of power, the appropriation of a vocabulary turned against those who had once used it, a feeble domination that poisons itself as it grows lax, the entry of a masked 'other'" ("Nietzsche" 154). The counter-nostalgic authors in this study appropriate dominant "vocabulary" to highlight history's messy *events*, rather than its comfortable homes. McKay's deliberate back-and-forth between his characters' reminiscences of their pastoral childhood homes and their harsh living and working conditions in the present are a case in point. Zitkala-Ša uses a similar tactic as she inverts the civilization-savagery binary and identifies her childhood home as a site of culture and "wild" freedom. Aldo Leopold and Rachel Carson narrate environmental losses and caution against a lack of nostalgia while invoking pastoral origins as counterpoints to the damages humans are inflicting on the natural world and on our own communities. N. Scott Momaday exploits countercultural "back to nature" nostalgia to fuel his critique of colonialism, violence, racism, and government relocation projects of the period. Later in the century, DeLillo considers the homesickness that permeates the everyday lives of Americans living in a postnatural world, and he exposes some of the losses and risks generated by a late-capitalist economy. Ruth Ozeki imagines diverse fictional communities based on a nostalgic agrarian ideal and enlists these unlikely allies in her twenty-first-century critiques of late capitalism, global agribusiness, and ideologies of racial and genetic purity.

All of these authors maintain complicated relationships to the past and skepticism toward the notion of progress. Boym reminds us that "nostalgia, like progress, is dependent on the modern conception of unrepeatable and irreversible time" (13). However, counter-nostalgia is irreverent of the notion that time is "unrepeatable." Instead, counter-nostalgic narratives are often attracted to seasonal or cyclical conceptions of time rather than linear ones, as in Momaday's *House Made of*

Dawn or Ozeki's *All Over Creation*. The past is not a truthful origin but a beginning, in Said's sense of "impl[ying] return and repetition rather than simple linear accomplishment" (xiii). Counter-nostalgia inverts the idea of progress, maintaining the concept of irreversible time only insofar as it recognizes "real" historical events at a broader scale—the displacements, forced migrations, and acts of violence that have resulted in both U.S. hegemony and a faltering democratic project within the nation itself. Just as racism, imperialism, and violence tend to repeat themselves in the present, the nonhierarchical communities for which counter-nostalgia longs might also be repeated. By recognizing history as nonlinear and events as complex—but continuing to long for them in all their complexity—counter-nostalgia has the potential to challenge the logics of "feeble domination" that govern both past and present.

Each of the following chapters makes a unique argument about a counter-nostalgic literary text as it touches down on specific features of the rocky landscape of American history. Brief interchapters set up and contextualize the full-length chapters through close readings of cultural texts. These interchapters encapsulate the more dangerous tendencies of their period's nostalgia even while some—like the third interchapter, on Ansel Adams's project *Born Free and Equal*—contain the seeds of counter-nostalgia within otherwise hegemonic ideological positions. The main chapters offer literary examples of how counter-nostalgia reappropriates, redirects, or otherwise intervenes in dominant nostalgic trends. By framing my readings of the literature with the culturally focused interchapters, I hope to sketch each historical moment as a cross-section of aesthetic, cultural, and political forces—what Foucault calls a "profusion of entangled events" ("Nietzsche" 155).

Although I do not attempt a comprehensive overview of the time period in question, I do suggest trends, identify continuities, and note disjunctures and shifts in American nostalgia for nature. For instance, readers will discover peaks in nostalgia at the national scale at the turn of both centuries—first following the frontier's closing, and again as the twentieth century draws to an end. Pastoral nostalgia remains a strong presence throughout the twentieth century and into the twenty-first, with particular appeal in the regionalist backlash to modernity and in 1960s counterculture movements and their loosely defined "back to nature" impulse. We will also see how, in the late 1980s, an emergent "end of nature" discourse points toward different objects of longing—to things like originality, unmediated experience, a unified self, and the cohesion of signifier and signified—even as traditional American nature narratives continue to provide jumping-off points for embarking on these emotional escapades. The nostalgia accompanying "end of nature" anxieties becomes, for some, an affective "check" to the sense of having crossed a line in human-nature relations and stepped into a "postnatural" world.

With attention to Roosevelt, Leopold, Carson, McKibben, and Edward Abbey, the book also keeps tabs on environmentalism's slow momentum during the period in question—a momentum that ebbs and flows with economic prosperity.[14] Environmentalism grapples with changing conceptions of nonhuman nature, which undergo a sort of pendulum swing in the twentieth century, moving from a primarily materialist understanding of the world based on a clear human-nature separation, to an antithetical view—emerging with postmodernism and debated primarily within intellectual circles—of nature as socially constructed rather than materially real. Like pendulums eventually do, this one comes to center by the twenty-first century, leaving most intellectuals in agreement that nature can only be understood as *both* materially real and inevitably conflated with the social.

By foregrounding counter-nostalgic narratives about the most powerful American understandings of nature—the frontier, the pastoral, wilderness, and postnatural nature—my goal is to push beyond the pendulum stop that defines nature as both real and socially constructed, toward new ways of talking about the effects nostalgia has historically helped produce, as well as what future natures and future cultures it might help imagine. The problems with nostalgia are important to be aware of, but counter-nostalgia offers more fertile ground for rejuvenating conversations about nostalgia. As Boym suggests, "The study of nostalgia might be useful for an alternative, nonteleological history that includes conjectures and contrafactual possibilities" (351). Beginning with the premise that "homesickness is a great teacher," my "nonteleological history" of nostalgia for nature uncovers in American literature latent possibilities for a world that is more socially and environmentally just (Stegner, "Finding the Place" 17).

In 1916—the year the National Park Service was formed—Yosemite National Park held its first Indian Field Days. This inaugural event brought together nearly 150 Indians from the Yosemite region and approximately 1,500 park visitors for a daylong celebration of Indian culture. Rugs, jewelry, and baby cradles made by regional tribes were on display at the dramatic Yosemite Falls pavilion, and competitive contests—such as potato races and tug-of-wars—contributed to an event that was "part rodeo, part pageant, and part craft fair" (Cothran 195–98). NPS judges, some wearing "Indian" attire themselves, granted awards for the "Best Indian Warrior costume" and the "Best Indian Squaw costume"; there was also an Indian Baby Show, which rewarded the "healthiest"-looking babies (Cothran 200).[1] By 1929, the last year of the Field Days, a promotional poster (see Fig. 2) advertised both adventure and economic opportunity: "EXCITING HORSE RACES," a "BASKET AND BEADWORK EXHIBITION," "Indian ceremonial and war dances" and (in bold letters) "$1500 IN PRIZES." In case visitors were daunted by the big spenders from San Francisco who would flock to this "big sale," the poster assured its audience that "small" and presumably more affordable items would be "the best sellers." The top of the poster promised a cast of performers worthy of Buffalo Bill's Wild West Show: a military band and a U.S. Cavalry troop along with "hundreds of Indians, Rangers and Cowboys." These were sure to be "the best Indian Field Days ever."

The Field Days were initiated as part of a park strategy to promote tourism in Yosemite during the late summer season, when visitation

Indian Field Days

September 6 and 7, 1929

A military band and a troop of United States Cavalry are expected to join with hundreds of Indians, Rangers and Cowboys to make these the best Indian Field Days ever held in Yosemite.

$1500 IN PRIZES

Indians wearing their own costumes that meet requirements of the judges (war bonnet or feather headdress; buckskin jacket, pants and moccasins or buckskin dress and moccasins) will receive an additional $5 for the two days. Indian men stripped and painted as warriors will receive $2 for the two days.

EXCITING HORSE RACES

Including Mounted Potato Races; Roman Races; Musical Chairs; Bending Races, etc., etc. Trick Roping.

BASKET AND BEADWORK EXHIBITION

A special half-day will be devoted to judging, showing and sale of Indian Baskets and Beadwork. Buyers from San Francisco and other cities have been invited to attend this big sale. Small baskets, watch fobs, necklaces will be the best sellers.

Indian Ceremonial and War Dances

A most interesting program has been arranged by the well-known Directors:

FOREST S. TOWNSLEY	HERBERT EARL WILSON
Chief Ranger	Chief Lecturer

YOSEMITE NATIONAL PARK

SUN-STAR PRINT

FIGURE 2. Promotional poster for the Yosemite Indian Field Days, circa 1929. (Yosemite National Park Service Library)

typically dwindled along with the park's waterfalls. By employing Indians to participate in the events, the NPS also hoped to benefit Indians financially and culturally by helping them become "productive citizens of the United States" (Cothran 199). To a degree, these goals may have been achieved. Brian Bibby credits the Field Days with fostering "greater appreciation for Native arts" and supporting an "economic base" that allowed some Indian artists to make a living by basket weaving (99). Boyd Cothran concurs, emphasizing that Indians were sometimes able to exploit this new "economy of authenticity" to earn more money for their products (195).[2]

But while the Indians involved may have reaped some benefits, the NPS controlled the Field Days both materially and ideologically. The specific events included each year were contingent on political realities and the need to attract tourists. For instance, the Wild West extravaganza rhetoric in the 1929 poster reveals a deliberate strategy by Chief Ranger Forest S. Townsley, who tried to draw a bigger crowd by emulating the Wild West Shows that were popular at the time (Cothran 198). Adventure and consumption were also calibrated according to non-Native gender norms of the period; the more militaristic and rodeo-inspired events, which "tested the virility of male bodies," took place alongside the crafts fair, constructed as a feminized space of consumption (Cothran 203).

As Mark David Spence explains in *Dispossessing the Wilderness: Indian Removal and the Making of the National Parks*, "Native people remained the central attraction of [the Field Days] throughout the 1910s and 1920s, but only through their confirmation of popular white conceptions of how Indians were supposed to look and behave" (117). Continually subjected to the adjudication of the NPS and the touristic gaze, the definition of "authentic" Indian culture was always changing. In the words of the 1929 promotional poster, "Indians wearing their own costumes that meet requirements of the judges" would receive "additional" compensation, and men "stripped and painted as warriors" would also be paid well. Tourists and park officials could pose with the Indians for photo ops or dress themselves in Native garb—"playing Indian" to demonstrate allegiance to the nation.[3] Indian clothes were thus rendered "costumes," a designation that celebrates only on special occasions and so implicitly memorializes the culture they represent. That Native attire could be worn by Indians and white tourists alike suggests a facile transferability of Indian culture to white Americans. Tourists at the Field Days could purchase souvenirs— photos, artwork, and perhaps a basket or a necklace—to certify their authentic experience to the rest of the "civilized" world.

Paradoxically, the expectation was that Indians would both continue to fulfill externally imposed criteria for "authenticity" *and* continue to assimilate—to become "industrious citizens" of the United States, as the 1924 Indian Citizenship Act mandated (Cothran 199). Just as most mandates for assimilation are foreclosed by the very racism that initiates them, these demands were mutually exclusive. The primary ideology that informs these paradoxical demands is the classification of Indian culture and Indians themselves as close to, or part of, nature. The National Park Service identified the Yosemite-area Indians with the region's other natural resources and, like the flora and fauna that resided in the park boundaries, "managed" them primarily for the sake of tourism. Native populations became part of the manufactured façade of the park while "unsightly" realities, such as their often dilapidated housing areas, were kept out of the public eye (Spence 121). During the years of the Indian Field Days, park managers also worked to keep undesirable behaviors, such as gambling, drinking, and theft, "in check, much like a tree that threatened to block an especially photogenic vista" (Spence 120). Offending Indians could be fined, imprisoned, banned from the park, or sent to a government boarding school. As long as they contributed to the pleasure of tourists, lived up to stereotypes about their culture, and conformed to park-mandated standards of "morality," then Yosemite's Indians would not be forced to leave their homes—at least not immediately. After the last Indian Field Days in 1929, park officials implemented a gradual removal plan, a policy of "casual neglect" that would eventually achieve the goal of a "pure" Yosemite, free of its native occupants, but would not draw criticism from the public (Spence 128, 125).[4] By 1996, the last Yosemite Indian resident had left home.

Underscoring the expulsion of Indians from park lands were compelling and often misleading narratives, some of which are maintained to this day. Among these is the popular misconception that, although Indians were the "first 'visitors' to park areas" they stopped using those areas long before the parks were formed (Spence 131). In actuality, Indian tribes considered many of the lands that are now national parks home and did use these areas for a variety of activities, such as hunting and gathering, or hosting religious celebrations.[5] Understandings of nature as "pure" and uninhabited enabled park preservation and Indian removal. Indians were, in a sense, dispossessed *because* of their association with nature; identified with (or, more accurately, as) natural resources, they were rendered part of the scenery rather than sovereign beings with rights to the land they inhabited. Whether understood as markers of wilderness or as trespassers on national property—or, as I will show in the next chapter, as both—more Indians ended up in Yosemite National Park's museum than in the public lands.

Many of today's photographs from the Field Days show Indians holding "fugitive poses," to use Gerald Vizenor's phrase for the complex and myriad ways that art, photography and visual images "capture" Indian people in ways that mark "the absence of native memories and the actual landscape" (152). As Drucilla Wall, who is inspired by Vizenor, puts it, the "dominant culture wishes the difficult and complex Native to disappear so that the constructed, controlled, and purely simulated Indian can conceal Indian people rather than reveal them" (103). Seen in this light, the Indian Field Days seem the product of a dominant culture that is adept at concealing less powerful cultures even when it appears to be celebrating them. The Field Days illustrate how nostalgia—when linked to national identity and publicly consumed—can translate into collectively reinforced stories that in turn influence real events. Representations of Indians that locate Native culture in a nostalgic, fictional prehistory dovetail with myths of pristine, unoccupied nature and, together, enable many Americans to overlook current problems faced by the country's indigenous inhabitants.

The Indian Field Days and events like them[6] have been overshadowed by the more popular images and histories of the natural world promoted by the NPS and other nature management institutions. But the Field Days are not an isolated incident. On the contrary, they are at once emblematic of the peculiar mix of patriotism and newfound love of dramatic natural landscapes particular to the modern period and indicative of a set of still-circulating ideologies about nature, indigenous people, and liberal democracy. The American democratic agenda privileges a liberal formulation of equality that presumes "humans share the same nature, the same rights, and the same terms of regard by state institutions" (Brown, *States* 153). Such logic guided federal Indian policy later in the century, as manifested in problematic programs like termination and relocation. Fueled by a similar kind of liberalism, the ideal of the "public park" as a democratic space for all Americans to enjoy has been fundamental to the Park Service's bureaucratic ethic. However, as the Field Days suggest, this ideal permits practices that are far from democratic. While perhaps not as appalling as the violence and bloodshed involved in wars with other tribes, the physical incorporation of these Indians into Yosemite's scenery—followed by their passive-aggressive expulsion—shows how parks were founded on strategic exclusions and the formulation of an abstract, white citizen-tourist who could consume and still reign supreme over nature and the people identified with it.

The Field Days lasted only fourteen summers, but the cultural exploitation evident in these events continues in celebrations such as Thanksgiving (a holiday that tends to gloss over conflict between European settlers and native inhabitants), Columbus Day (a dishonest origin myth that, with its rhetoric of "discovery," erases Native people's presence from North America), and the many classrooms nationwide that continue to host "pioneer days" that reify the "innocence" of the frontier.[7] An updated liberal ideology that perceives American Indian tribes as slices of multicultural America threatens to elide historical conflict and memorialize present-day concerns out of existence. Stereotypes of the wise old Indian chief and the spiritual healer—both educated in nature's school—permeate mainstream culture, often with the effect of romanticizing Indians and silencing contemporary conflicts. And yet, the extreme poverty on many reservations, the vast number of pending tribal lawsuits contesting treaty violations, and the enormous amount of land still in dispute leave no doubt that the effects of conquest are still being felt by many tribes and that injustice remains all too commonplace in the U.S. government's treatment of the country's original inhabitants.

As I will discuss in chapter 1, the modern period juggled confusing, sometimes contradictory, conceptions of Indians and nature. Nostalgia was a complicating force directing these conceptions in different ways, depending on whether one identified with the national longing to preserve dwindling natural resources or whether one was reacting to modernity as a displaced resident of a homeland. The next chapter focuses on the now-canonized *American Indian Stories*, by Zitkala-Ša, to show how her young narrator pits her own nostalgia, attached to her tribal homeland of South Dakota, against the national nostalgia, exhibited in the Field Days, that erases or incorporates Native presence. Not only does her work remind readers that Indians remain a real presence in the American West, but her stories also undermine ideas about Native "savagery" and depict, instead, a civilized and highly cultured tribal community. The pastoral ideal for which Zitkala-Ša's young narrator longs precedes and confronts the violence brought by nineteenth-century frontiering and its legacy in the twentieth.

Publishing at a time of cultural transition as many tribes moved from a primarily oral to a written literary tradition, Zitkala-Ša wields language with a seemingly calculated ambivalence that reveals the difficulty of articulating one's identity while negotiating the expectations of a non-Native publishing and reading world. Her stories anticipate more contemporary writers who continue to manipulate national rhetoric—including nostalgic stories featuring overdetermined "natural" Indians—to their own ends. Writers like N. Scott Momaday (the subject of chapter 4), Leslie Marmon Silko, Linda Hogan, and Sherman Alexie warrant attention for the ways they continue to negotiate the relationships between nostalgia, nature, and Indian identity—often in ways that work against the always evolving myths about Indianness. Zitkala-Ša's counter-nostalgia should be understood as a precursor to these other writers, although the context her work responded to was a particularly modern one.

1 / Longing for Wonderland: Zitkala-Ša's Post-Frontier Nostalgia

Indians and nature have been versatile, often contradictory, foils for constructions of white American identity since European settlement. Indians have a long and distinctive history of being both quintessentially "American" and the very antithesis of national identity. In *Playing Indian*, Philip J. Deloria describes how, for instance, Revolutionary War–era Indians were "noble and customary, and they existed inside an American society that was not British. But Indians were also savage, existing outside of a British society that included both colonists and officials" (26). The nineteenth and early twentieth centuries were a time of especially dynamic change, as constructions of "savage" Indianness evolved in tandem with conceptions of wilderness. Sometimes Indians were the "natural" occupants of wilderness areas; at other times they were a "problem" for management—a blemish on natural landscapes that needed to be erased to create "pure" natural spaces. In the nineteenth century, whether Indians were romanticized or ostracized depended largely on land availability. In the early part of that century, Indians were often depicted as "picturesque and 'noble,'" their lives idealized in the face of growing unease about industrialization, urbanization, and immigration. By the end of that same century, as "free land" in the West became scarce and indigenous people were framed as trespassers on desirable property, Indians were more frequently described as outlaw tribes who had "regressed into 'treacherous, bloodthirsty savages'" (Spence 30). Far from a clean break or an absolute paradigm shift, both depictions—the noble Indian and the trespasser (who could safely be deemed a bit less "savage" with the end of the Indian wars)—persisted into the early twentieth century, informing national park management and public perception.

As spectacular geography replaced Native presence as the primary indicator of wilderness in the American mind, situating Indians as both "self" and "other" enabled white Americans to affiliate themselves with the natural, "savage" elements of Indian culture—a kind of cultural imperialism that accompanied the now trendy tourism of nature—but still justify poor treatment of these "others." In the modern period, both nature and Native Americans were often posited as preindustrial antidotes for a quickly changing nation and, so, rendered "past tense"—origins, of sorts, to which the American public could return for unreflective consumption and imaginary authenticity (Wall 103). "Playing Indian" in modern America, as tourists at the Field Days did, promised an authentic connection to the nation's "origins" by "help[ing] preserve a sense of frontier toughness, communal warmth, and connection to the continent," especially to its coveted natural world (Deloria 129).

Arguably "the nation's most sacred myth of origin," nature, like Indianness, has a long history of being alternately respected and romanticized, or feared and tamed (Cronon 77). As William Cronon explains in "The Trouble with Wilderness; or, Getting Back to the Wrong Nature," wilderness is not just a material reality; rather, popular perceptions of wilderness have always been socially constructed and historically contingent.[1] Throughout much of the seventeenth and eighteenth centuries in the United States, wilderness, stemming from biblical references, was "a place to which one came only against one's will, and always in fear and trembling" (Cronon 71). By the end of the nineteenth century, however, this understanding of wilderness had begun to change drastically. Cronon notes that rapid industrialization, combined with the nineteenth-century emergence of the American sublime (adapted and popularized by writers like Henry David Thoreau and John Muir) and the construction of the frontier myth (by Frederick Jackson Turner, Theodore Roosevelt, and others), contributed to a reversal of the earlier wilderness ideology. As industrialization marched steadily forward, more Americans cultivated an anti-modern nostalgic backlash to help alleviate the anxieties accompanying technological, economic, and social change. Wilderness was no longer a scary place in need of taming, but a valuable asset in need of protection.

A major shift in American environmental values had occurred. Nostalgia for nature had been catapulted into the forefront of the national imaginary, and the nation began to embrace a new ethic of preserving its dwindling natural resources. Perhaps the largest contributing factor to this shift was the declaration by the U.S. Census Bureau, in the year 1890, that the frontier was "closed": there was no more land for westward expansion. Three years later, Frederick Jackson Turner identified the frontier as central to national identity in his well-known and much-contested essay "The Significance of the Frontier in American History." With the frontier's closing came the recognition that American nature—a unique cultural asset, often invoked to prove the exceptionalism of "nature's Nation"—was perhaps being tamed a bit too quickly. Up until this time, nostalgia for nature had existed in diffuse literary and artistic cultural enclaves—for instance, in the work of the transcendentalists or the Hudson River School. But nineteenth-century nature was still considered an infinite resource for the nation, and questions about how it might be put to use superseded questions about how it might be left alone. The closing of the frontier, and the concomitant sense that this "resource" was running out, helped solidify what had been relatively minor and disparate nostalgic stirrings into a broader, more dominant, national nostalgia for nature.

Frontier nostalgia in Turner's essay relied on problematic assumptions and rhetorical strategies—including erasing the country's indigenous inhabitants in order to construct a West with "free land" for the taking— and other scholars have detailed the many problems with his "frontier thesis" more thoroughly than I will here. One aspect of the thesis that is crucial for my study is Turner's formulation of the frontier as an origin to which Americans could "return" again and again to establish a national character: "American development has exhibited not merely advance along a single line but a return to primitive conditions on a continually advancing frontier line, and a new development for that area. American social development has been continually beginning over again on the frontier. This perennial rebirth, this fluidity of American life, this expansion westward with its new opportunities, its continuous touch with the simplicity of primitive society, furnish the forces dominating American character" (187). This kind of "beginning over again" sounds like Said's theory of beginnings, especially insofar as it seems to disrupt the idea of "advance along a single line." However, while Said imagines beginnings that destabilize both past and present, Turner's "perennial" return works not to reevaluate the present but to reconfirm it as the natural endpoint of a kind of teleological progress. Unlike the authors in my study, whose work follows Said's model by calling into question such progress, Turner situates "expansion westward" along the frontier as a reliable and static national origin myth.

Of course, this origin myth was largely a bourgeois, anti-modern narrative; its nostalgia was felt strongly by some Americans but hardly registered by others. When John Muir wrote of the "thousands of tired, nerve-shaken, over-civilised people" who were "going home" to the mountains, it hardly needs to be said that such a home would not have been "universally appealing" (qtd. in Outka 156). Exemplifying what Renato Rosaldo has called imperialist nostalgia, lamentations of "lost" wilderness typically came from elite white males—the people who profited most from the exploitation of the nature whose loss they mourned. Not surprisingly then, this nostalgic longing was complex, dichotomous, and often contradictory. A split tradition of post-frontier nostalgia emerged and was re-coded in two different versions of American history that sought to explain national identity in the modern present. Along with this nostalgia, national rhetoric situating savagery or primitivism against the forces of civilization evolved in new directions during the modern period and beyond. Because this frontier rhetoric is so integral to the work of the writers I analyze in this chapter and throughout this study, I will spend some time here detailing its emergence.

On one hand, the American frontier past was coded as primarily a pastoral, democratic space, occupied by a harmonious community that lived and worked on the land. This version of the frontier remained truer to Turner's idealized national history. Richard Slotkin explains that Turner's nostalgic vision glorified the yeoman farmer and understood "the past as a place in which, once upon a time, our political life was regenerated and purified"; the corrupt present, by contrast, could no longer profit from the frontier's revitalizing effects ("Nostalgia and Progress" 612, 636). In this version of nostalgia, the negative effects of the frontier's taming—such as Indian removal—were quietly overlooked in favor of a neo-utilitarian ethic concerned primarily with appreciation of the natural world. Violence, even while it continued in the present, was downplayed, couched safely within the "progressive" rhetoric of Manifest Destiny or the liberal ideology of uplift. As Paul Outka argues, the sublime landscapes of the American West—especially as linked to (white) national identity via Turner's frontier myth—provided a natural space in which "the racial trauma that had organized the national geography for much of the nineteenth century could be left behind" (154). In the modern United States, a new "cultural nationalism," based on touring the country's natural wonders, "grew out of a nostalgic ideal of America as nature's nation" (Shaffer 146). The Indian

Field Days demonstrate how tourism erased violent histories even as it became, in effect, a new form of pioneering—a way to experience the frontier in small, safe doses.[2]

On the other hand, in an alternate version of the turn-of-the-century frontier story, nostalgia for the more traditional frontier remained prominent—nostalgia for the violent West of the boom town and the gold rush, now popularized by dime novels, by Buffalo Bill Cody's Wild West Show, and by Western American fiction like Owen Wister's *The Virginian*. This was the West of the cowboy, a nostalgic national symbol whose popularity coincided, ironically, with the end of the frontier that had spawned him and nurtured his way of life.[3] This West was also the proving ground for the figure Cronon describes as the "mythic frontier individualist": a racialized, masculinized subject position that values and romanticizes "unspoiled" or "savage" wilderness as the site of identity formation (78). In this strand of nostalgia, the frontier's violence was essential for national progress and, as such, was naturalized and even celebrated through its performance (in the popular Wild West Show, for instance) and its canonization in Western literature. Indians and other "uncivilized" groups were implicated in this myth of the West as well, usually as "natural" foils for white identity formation.

Perhaps the man who best embodies this second, more violent manifestation of the frontier is Theodore Roosevelt. Slotkin explains how Roosevelt developed and popularized a particular variation of Turner's frontier myth. While Turner's work downplayed the frontier's violence, Roosevelt's sense of frontier history emphasized not only the "egalitarian democracy" fostered by frontier life but also "the course of savage war" that helped created a "class of those invested with heroic, history-making capacities"—a "race of heroes" of which Roosevelt counted himself a member (*Gunfighter* 54). Slotkin concludes that the balances each man struck between nostalgia and progressivism were different, since each embraced a slightly different myth of the frontier: Turner's was "thoroughly nostalgic in its contrast of happy past and troubled present," but Roosevelt's adaptation valued the enduring potential of the frontier in the present. For Roosevelt, positive "effects on racial morale" could and should be maintained via "a disciplined program of preaching, myth-making, exercise, and conquest" that drew on historical struggles to further national agendas and revitalize national identity. In other words, Roosevelt's frontier was "not an alternative to the present, but was its justification"—a national resource to be mined in the service of imperialist projects (Slotkin, "Nostalgia and Progress" 636).

We might say, then, that Turner embodied one pole of the frontier's new split—a pastoral and less outwardly violent pole, which emphasized a break with the past and foregrounded environment rather than race as the key factor in shaping national identity—while Roosevelt embodied the other, in which a "new class of hero-leaders" that included the "wilderness hunter and Indian fighter" kept the "spirit of the frontier" alive (Slotkin, "Nostalgia and Progress" 611, 636). This comfortable binary is complicated, though, by Turner's frequent association with violence in contemporary, especially scholarly, discourse and Roosevelt's widespread association with nature preservation. A self-made "frontier individualist," Roosevelt is also well known and respected by many of today's environmentalists for his substantial contributions to nature conservation. And for good reason. The National Forest Service was created under his guidance, and he set aside millions of acres of land for forest reserves and national monuments. But if Roosevelt's nostalgia was beneficial for some environments, it was detrimental to Americans who did not occupy the identity category he privileged—the white, middle- to upper-class, heterosexual male.[4] For one thing, Roosevelt promoted both nature's preservation as an antidote to excessive civilization and the tourism-driven development that, ironically, molded that nature into a "reflect[ion of] the very civilization its devotees sought to escape" (Cronon 78). Moreover, Roosevelt's prescription for Americans to "get back to nature" was an elitist one, which ignored historical and cultural differences between people. The brief, rejuvenating sojourns into nature he advocated were only available to those with adequate leisure time, ample money, and the right skin color.

Ultimately, Roosevelt, like Turner, did draw on rhetoric and myths that were "thoroughly nostalgic"—and he did so in a way that early American theorists of nostalgia had foreclosed. Swiss doctor Johannes Hofer had admired nostalgia as an indication of excessive patriotism, but American doctors of the eighteenth century saw the "disease" as a sign of an unhealthy country and initially repudiated the idea that it might exist in the United States. Specifically, the American military doctor Theodore Calhoun considered nostalgia to be "a shameful disease that revealed a lack of manliness and unprogressive attitudes" (Boym 13). But by the early twentieth century, Roosevelt had claimed frontier nostalgia as not just available but a patriotic resource that helped bolster confidence in the nation's "manly" progressivism ("Nostalgia and Progress" 634). Perhaps because Roosevelt saw himself as a member of the "race of heroes" evolved from the rigors of the frontier, elitism and racism infused both his domestic and foreign policy. Roosevelt posited nature as an antidote to "race suicide": the fear that the white race was dying out due to excessive civilization, leaving it unfit to compete with more "primitive" races. In response to this perceived threat, Roosevelt lauded male virility, which could be regained through the patriotic duty of contact with wilderness. Not surprisingly, then, he advocated extending the U.S. frontier abroad, through imperialism, and he celebrated conflict and conquest as character-building traits.

Gail Bederman explains that, for Roosevelt, "regression to savagery was only temporary and proved the Americans' racial superiority" (182). The term "savage" could apply to African Americans as well as to Indians, for Roosevelt, since he considered both to be "uncivilized" (181). Thus, being "close to nature" could function as either a disparaging association, if you were a person of color, or as a desirable connection—provided you were a white male and only temporarily dabbling in the wilderness for the ultimate benefit of civilization. A comparable double standard informed national park visitation. For instance, George Bird Grinnell, an influential preservationist who helped designate Glacier National Park, encouraged Americans to "'uncivilize' themselves a bit and return to the mountains on a regular basis," whereas he instructed Blackfoot Indians "to become 'civilized'" and assimilate into the American mainstream (Spence 78).

Indeed, some of the criticisms I (and others) have made of Roosevelt could just as easily be made of the newly formed NPS.[5] If nature in its pristine state was the antithesis of civilization, then groups of people who were considered closer to nature were also antithetical to the (white) civilized world. Moreover, if nature was, by definition, the place where humans were not, then identification with nature meant certain groups of people were effectively dehumanized. These cultural logics indicate the powerful effects of the period's progress ideology, dependent as it was on an opposition between savagery and civilization, with its sense of inevitable movement toward the latter. They also suggest that turn-of-the-century racism was, to some degree, predicated on nostalgic constructions of nature.

At their most extreme, concerns about preserving the white race emerged in Southern literature of the period that promoted identification with regional landscapes combined with a racialized nostalgia for exclusively white communities. Thomas Dixon Jr.'s *The Clansman: An Historical Romance of the Ku Klux Klan* demonstrates this nostalgia at its worst; it anchors white supremacy in the natural world in order to legitimize and promote class- and race-based violence. Although Dixon's nostalgia might be an extreme case, the blatant racism of his "romance" did not prevent it from being made into the popular motion picture *Birth of a Nation*, a film still acknowledged, in spite of its racism, as an important part of film history. A more mainstream instance of a comparable form of nostalgia might be *Gone with the Wind*, a film notable for its celebration of Southern landscapes and its nostalgia for the passing of the South's way of life, including the racial hierarchies that enabled some to enjoy leisurely lives within the plantation system. As I will discuss in later chapters, the Dixonesque strand of nostalgia for nature was later picked up by the Southern agrarian regionalist movement and represented by the anthology *I'll Take My Stand*, as well as (in less overtly racist forms) in regional political movements like the Sagebrush Rebellion of the 1970s. This strand of nostalgia, while not dominant, illustrates the dangerous tendencies of nostalgia to draw racial boundaries and foster destructive ideologies.

Racial boundaries were, of course, central to turn-of-the-century nation-building projects that relocated and reproduced frontier violence via American imperialism. Within the nation's boundaries, Richard White explains how "descent from true Americans" became the new standard for citizenship once the frontier experience was no longer an option (47). Of course, new immigrants could claim neither frontier experience nor native ancestry; thus they became "dangerous" and "unassimilable" in the eyes of those who, like Roosevelt, prized "true Americanness" (White 47). Patricia Limerick identifies a related effect of the frontier's closure on ethnic minorities as she remarks on the role of nostalgia during this time period: "When Indian war dances became tourist spectacles, when the formerly scorned customs of the Chinese drew tourists to Chinatown, when former out-groups found that characteristics that once earned them disapproval could now earn them a living, when fearful, life-threatening deserts became charming patterns of color and light, ... the frontier could be considered closed, even museumized" ("Adventures" 74). In effect, the closed frontier and its accompanying nostalgia cemented racial difference in the national imaginary. People of color and other "out-groups" could be included in the nation only as tourist attractions or as emblems of disappearing cultures. These people's histories—including their contributions to building the nation—were effectively "museumized" or erased. Nostalgia aided in legitimating these unfortunate erasures, but it was also a key tool in resisting them.

* * *

The dominant nostalgic narratives embedded within and spread by the National Park Service and political figures like Roosevelt, combined with the even more extreme versions of nostalgia found in texts like Dixon's, left little space for writers of the time to rewrite nostalgic nature stories for alternate purposes. However, within the "hazardous play of dominations" perpetuated by hegemonic narratives, there is always room for exploitation (Foucault, "Nietzsche" 148). One author who successfully wrote about nature counter-nostalgically is Zitkala-Ša, a Yankton Dakota writer and activist whose poignant and often critical autobiographical stories and Lakota-Dakota legends were published during the early twentieth century. Born on the Yankton reservation in South Dakota, she left home at a young age to pursue a boarding school education at White's Manual Institute and Santee Normal Training School. She later attended Earlham College (which was all-white), taught briefly at the notorious Carlisle Indian School, then redirected her energies to political activism. Her three-part autobiography, which was reissued in *American Indian Stories* in 1921, was first published in the *Atlantic Monthly* in 1900. As Jeffrey Myers points out, this meant she was publishing at the same time, even in the same journal, as W. E. B. Du Bois—who had just theorized "the problem of the color line"—and Muir, who was championing nature preservation (Myers 116). Like these other writers, Zitkala-Ša intervened in the broader discourse about race and nature at the turn of the century. She wrote to preserve her tribal culture—and, as her pan-Indian activism indicates, all tribal cultures—to locate Indians squarely in the Western landscape, and to redeem these "savages" in the eyes of her readers.

Hers was no easy task. As Foucault argues, to successfully write history—itself a "system of rules" enabling both domination and resistance—one must be "capable of seizing these rules, to replace those who had used them, to disguise themselves so as to pervert them, invert their meaning, and redirect them against those who had initially imposed them . . . so as to overcome the rulers through their own rules" ("Nietzsche" 151). In this sense Zitkala-Ša was able to redirect the rules of her time concerning nature, nostalgia, and American Indians so as to present Indian concerns to white readers in a language they would be inclined to hear. Though she does not necessarily blur racial categories— she inverts the existing binary between Native and non-Native but only rarely deconstructs race itself—she certainly questions who the "true Americans" are as she writes her own "out-group" back in to the natural and cultural landscape. By counter-nostalgically identifying Indian culture with nature and presenting white civilization as "unnatural," Zitkala-Ša's *American Indian Stories* capitalize on contemporaneous fears about overcivilization and industrialization in order to humanize American Indians, complicate the progress narrative implied by Turner's frontier thesis, and call into serious question the presumed benefits of assimilating to white American culture.

Many anthologies today include Zitkala-Ša's work. Most often, this inclusion is framed by her cultural exile, the political pressures to which she was subject, and her ability to create literature in the face of these pressures. Yet as Jessica Enoch points out, many anthologies fail to accentuate her "rhetorical sovereignty and pedagogical resistance" in the face of the "systematic silencing" of her work that plagued her career; instead, she is most often presented as simply an example of American literary "multiculturalism" (13). My reading of Zitkala-Ša foregrounds elements of *American Indian Stories* that other critics have either not explored or have underemphasized: her inversion of the civilization/savagery binary (which, because of its close connection to frontier ideology, I shorthand as frontier rhetoric); her reappropriation of dominant stereotypes and deliberate identification of Indians with nature; and her tactical use of nostalgia to achieve her literary and extra-literary goals.

Myers's recent work on Zitkala-Ša comes closest to addressing these concerns. He reads her writing as "an ecology that brings together environmental awareness with social justice"; he suggests she imagines common ground for Native and non-Native people to come together to foster "a multicultural, ecologically sustainable inhabitation of North America" (114). In Myers's mind, *American Indian Stories* and *Old Indian Legends* must be read as "two parts of a whole work, a conglomeration of Native American and European literary traditions" that "speak in different voices about twin concerns: Euroamerican racism toward American Indians and Euroamerican destruction of the natural world" (114). Like Myers, I highlight the environmental dimensions of Zitkala-Ša's work, especially as they connect to her joint critiques of assimilation and racism. But I focus on *American Indian Stories*, especially its autobiographical stories, as not only adequate for addressing these related issues together but also more appropriate for contextualizing her work within the nostalgic frontier rhetoric circulating at the time. I do not disagree with Myers's claims—indeed, he productively extends scholarship on her work—but my focus on *American Indian Stories* enables an investigation of how nature, Indians, and frontier rhetoric were interarticulated in dominant culture as well as how Zitkala-Ša manipulated and reworked these intertwined narratives via counter-nostalgia.

Zitkala-Ša emerged on the literary and political scene just as the ideologies I have been describing were beginning to inform national organizations and institutional rhetoric. As Indians faced the loss of their distinctive oral traditions, the partitioning of tribes on reservations, the fragmentation of tribal communities, and declining populations, some Indians began to create written records of their tribal legends, folktales, and personal stories (Fisher v.). Zitkala-Ša was among the earliest American Indian writers to begin making the transition from oral to written culture,[6] and her writing negotiates the tensions between traditional Indian culture and the expectations of assimilation into white America—tensions between "the remembered past and the alien present" (Fisher vi). Further, as the "darling" of white readers of *Harper's* and *Atlantic Monthly*, where she initially published many of the essays that would later make up *American Indian Stories*, Zitkala-Ša's ability to keep her writing in print hinged on meeting the criteria for "attracting attention" determined by her audience (Fisher vii). She wrote and published amid mounting pressures to work within the confining expectations of the ethnographic narrative: to write on behalf of the concerns of her "race," to represent those concerns accurately, and to subjugate creative endeavors to more political pursuits.

Even within the rigid guidelines of these expectations and the overwhelming material limitations facing Indians at the time, Zitkala-Ša was able to find a surprising amount of creative leeway through which to make political statements. Partially adopting the genre of sentimental autobiography allowed her some writerly freedom, extended her audience appeal, and enabled her to embed a political critique within her ostensibly sentimental stories. But her adoption of sentimental autobiography is incomplete and so ambivalent, in a sense, as she refuses to fulfill the generic contract of the narrator's ultimate resolution into a whole, complete individual.[7] Most of Zitkala-Ša's stories are ambivalent; sometimes the same story will both celebrate and decry the white "civilization" to which she was expected to conform. Often characterized as an inevitable result of trying to engage white audiences, her ambivalence can also be read as tactical, contrived, and deliberate. Julianne Newmark, for instance, suggests that the "gaps between words" (342) produce a discord within the text, which Zitkala-Ša exploits to make her critique of white civilization. In my reading of her stories, the stories' nostalgic gaps between past and present become a central, and very powerful, rhetorical strategy. Far from embracing assimilation or merely lamenting her position between two cultures, I suggest Zitkala-Ša deploys counter-nostalgic ambivalence to emphasize the "breech" between two binary positions—past and present, Indian culture and white (over)civilization, Western landscapes and the industrialized East—and coax the reader into identifying with the former over the latter. By revising her white audience's expectations of the "return home," Zitkala-Ša's stories represent Indian cultures as civilized and Indians as fully human.

White readers, in effect, are tricked into longing to return to a natural home that not only is not what they imagined it to be—an unpopulated Eden—but was never *their* home in the first place. What is found at the nostalgic origin is the violent uprooting of a cultured, civilized people, and a history of inequity. Zitkala-Ša's contrasting depictions of the West and the East force white audiences to see themselves as the "savages" and Indians as the original inhabitants of "Eden." As Enoch argues, Zitkala-Ša "inscribes a kind of white savagery" through her descriptions of the Carlisle School and so "break[s] down the false dichotomy that . . . define[s] Indian culture as savage and white 'American' life as civilized" (Enoch 7). Indeed, for Zitkala-Ša, white civilization has become so *over*civilized that it embodies the worst of the "savage" characteristics typically attributed to Indians at the time. However, most readings of her work, including Enoch's, do not ground the analysis of her frontier rhetoric in contemporaneous understandings of the natural world; nor do they grapple with Zitkala-Ša's identification of Indians with nonhuman nature, which was still characterized as the antithesis of (indeed, antidote to) civilization during this time period. Introducing nature and nostalgia into the savage/civilized dichotomy enables a richer understanding of how her stories work.

Throughout the stories, Zitkala-Ša identifies Indians with nature through formal linguistic strategies (like metaphor) and by emphasizing, rather than downplaying, the widespread conception of Indians as closer to nature. She foregrounds then condemns the ways in which this conception has led to exploitation by whites as she longs for her lost community's positive experiences in and with the natural world. She achieves her critique through a twofold process of linking the white "civilizing machine" with images of homogeneity, antiseptic formalities, empty ritual, even death, and contrasting this civilization with her tribe's culture, which she depicts, nostalgically, as natural, happy, and free (66). Her argument also works by invoking nonhuman nature as a moral authority—a source of cultural righteousness and ancient beauty that she sets in opposition to excessive civilization.[8] Such a definition of nature is consistent with the one popularized by Roosevelt and the National Park Service and, so, would have been recognizable to her audience.

Even while she toys with dominant understandings of nature, though, Zitkala-Ša insists on her own definitions, which she grounds in white conceptions only enough to effectively engage her audience. Displaced from her home at a young age, she becomes an exile, for whom everything that happens in her new environment "occur[s] against the memory . . . of another environment" (Said, "Reflections on Exile" 186). Once she leaves her reservation to begin her education, she is "at home" neither in white culture nor in Dakota culture. Culturally homeless, she also suffers, in Said's words, from "the loss of contact with the solidity and satisfaction of earth: homecoming is out of the question" ("Reflections" 179). My reading of Zitkala-Ša's stories thus attends to the role of the actual landscape rather than just the metaphorical one, as I tease out the roles both nostalgia for her Yankton reservation and antipathy toward the bleak environment of the "civilized" East play in her stories.

Her love for the South Dakota landscape is apparent in many of the stories and essays in the collection. As a child growing up "in the lap of the prairie," she feels a strong connection to her home region (22). She and her friends run and play "like little sportive nymphs on that Dakota sea of rolling green" (23). As a student at the boarding school, she dreams of the "Western rolling lands" where she grew up (65). When she returns home to recruit new students for the school, she shouts aloud with apparent pleasure upon seeing the wigwams situated amid the "old familiar sky lines of rugged bluffs and round-topped hills" and the sunflowers, plum bushes, and other plants that dot "this nature's garden" (87–88).

But her understanding of "nature" goes beyond landscape or "garden" to include a worldview that encompasses relations between all species. Her essay "The Great Spirit" (originally titled "Why I Am a Pagan") explains why she prefers "excursions into the natural gardens where the voice of the Great Spirit is heard" to the "dogma" of Christianity (107). The essay begins with joyful expressions of her love for nature's aesthetic properties but goes on to describe an even more powerful understanding of the more-than-human world that infuses the entire collection, including the autobiographical stories. She starts with a description of her exuberance over the "loving Mystery" of nature on a summer day, as she sits on the bank of the Missouri River (101). She immerses herself in the day's beauty: the shifting shapes of clouds, the "soft cadences of the river's song," and the nearby prairie flowers that "soothe [her] soul"

(101). As Myers points out, the "lyrical" language of this passage resonates with the British romantic tradition—most directly, Wordsworth's
poetry—as well as with Muir's brand of nature writing, with which she
could have conceivably been familiar (Myers 119).

If she has had a sublime encounter with nature here, it is not one that
leads her to retreat into comfortable divisions between humans and
nature.[9] To the contrary, once she returns to her cabin and her writing
desk—"buoyant with good nature" after her time outdoors (103)—she
expresses her feelings of "keen sympathy with [her] fellow-creatures"
(104). Interestingly, racial categories dissolve for her as she sees the world
as consisting of a "living mosaic of human beings" that renders not just
her tribe but all of humanity "one large family" (104–5). Unlike in the
autobiographical stories, where her negative depictions of "palefaces"
and the boarding schools tend to reinforce racial boundaries, in this
essay she indicates that we all participate in a kind of "kinship to any
and all parts of this vast universe" (102–3).[10]

The first section of *American Indian Stories*, "Impressions of an Indian
Childhood," makes a point of illustrating these beliefs as they play out in
the everyday life of Indians on her reservation in South Dakota. Zitkala-
Ša's home is cultural as well as natural; "her tales of Indian home life
are marked by descriptions of art, etiquette, and social code" (Enoch 6).
These early stories emphasize the feelings of kinship, the respect for others' space, and the familial caretaking and hospitality that characterize
her tribal community. Her mother trains her to follow the tribe's rules
of etiquette; in return for good behavior, she is treated "as a dignified
little individual" (Zitkala-Ša 20). In "The Coffee-Making," for instance,
Zitkala-Ša tells of her humble efforts to "play the part of a generous host-
ess" by doing her best to make coffee for a tribal member who stops by
unexpectedly when her mother is out (27). Although her coffee is hardly
deserving of the name, neither the visitor nor her mother makes her feel
embarrassed for its poor quality; rather, they reward her efforts with "the
utmost respect" (29).

The "social codes" her stories depict include children as worthy of
respect, women as trusted authority figures, the role of hospitality in fostering community, and the important rule not to "intru[de] . . . on others"
(8). Beginning the collection with the story called "My Mother," which
emphasizes her mother's sorrow and anger at the "palefaces" and their
devastating effects on tribal culture—including various "intrusions" like
land theft, forced migrations onto reservation lands, and the diseases that
killed both Zitkala-Ša's uncle and sister—foreshadows the losses she will

soon face. We are not surprised, then, by her experiences at the boarding school, where she is objectified, tossed around like a doll, and perpetually subject to intrusive treatment by her white "benefactors." This treatment, like the federal government's treatment of tribes, breaks each of the tribal norms she so carefully details in her opening stories.

Zitkala-Ša's representations of tribal life are clearly culturally specific, distinctive to the Dakota tribe. However, they can also be seen as pastoral insofar as they reveal a community that lives and works in harmonious connectivity with a bountiful nonhuman nature. The home she writes into existence resonates with dominant nostalgic narratives that position the pastoral as a counterpoint to excessive civilization. The role of labor in close proximity to nonhuman nature also renders her text, broadly speaking, pastoral. As Greg Garrard notes, an emphasis on a "working rather than an aesthetic relationship to the land" is common to American pastoral formulations, rooted as they are in Jeffersonian agrarianism (*Ecocriticism* 49). The early stories of tribal life nearly all depict work— women's work, since we follow women's lives more closely—including tasks like gathering water, preparing food, drying corn, pumpkins, and fruits, and creating beadwork for moccasins and other items. Given that much of this labor reflects her tribe's cultural priorities, to situate the stories squarely within an American pastoral tradition would be unfair. Yet Zitkala-Ša's descriptions of tribal life would have resonated with white readers whose expectations about the West included the belief that frontier expansion had remade environments into pastoral communities like the one she describes.

Contrary to the frontier myth, her pastoral community actually precedes the frontier and its violent, colonial project. By situating Indians as inhabitants of the American West prior to pioneer settlers' intrusion and by emphasizing her tribe's various codes, Zitkala-Ša challenges the frontier ideology that would declare her a savage in need of civilizing. At the same time, she debunks the myth of a "pure," unspoiled natural world that is devoid of human impact—a myth upon which the NPS and much contemporaneous environmental rhetoric relied. The natural home for which she is nostalgic is most definitely inhabited, and any Edenic qualities it possesses stem from human interactions with their environment, not from the absence of humans. Unlike tourists dabbling in nature as an antidote to excessive civilization, Zitkala-Ša shows that an everyday life balancing nature and culture is a more realistic and satisfying option. Rather than replicating the romanticization of Indians as a national symbol of "wildness" or the museumification of Indian culture perpetuated by the national parks, she constructs her natural home as structured, egalitarian, welcoming to all living things, and, most important, still functioning in the present. If the state of this home has declined since colonization began, and if Indians are, in that sense, "vanishing," it is because of the violent displacement and cultural loss imposed on them by non-Natives under the pretense of assimilation.

Zitkala-Ša thus dismantles the common equation of nature with savagery and reconfigures Indian life as "civilized" in its own right. Furthermore, Indian culture, for her, is a more "natural" and healthier form of culture than white civilization, which her stories critique for being alienated from nature and, as such, extremely *uncultured*. In the world of her stories, Roosevelt's fears of excessive civilization have come to pass: whites are pale, weak, anonymous automatons carrying out empty routines. A central metaphor reflecting this state is the telegraph pole—an example of the "unnatural nature" created by white civilization.[11] On her way to school in the East, Zitkala-Ša observes that "along the edge of a road thickly bordered with wild sunflowers, some poles like these had been planted by white men . . . and, hearing its low moaning, [she] used to wonder what the paleface had done to hurt it" (48). Later, she invokes the telegraph pole metaphor again, describing herself as "a cold bare pole . . . planted in a strange earth" (97). In Foucauldian fashion, the civilizing machine carves such poles through institutional discipline:[12] the uprooting and transporting of Indian bodies to the East; the physical alteration of those bodies; the partitioning of individual students; and finally, the indoctrination of the students into new cultural norms at the expense of the old. As the founder of the Carlisle School, Captain Richard C. Pratt, infamously put it, this was a process of "killing the Indian and saving the man."

In *American Indian Stories*, the civilizing machine is faceless, powerful, even violent—a combination of spectacle and surveillance in which individual students could be visibly, corporeally punished as "examples" even while institutional power was "permanent, exhaustive, omnipresent . . . capable of making all visible, as long as it could itself remain invisible" (Foucault, *Discipline and Punish* 214). The "iron routine" of the "paleface day" contains a variety of disciplinary mechanisms, including rote learning, military-style drills, an unsympathetic approach to physical illness, and the separation of the students from each other, as they were separated from their homes and families. Many critics have noted the humiliation expressed in Zitkala-Ša's description of her first haircut at school as a powerful example of its "cold" discipline, after which she writes: "Then I lost my spirit" (56). The school and its teachers are described at various points in terms of military barracks and prisons, and Zitkala-Ša slowly realizes that "the large army of white teachers in Indian schools had a larger missionary creed than [she] had suspected" (95). Thrust into the cells of this educational panopticon, she shows her readers how racist white power functions to rob its victims of their spirits through routine, isolation, and the oppressive structure of the institution's physical space.

In addition to depriving her of her language and other cultural elements, alienating her from the nonhuman nature that had been central to her tribal home is also crucial to this "missionary creed." Zitkala-Ša often notes the absence of nature in her new environment. Through indoctrination into white culture, she has "lost all consciousness of the nature world about [her]" and is left feeling that "even nature seemed to have no place for [her]" (96, 69). Given her model of nature as encompassing all life forms without prejudice, the "even" here has significant impact: the loss of nature equates to a loss of spirit and identity that is akin to death. If the "palefaces" are telegraph poles—homogenous tools sculpted out of, but ultimately separate from and fundamentally unlike, the natural world—then she herself becomes one such tool, especially later in life when she becomes a teacher.

The primary way Zitkala-Ša deals with her cultural and geographic alienation in these stories is through nostalgia—for the landscapes of the West, for her home, and for her mother, from whom she has become estranged. Dorothea M. Susag recognizes Zitkala-Ša's nostalgia, suggesting that while we might read in the stories a "nostalgic respect for a 'vanished' way of life," her writing "powerfully surpasses nostalgia" in the final analysis (21). While I concur with Susag's reading of Zitkala-Ša's stories as humanizing and empowering, I argue that it is *through*, rather than in spite of, nostalgia that the stories achieve their counter-hegemonic effects. Here, Susag displays the prevalent tendency among academic writers to dismiss nostalgia as an inherently conservative or politically impotent narrative. D. K. Meisenheimer Jr. reveals similar assumptions when he writes of Zitkala-Ša's work: "Just as there is no self-pity in Zitkala-Ša, there is no nostalgia" (121). To be fair, Meisenheimer is situating her stories within the genre of regionalism, which he defines as partly "elegiac ethnography"; his essay, then, is invested in formulating progressive potential for regionalism as it attempts to recuperate a "less tragic reading" of her work than the genre typically allows. Yet his definition of regionalism as inherently nostalgic—and nostalgia as inherently "tragic"—limits his reading of Zitkala-Ša's work (not to mention his understanding of regionalism), to the point of refusing to acknowledge the presence of a nostalgia that is everywhere in her stories.

For Susag and Meisenheimer, as for many critics, nostalgia is "naturally" a narrative that longs for, romanticizes, and eulogizes the past, but not a narrative that imagines a future, resists dominant power structures, or enables a critique of oppressive forces. However, it is not necessary—or necessarily desirable—to "surpass" nostalgia, or deny its existence, in order for a text to resist oppression. Rather, as Zitkala-Ša's stories indicate, counter-nostalgia can invert, complicate, and ultimately challenge dominant cultural narratives. In her deployment of nostalgia for nature, Zitkala-Ša picks up on the larger national trend of nostalgia for the landscapes of the American West after the closing of the frontier. White readers of the time would identify with the anxieties about development expressed in these stories and the concomitant loss of intimacy with nature feared by Roosevelt and others. While these dominant nostalgic narratives contributed to the displacement of American Indians in the West, Zitkala-Ša is able to speak to her audience through these very narratives, by carefully inverting them to contest the mistreatment they also justified.

Two key examples of such inversions are her chapters "The Big Red Apples" and "Land of the Red Apples," which combine a rewriting of the Christian Garden of Eden origin story with a reversal of Turner's frontier narrative. In these chapters Zitkala-Ša casts white civilization as the serpent that corrupted humanity and repositions Eden in the prefrontier West. In "The Big Red Apples," the final chapter in the larger section, "Impressions of an Indian Childhood," the trajectory of Western migration is geographically as well as symbolically reversed. Rather than positing the West as the new frontier, the "wonderful Eastern land" is situated as the new land of plenty—home of civilization, progressive technologies, and orchards where the young Indian children "could reach out [their] hands and pick all the red apples [they] could eat" (42). Here, Zitkala-Ša rewrites Turner's frontier narrative: in her Edenic temptation story, East, rather than West, is the promised land. For the young Zitkala-Ša, the East promises a land of abundant resources, "a more beautiful country," and most important, freedom to "roam among [the orchards]" (39, 42). Both physical landscape and the lure of plentiful nature help tempt her away from a home she loves dearly, even in spite of her mother's discouragement. In anticipation of happy times to come, she sets out eagerly for "the Wonderland" (40). With a word that ironically echoes common descriptions of American national parks as the nation's "Wonderlands," the text reminds us that these are lands from which Indians were expelled.

In case readers are tempted to identify with this sympathetic child's wide-eyed excitement about her journey East, Zitkala-Ša gives us plenty of hints that this mythical place will not live up to the image the palefaces have marketed. Her mother warns her not to heed "the white man's lies," since "their words are sweet, but . . . their deeds are bitter" (41). While her mother is often a voice of outspoken critique in the stories, an even more overt foreshadowing sentiment comes from Zitkala-Ša herself. Reminding the reader of the stories' retrospective narration and warning the reader of conflict to come, she writes, "Alas! They came, they saw, and they conquered!" (41). Rewriting Julius Caesar's often-quoted declaration of victory, she locates empire as central to the origin story of the West and applies this violent rhetoric to the U.S. assimilationist project. This statement situates American Indians as the victims of empire and sets the stage for the "Fall" that assimilation mandates.

Indeed, once she gets on the "iron horse" that is to transport her East to "Red Apple Country," disillusionment sets in quickly. Instead of a pleasurable ride, she is confronted by "throngs of staring palefaces" with "glassy blue eyes" that discomfit and "scrutinize" the children (47). Several white children sitting near her gawk rudely and "point . . . at [her] moccasined feet" while their mothers add fuel to the fire by "attract[ing] their children's further notice to [her] blanket." Rendered an exotic commodity subject to the white gaze, the narrator is kept "embarrassed . . . constantly on the verge of tears" (48). Missionaries try to appease the anxious children with candy—like the mythical apples, bait for the eager "pioneers." Throughout the stories, whites are cast in the role of Eden's serpentine devil, whose apple tempts the children with the promise of knowledge through civilization. Like Eve, Zitkala-Ša is exiled from her home after succumbing to temptation; unlike Eve, she does not feel shame at her "naked" exposure to the "semblance of civilization" that was supposed to be her salvation, but instead depicts the serpent as the guilty party (99). Portraying herself in sympathetic terms, Zitkala-Ša is "as frightened and bewildered as the captured young of a wild creature" (45). In contrast to a young girl's fear and naïve expectations, the white colonizers' treatment of the hopeful child and her companions comes across as merciless.

In "The Land of the Red Apples," the first chapter in "The School Days of an Indian Girl," the reader is privy to Zitkala-Ša's disappointment upon arrival. Having found only "whitewashed room[s]," "throngs of staring palefaces disturbed and troubled by [her]" and a perpetual homesickness, she "dream[s] of roaming as freely and happily as [she] had . . . on the Dakota plains" (49, 47). As her situation at school worsens, Zitkala-Ša increasingly longs for home and for her mother. Upon arrival, when she is tossed playfully into the air by a "rosy-cheeked paleface woman," Zitkala-Ša reflects, "My mother had never made a plaything of her daughter. Remembering this I began to cry aloud" (50). Similar nostalgic moments abound, and Zitkala-Ša often connects them to her biggest mistake: "dar[ing] to disregard nature's warning with such recklessness" (85). In short, for the white man's "papers [she] had forgotten the healing in trees and brooks" (97). The youthful narrative voice and repeated assertions of nostalgia help align readers with the story's political critique.

Although her nostalgia is for "Western rolling lands and unlassoed freedom," the West for which she longs is not Turner's. Rather, the "unlassoed freedom" of her childhood stands in stark contrast to the "civilizing machine" of institutionalized learning and disciplinary authority—the civilization Turner's teleology celebrates for "taming" the American West (66). Her nostalgia is also, to a large extent, for nature more generally. "Like a slender tree, [she] had been uprooted from [her] mother, nature, and God," and she longs to return to the "trees and brooks" of her childhood (97). By contrasting nature with the "iron" Eastern civilization she despises, Zitkala-Ša associates Indians with "the natural" and repositions civilization as a negative, brutal force, which works, in a sense, "against nature." If there is a linear trajectory of degeneration for American Indians—a "Fall" from a natural origin—Zitkala-Ša is clear that it has been initiated by white violence and forced assimilation.

* * *

Eventually—older, disillusioned, and "worn"—Zitkala-Ša becomes a schoolteacher herself. Although she does decide to "spend [her] energies in a work for the Indian race," it is with a sense of conflictedness; she does not subscribe uncritically to ideologies of "uplift" (81). Her eventual resignation from her teaching job follows upon the recognition that "the encroaching frontier settlers" were still conquering, and she tires of looking for "latent good in [her] white co-workers" (96). Shifting the burden of judgment away from herself, the final story concludes with a challenge to readers to reconsider the presumed fruits of assimilation:

Examining the neatly figured pages, and gazing upon the Indian girls and boys bending over their books, the white visitors walked out of the schoolhouse well satisfied: they were educating the children of the red man! They were paying a liberal fee to the government employees in whose able hands lay the small forest of Indian timber. In this fashion many have passed idly through the Indian schools during the last decade, afterward to boast of their charity to the North American Indian. But few there are who have paused to question whether real life or long-lasting death lies beneath this semblance of civilization. (98–99)

These oft-cited, if somewhat uncharacteristic, final lines are indicative of the powerful critique Zitkala-Ša is able to weave into her writing. Indeed, their placement in the final story, "Retrospection," leaves little doubt as to her position: "real life" is not found in the Eastern schoolhouse but in the West, at home, close to nature. By identifying herself and all American Indians with the "lost" nature that has been harvested for profit and development—the "small forest of Indian timber"—she links her people with popular understandings of nature as a commodity and generates sympathy for both. The passage also echoes other references in the stories to Indians as natural resources that have been exploited and mistreated. One poignant example occurs in "The Cutting of My Long Hair." After she endures her first haircut—one of many "extreme indignities" she suffers at school—she explains she has become "only one of many little animals driven by a herder" (56). Later, she describes herself as one such "herder" when she is "turn[ed] loose to pasture" to recruit new students in the West (85). "Retrospection" and these other references critique the utilitarian ethos, embodied by the NPS and a hallmark of the Progressive Era, that treats both nature and Native people as exploitable, consumable resources.

Moreover, in the final story's dramatic depiction of busy schoolchildren dutifully learning to assimilate, Zitkala-Ša describes a touristic gaze much like the one inflicted upon the Yosemite Indians at the Field Days. These "examiners" inflict a comparable othering of Native American culture that enables distance, objectification, then domination. Just as the Yosemite tourists were "well satisfied" at seeing their tax dollars at work in protecting both nature and culture, these "charitable" donors to the Indian schools participate in liberal notions of uplift that glorify the civilization Zitkala-Ša calls into question here. Thus, the phrase "liberal fee" becomes suggestively political: liberalism, as represented through the Indian school's benefactors, is critiqued in this passage for perpetuating cultural loss and homogeneity within capitalism's hegemony. Through its assumption of a universal, national citizen, and its efforts to compel all Americans to fit that mold, the Indian school extracted a "fee" from its students that was, indeed, "liberal."

Zitkala-Ša leaves her readers to wonder: At what cost is this "civilization" attained? And is it perhaps only a "semblance" of life that has been achieved? By this point in the stories, the reader has learned to identify the schools with a repressive disciplinary system that is cold and harsh to the point of inhumanity and to understand the schools as an example of "liberal strategies of government . . . that promise to create individuals who do not need to be governed by others, but will govern themselves, master themselves, care for themselves" (Rose 45). Understanding the schools in this light, the reader is prepared for Zitkala-Ša's message that, despite advertising themselves as an avenue to Americanization, the Eastern schools yield only "lost freedom" rather than the promised fruit of educational opportunity (52). The carrot of freedom-through-assimilation (enforced by the stick of disciplinary institutions) is revealed as an illusory reward. Racism prevents Indians from ever achieving a "civilized" American identity, and assimilation is revealed as a false promise.

A particularly poignant illustration of this racism occurred in Zitkala-Ša's own life when she represented Earlham College at the Indiana State Oratorical Contest in 1896. There, she was taunted by a large banner with a hand-drawn image of an Indian woman on it, labeled with the derogatory word "squaw." Zitkala-Ša was able to overcome these insults in life (she won second place in the contest) and in her stories where, to her credit, she turned the rhetorical tables on the offending racists by lamenting their "worse than barbarian rudeness," thus describing them as the "savages" they would accuse her of being (79). This real-world example of deploying frontier discourse mirrors the effective rhetorical reversals so prominent in *American Indian Stories*.

Claiming that not just freedom but also "real life" has been lost, Zitkala-Ša's counter-nostalgic stories disrupt the period's dominant nostalgia for "vanishing" Indian culture and locate Indian experience in real time and real space rather than in museumified parks, tourist scrapbooks, or a distant prehistorical era. Yet despite her powerful claims, the extent to which Zitkala-Ša subverted dominant narratives remains contested. As with her isolated acts of rebellion at the school, where the disciplinary mechanism of the educational institution continually attempted to "neutralize the effects of counter-power" that challenged the school's authority, it is questionable to what degree her stories' "counter-power" was defused by the school or absorbed by her white readers (Foucault, *Discipline* 219).

The Carlisle School tried to deflect Zitkala-Ša's attacks by "saying that her critique is true of all institutions" and claiming "that anything white America does for the Indians is better than the 'barbaric' state in which they are living" (Enoch 12). Far from being "true of all institutions," though, the kind of power functioning at the Indian schools was geared toward particular ends: the schools did not just train young Indians to blend into "the American 'melting pot'" but also "to adopt the work discipline of the Protestant ethic and to accept their proper place in society as a marginal class" (Lomawaima 211). A distinct history of oppression—legitimated in part by nostalgic nature narratives—differentiates the treatment of Indians from other objects of disciplinary institutions.

Even as Zitkala-Ša struggled to rewrite dominant narratives, the schools helped solidify Indians' marginality. While being "systematically divested of their land and other bases of an independent life," Indians were expected to be grateful for the opportunities the schools offered (Lomawaima 211). Much like freed slaves who were considered "uppity" if they did not continue to serve and demean themselves in front of whites, Zitkala-Ša was condemned as ungrateful for her Indian education. Appearing in a 1901 edition of the *Red Man*, one of two newspapers published by the Carlisle Indian School, a telling review of her story "The Soft-Hearted Sioux" was prefaced with this reprimand: "All that Zitkalasa [sic] has in the way of literary ability and culture she owes to the good people, who, from time to time, have taken her into their homes and hearts and given her aid. Yet not a word of gratitude or allusion to such kindness on the part of her friends has ever escaped her in any line of anything she has written for the public. By this course she injures herself and harms the educational work in progress for the race from which she sprang" (qtd. in Enoch 117). Implying that Zitkala-Ša did not "know her place," this reviewer dismissed her story on moral grounds because it called into question the disciplinary goals of the Carlisle School. Through its journalistic propaganda in both newspapers—the *Indian Helper* and the *Red Man*—the Carlisle School enforced the same view. "Insolence" was often pointed out as something for "his boys and girls [to] guard against," lest they be reprimanded by "the Man-on-the-bandstand"—a symbolic representation of the school's central authority as well as a physical statue recreating that authority, visibly, on the school grounds (Enoch 122).

Likewise, there were advantages and disadvantages that came with being considered the "darling" of her enthusiastic white audience. The following account, which appeared in a 1900 *Harper's Bazaar* column called "Persons Who Interest Us," foregrounds some of the challenges she faced: "A young Indian girl, who is attracting much attention in Eastern cities on account of her beauty and many talents, is Zitkala-Sa [sic]. . . . Zitkala-Sa is of the Sioux tribe of Dakota and until her ninth year was a veritable little savage, running wild over the prairie and speaking no language but her own" (qtd. in Fisher vii). Considered noteworthy partly on account of her physical beauty—defined in opposition to her "savage" youth—Zitkala-Ša achieved popularity according to criteria determined by her white audiences. There was always the threat that if she did not conform to these standards—both in writing and in physical appearance—she would be silenced. Within the rigid ideological structures presented by the "Us" of *Harper's* elite readership, it is impressive that Zitkala-Ša achieved the amount of success she did, and the apparent ambivalence in many of her stories comes as no surprise.

Yet it is clear that, even in the face of such powerful forces, Zitkala-Ša revises the dominant frontier narrative. It is not a savage wildness that has been overcome by the assimilation process, but "wild *freedom*" that has been captured and snuffed out by cultural imperialism and violent conquest (8, my emphasis). Rather than longing for an idyllic past that has mysteriously disappeared, *American Indian Stories* longs for a historically rooted, "re-placed," tribal community. Her longing details how her loss came about and expresses how much was lost through the violent displacement enabled by frontier rhetoric. This loss is precisely what generates resistance; through displaying her own nostalgia for nature and exploiting that of her audience, Zitkala-Ša effectively makes her critique. Literature, particularly the genre of sentimental fiction within which she was working, provides the ideal outlet for the manipulation of readers' emotions in the service of fostering critical thinking about past and present. By the end of the stories, readers have been forced to ask "questions concerning [their] native land, native language, [and] the laws that govern" them; the natural "home" for which readers may long has become far more complicated (Foucault, "Nietzsche" 162). Capitalizing on the modern period's widespread frontier nostalgia and inverting that nostalgia through redefinitions of both nature and Indian culture, Zitkala-Ša's stories achieve a measure of resistance to white norms.

She also attempted to bring about reform through existing political organizations as well as the one she founded in 1926: the National

Council of American Indians. She served as president of this organization until she died in 1938. Prior to that, she worked as secretary of the Society of the American Indian from 1916 until its dissolution in 1920. Zitkala-Ša's marriage to Raymond T. Bonnin also involved her in politics, since her husband worked as a lawyer for the Bureau of Indian Affairs. *American Indian Stories* includes her most overtly political text, "America's Indian Problem." This final piece in the collection overturns the myth of Europeans as compassionate protectors of Indians through an examination of the Bureau of Indian Affairs that highlights its "sham protection," its "fraud, corruption, and institutional incompetence," and its erroneous characterization of native residents as "wards" of the state rather than sovereign citizens (192–93). She directly addresses white women activists and attempts to enlist their support in helping American Indians "have [their] day in court" (186). In fiction and in her life, Zitkala-Ša's work undermined white civilization as a reliable touchstone and began to carve out a self-determined natural, cultural, and historical space for American Indians.

Even though she formed her own family, Zitkala-Ša never reconciled with her mother, from whom she was alienated in the ways her stories describe. As such, loss and nostalgia underlay her personal life and political career much as they do her stories. Counter-nostalgic longing for a natural home, where all living beings are treated with respect regardless of gender, race, or other social constructions, provided Zitkala-Ša with a model for socially just societies—societies that are unrealized in the present and, so, are relegated to the future even as they draw on the past. Like all pleas for social justice, hers resounds "only for those ears that are bent with compassion to hear it" (68).

"PLUCKED UP BY THE ROOTS":
THE NOSTALGIC TRAJECTORIES
OF THE SOUTHERN AGRARIANS

"It is out of fashion these days to look backward rather than forward," admits John Crowe Ransom at the start of the opening essay in *I'll Take My Stand: The South and the Agrarian Tradition* (1). For Ransom and the other Southern agrarians, looking backward was a radical, if not a fashionable, way to counter a modernity they accused of breeding alienated individuals who had lost touch with community and place. These writers found an ideal "extended metaphor" in the American South, home of "a society, they felt, in which leisure, tradition, aesthetic and religious impulses had not been lost in the pursuit of economic gain" (Rubin xi, viii). Along with Robert Penn Warren, Allen Tate, and Donald Davidson, Ransom was one of the "Nashville Fugitives," a group of writers at Vanderbilt University who began publishing poetry and criticism in the *Fugitive* and other publications in the early 1920s that lamented the debased state of life and the fine arts within an increasingly industrial and materialistic nation. The Fugitives joined forces with the Southern agrarians—writers, teachers, and other "men of letters"—to publish *I'll Take My Stand* in 1930 (Rubin xi).

The agrarians constructed Southern tradition out of two basic principles: first, a respect for nature—coded as white—and second, an explicitly anti-industrial and anti-national political agenda. Writing against what they saw as an "industrial regime," the agrarians prized a regional culture that valued "regard for a certain terrain" (the Southern landscape); tradition, identified with white European cultural heritage and tied to the aristocratic South; leisure, the presumed result of cultivating tradition; and labor, which should take place in nature and proceed "leisurely" (1). The South was a "lost cause" that was worth fighting for, even if it was likely to be a difficult, even unwinnable battle (2).

Most notably for my study, *I'll Take My Stand* yokes nostalgia to a highly racialized ideal of nature as it sounds its call to arms in support of "the Southern tradition" (x). In his provocatively titled essay "Reconstructed but Unregenerate," Ransom recommends physical and cultural "rootedness" as the best prescription for a country sickened by industrialization. He decries progressives as having lost touch with traditional values by obsessively looking forward. According to Ransom, "The progressivist says in effect: Do not allow yourself to feel homesick" (6). Thus, nostalgia—feeling homesick—becomes, for Ransom and the other agrarians, a necessary corrective to progressive values and, as such, an inherently conservative emotion and narrative. Ransom defines nostalgia as follows:

> Memories of the past are attended with a certain pain called nostalgia. . . . Nostalgia is a kind of growing pain, psychically speaking. It occurs to our sorrow when we have decided that it is time for us, marching to some magnificent destiny, to abandon an old home, an old provincial setting, or an old way of living to which we had become habituated. It is the complaint of human nature in its vegetative aspect, when it is plucked up by the roots from the place of its origin and transplanted in foreign soil, or even left dangling in the air. And it must be nothing else but nostalgia, the instinctive objection to being transplanted, that chiefly prevents the deracination of human communities and their complete geographical dispersion as the casualties of an insatiable wanderlust. (6)

For Ransom, nostalgia operates as both a narrative tool—to manipulate readers into sharing the author's political beliefs—and a collectively shared sentiment, which readers might choose to adopt. Ransom recovers nostalgia as a productive emotional experience that grounds an individual or a culture in the conservative values of home, family and community. He presumes nostalgia will "cure" victims of progress by causing them to appreciate the values of staying, or returning, home. More than that, his definition links nostalgia with mobility: Ransom posits nostalgia as a much-needed antidote not just to progress itself but also to the migrations—both actual and symbolic—that unchecked progress spurs.

Ransom picks up on nostalgia's historical meanings—its original "diagnosis" in soldiers and exiles—when he describes the emotion as a homesickness felt by displaced people. Yet there is a strange paradox embedded in his definition. How can this "growing pain" be both the result of an alluring "march" toward "some magnificent destiny" *and* a backlash against the invasive act of being "plucked up by the roots" from one's "origin"? How can it be both an unfortunate repercussion of "an insatiable wanderlust" *and* a resistance to being "transplanted in foreign soil"? This contradiction involves a fundamental difference in agency and intentionality. That is, Ransom's explanation contains a tension between nostalgia that results from deliberate action—the consequence borne by the marchers and insatiable wanderers—and a passively afflicted nostalgia, suffered by the uprooted transplants. Indeed, we might say there are two different versions of nostalgia at work here, and two different groups of people experiencing this "originary" longing.

On the surface, Ransom's prose assumes "wanderlust" is a trait common to all modern individuals, albeit a trait one can and should keep in check. Many of his white readers would share the assumption of a common "magnificent" destiny, whether or not they shared Ransom's wariness of this temptation.[1] But the experiences of the passive nostalgics—the ones whose nostalgia was sparked as they were "plucked up" and either "transplanted" or "left dangling in the air"—are also invoked by Ransom's argument. Perhaps unintentionally, Ransom's dual account of nostalgia calls to mind others who were forced to leave home: the uprooted slaves upon whose labor the "leisure" of the Southern aristocracy depended. Just as Ransom conflates labor and leisure—after all, labor *was* leisurely if you were a member of the Southern aristocracy during slavery—he confuses voluntary travel with the forced migrations of the slave trade and the migrations of blacks out of the South during this time.

Of course, the degree to which South-to-North migrations were "forced" is debatable. Many historians characterize the Great Migration as a demonstration of agency on the part of Southern blacks.[2] Still, it seems important to recognize the constraining forces—economic and otherwise—directing this migratory flow, even as we celebrate its landmark power. Ransom's rhetoric becomes even more interesting when we take into account the historian James Grossman's observations that many Southern whites attributed the Great Migration "to 'the Negro's love of travel' or 'wanderlust'" (56). This "travel" narrative fueled white hopes that black migrants would return to the South to resume their "natural" role as the region's primary labor force. In reality, few migrants did return (Grossman, "Black Labor" 56). Although both white and black communities had natural connections to Southern landscapes according to this formulation, whites linked themselves to the leisurely enjoyment of nature, while the role of blacks was tied to labor. In effect, the "natural home" narrative reified both nature and African Americans as (still) the property of white Southern aristocrats.

Ransom's essay suggests close ties between race and region, but it only alludes to another kind of nostalgia that emerges more clearly in some of the other pieces in the collection. For instance, Stark Young's capstone essay, "Not in Memoriam, but in Defense," makes mention of "the nostalgia for one's own blood," a phrase that leaves little doubt that the Southern culture for which these authors are nostalgic is understood as a natural expression of whiteness (336). Even for Ransom, those whose "blood" renders them subordinate to this elite group are a spectral presence; they slip into the text unannounced, despite his determination to erase the violence inherent in slavery. When African Americans do receive mention, Ransom justifies their position in the Old South by claiming that "people were for the most part in their right places. Slavery was a feature monstrous enough in theory, but, more often than not, humane in practice." He insists that "all were committed to a form of leisure, and that their labor itself was leisurely" (14). Given the racism so deeply embedded in this text, it is not surprising that Ransom seems unaware of his paradoxical definition of nostalgia, that he claims to speak for "all" Southerners, or that he neglects to explore the nostalgia resulting from the historical or present-day trajectories of those whom his Southern practices uprooted.

Although Ransom and the other Southern agrarians might be considered extremists in their racist conceptions of the past, the nostalgia they cherished was powerful in its time and beyond. Like most traditions, theirs was carefully crafted. Part of the anthology's appeal lies in the way it tells the story of that cultural tradition. Their simple, inspirational tale of an essentially good community helps generate longing for a South in which everyone is "in their right place."[3] Imagining an origin that is coherent, reductive, and romanticized allows these writers to sublimate the extremely problematic realities underpinning such a story—in this case, white supremacy, forced migration and enslavement, and the centrality of black labor to the South's "way of life." Their traditional South was "a society that perhaps never existed" but, in their minds, "*should have existed*" and so might serve as a model for the future (xiv, original emphasis). While some of the contributors admit they "can never go back" to this way of life, the nostalgic origin still works as an ideal, as a guide for present-day beliefs (Young 328).

Like Thomas Dixon Jr.'s *The Clansman*—but without the violent struggle—*I'll Take My Stand* constructs a narrative of homeland defense: the South is being attacked by Northern-led industrialism, which is threatening to deprive the region of its cultural heritage. Their manifesto retaliates against this perceived invasion by conjuring an ideal of a lost pastoral environment in which humans and nature coexist peacefully, aesthetic appreciation of nature is an integral part of everyday life, and leisurely labor allows ample time to enjoy the beautiful landscape. Their nostalgia aligns them with Turner's in that both told stories of national decline and contrasted a "fallen" present with an Edenic past. But unlike Turner and most other early-century proponents of nostalgia for the lost frontier, the agrarians were not nationalistic; nor were they primarily interested, like Roosevelt, in regenerating manliness by replaying the violence of the frontier. Although the agrarians did fear for their manhood—they end their statement of principles with the threat of "impotence" (xxx)—and they certainly shared Roosevelt's concerns about overcivilization, the rhetorical focus of *I'll Take My Stand* is on recreating a pastoral environment, not a frontier, to which to return.[4] This focus makes sense given their vested interest in minimizing the violence that enabled their "leisurely" Southern culture.

Contrary to progress-courting pioneers, who were fighting a losing battle—because "nature wears out man before man can wear out nature"—the agrarians claimed a harmonious relationship with nature, not a combative one (9). Theirs was a way of life "deeply grounded in the love of the tiller for the soil," where affection for a "spot of ground" was one of life's fundamental principles (18–19). Leo Marx points out that "the soft veil of nostalgia that hangs over our urbanized landscape is largely a vestige of the once dominant image of an undefiled, green republic, a quiet land of forests, villages, and farms dedicated to the pursuit of happiness" (Marx 6). It is precisely such a "green republic" that the agrarians construct and romanticize, and the end result is a nonfictional example of what Marx calls the sentimental pastoral (5). Given the history of agrarianism in the Southern United States and the popularity of early-century regionalist movements, tapping into the widespread modern nostalgia for the pastoral was a timely tactic for this expository manifesto.

While the violence embedded in frontier narratives is comparatively easy to pinpoint, the violence in pastoral narratives can be as harmful, but less obvious. Just as the frontier requires the domination of nature and those people associated with it, the pastoral can justify (or obscure) social relations that are hierarchical, racist, and imperialist. What at first seem to be incompatible narratives—in this case, Ransom's nostalgic invocation of a lost pastoral world and his simultaneous brushing aside of those whose labor made that world possible—are integrally connected. If "in the pastoral economy nature supplies most of the herdsman's needs and, even better, nature does virtually all of the work," then the agrarians' "nature" is synonymous with slaves (Marx 23). As Jeffrey Myers argues in relation to the nation's best-known agrarian, Thomas Jefferson, "racial and ecological hegemony merge" in narratives (like *Notes on the State of Virginia*) that define white Americans in opposition both to people of color and to nature (19). The Southern agrarians' "stand" reminds us, then, how race and nature are, to use Myers's phrase, "converging stories."

Even today, a pastoral ideal continues to resound in some contemporary environmental writing. Agrarianism is sometimes still characterized in terms similar to those of the Southern agrarians. In *The Art of the Commonplace*, for instance, Wendell Berry posits a Jeffersonian agrarian ideal as an antidote to Americans' "general homelessness" (Wirzba vii). Although Norman Wirzba claims in his introduction that Berry's essays are "not nostalgic" (xix), there is a measure of carefully doled out longing in them. The cultural shifts Berry challenges are similar to the ones the Southern agrarians resisted: an unselfconscious embrace of progress, a loss of leisure time, an unnatural separation between humans and their environments, an increasingly specialized capitalist economy (which has become primarily knowledge-based in recent decades), and the sense that we have "cut ourselves off from [our] roots" (ix). But Berry's nostalgia is not for a way of life based on exploiting others. To the contrary, in "Racism and the Economy" he argues that the exploitation of African Americans through slavery was based not strictly on racism but on a desire to avoid hard work; he clarifies that "their labor promised to free us of the obligations of stewardship" (47). Berry's work thus highlights one of the realities the Southern agrarians' nostalgia overlooked: that slave labor enabled others' freedom.

Berry's belief that migration to cities was an instance of "dispossession" and a lost opportunity (50) aligns him with bell hooks, whose often-anthologized essay "Touching the Earth" also reminds us that "black people were first and foremost a people of the land, farmers" (hooks 173). She argues for the importance of reaffirming cultural traditions based on "renew[ing] our relationship to the earth" and "remember[ing] the way of our ancestors" (173). In moving to reconnect African Americans with nonhuman nature, hooks advocates an environmental justice ethic based on an awareness of blacks' agrarian history. Even though Berry self-identifies as "something of an anachronism" in contemporary America (4), he and hooks both insist that agrarianism is not an outmoded or archaic way of life but rather an ethic that can be lived out in the present.

Whether these new agrarian manifestos seem anachronistic or not today is debatable. But during the 1920s and '30s, when many regionalist writers and artists articulated similar values, they likely would have seemed timely, if perhaps a bit "out of fashion." The Southern agrarians were far from alone in valuing a strong attachment to place and a notion of nature as central to everyday life. Most interwar regionalists hoped to counter the negative aspects of modernization—overindustrialization, progress for progress's sake, poorly planned urbanization, the rise of consumer culture, and the emergence of a particularly modern brand of alienation—with an emphasis on folk culture and local heritage. The following chapter entertains the idea of the Harlem Renaissance as a kind of regional movement, albeit one that diverges from writers who demonized cities and glorified rural lifestyles. Even some urban-set novels, like Claude McKay's *Home to Harlem*—the subject of chapter 2—did not entirely abandon the pastoral or the nostalgia associated with it. Indeed, McKay deploys nostalgic memories of pastoral settings in the rural South and romantic ideals of Haiti (both of which may have been influenced by his own nostalgia for his Jamaican homeland) alongside celebrations of African primitivism to expose negative living and working conditions in the present. Like Zitkala-Ša, McKay identified himself and other black Americans with a more natural form of culture that countered modernist anxieties about becoming overly civilized. But while Zitkala-Ša refused to be labeled "savage" (indeed, she hurled the insult back at her oppressors), McKay tapped into, embraced, and revised modern narratives of "primitivism" that marked African Americans as the exclusive owners of desirable cultural traits. McKay also exhibits the simultaneously local and global dimensions of modernity when he takes nostalgia beyond national boundaries, where it can resonate at both personal and transnational scales. Juggling frontier and pastoral discourse, McKay's work attests to the flexibility and impact of pastoral nostalgia—even if the past it invokes is far from perfect.

2 / "Home Thoughts": The Transnational Routes of Nostalgia in Claude McKay's *Home to Harlem*

With the Western frontier now several-decades "closed," the "Great War" in the not-so-distant past, and increasing mechanization, industrialization, and mass production creating anxiety in the present, many modern authors shared Willa Cather's feeling that the world had "broke[n] in two" (*Not Under Forty* v).[1] Regionalist literature like Cather's reflected a widespread modernist nostalgia, but it was distinguished from other forms of modernism by its attempts to heal this sense of cleavage through rootedness in place and a "return" to an idealized, often pastoral, premodern society. Although most regionalists frowned upon pioneers for the same reasons Ransom and the Southern agrarians did, nostalgia for the frontier was sometimes an implicit subplot in regionalist fiction. As Robert L. Dorman explains in his survey of interwar regionalism, many regionalist writers invoked a revised frontier myth to highlight "the folk characteristics that pioneers displayed at special moments along that modernizing continuum of development . . . when culture and place melded, community flourished, a 'yeomanry' emerged." Interwar regionalists looked to these "special moments" to retreat "to a more humane and heroic past" (87).

Unfortunately, some aspects of the past are neither humane nor heroic. The nostalgia espoused by some regionalists risked re-naturalizing racial difference (and race-based inequalities) even through a seemingly benign celebration of pastoral nature.[2] Cather's *The Professor's House*, with its appropriative nostalgia for indigenous culture in the Southwest and its celebration of the masculine frontier explorer, is a case in point.[3] This

novel exemplifies how "backward looking" regionalist texts could reproduce hierarchical social dynamics and sustain the frontier ideology that
Zitkala-Ša and other writers of the early twentieth century were working
against. Although the pastoral region masquerades as a peaceful locale,
it often implies its precursor: the conquest of nature and the oppression
of people that accompanied the frontier's "taming."

There are, of course, limits to generalizing about any literary movement, especially one defined by dispersal, and I do not mean to imply
that all regionalist texts deal in these problematic forms of nostalgia.[4]
Moreover, recent studies have productively reconsidered regionalism, to
the point where it is questionable whether the category is still meaningful in any historical or formalist sense. New work by literary scholars,
architecture theorists, and "New Western" historians advocates a "critical regionalism," which suggests, among other things, that attentiveness
to local-global nexuses is essential to understanding regions.[5] Many contemporary scholars are heeding historian Lewis Mumford's warning to
"never us[e] the word regional without mentally adding to it the idea of
the universal" (qtd. in Campbell, *Rhizomatic West* 51). This new scholarship tends to downplay physical environment and define regionalism
"less [as] a term of geographical determinism and more as a discourse or
a mode of analysis, a vantage point within the network of power relations
that provides a location for critique and resistance" (Fetterley and Pryse
11). As scholars and writers struggle to recast regional character in the
context of a rapidly homogenizing, increasingly technological, and easily commodified world, it makes sense to understand regions as contact
zones, rhizomes, or process geographies.[6]

Whichever terminology one prefers, regions are dynamic places
that should be characterized not just by their "roots" but also by their
"routes": the migrations, itineraries, and mobilities of the diverse people
that inhabit, pass through, and give meaning to any place. As James
Clifford suggests, "Travels and contacts are crucial sites for an unfin-
ished modernity" (2). This tension between "roots" and "routes" is an
especially useful one for thinking about a *regional* modernity in which
nostalgia was commonplace. Indeed, seeing literary regionalism as a site
of critique and resistance should involve a renewed attention to how nostalgia contributes to that critique.

Although it is not typically labeled "regionalism" per se—and should
not be casually treated as such—the Harlem Renaissance did engage
contemporaneous discourses about nostalgia as well as the pastoral
and frontier narratives that were central to regionalist ideologies. The

movement also participated in a broader, modern "Return to the Primitive," albeit on its own particular terms (Cooper xiii). In this chapter, I treat Harlem as a modernist region in that it engages contemporaneous discourses and anticipates current trends in regionalist theory. With its complex migratory patterns (routes) and its simultaneous location of a unique black culture (roots), both the space of Harlem and the literary-cultural movement it spawned can be productively understood in terms of both.

Of course, as Houston A. Baker Jr. and others have shown, the Harlem Renaissance differed from other modernist movements in important ways and must be seen as part of a distinct Afro-American historical, discursive, literary-intellectual tradition. Opting for the more "inclusive" term "renaissancism," Baker suggests that the movement was successful for its "heralding of a countermodernism . . . a drive unlike the exquisite disillusionment and despair of Britain and Jazz Age U.S.A." (123). Indeed, its approach to urban life contrasted with mainstream modernist—and most regionalist—literatures, which tended toward a view of cities as both producers and symptoms of modern alienation. The relative optimism of Harlem Renaissance writers, especially their enthusiasm for urban life, differentiates their work from the anti-urbanism that characterizes so many modernist texts.

Hopeful exuberance does not foreclose nostalgia, though. Although urban space may have been the primary site for "impetus, empowerment, and inspiration," rural nature, often nostalgically invoked in the form of pastoral environments, also had a part to play in Harlem Renaissance texts (Baker Jr. 122). Rural nature has, understandably, been a fraught, often fearful, space for African Americans.[7] Yet as Paul Outka shows in *Race and Nature: From Transcendentalism to the Harlem Renaissance*, some Harlem Renaissance writers felt enough distance from their Southern pasts to undertake "a careful embrace of the beauty of the rural landscape" in their work and to depict an "anguished longing" for connections to the natural world that have been lost (172). Despite these acknowledgments, Outka's study seldom mentions the "more positive relations to nature" that, as reviewer John Claborn notes, generate a counter-hegemonic "solidarity" through a "pastoral vision of nature" (88).

This pastoral vision does not have to be located in the American South. Some African American texts looked to Africa as the origin of a distinctive and positive black relationship to rural nature beginning at least as early as *The Souls of Black Folk*. In "Of the Faith of the

Fathers," W. E. B. Du Bois argues that blacks possess a historically rich culture, defined by religion, music, and a profound connection to nature that underlies both. In opposition to the "lie" of white culture and the "hypocritical compromise" he identifies as its "price," this essay in his seminal "singing book" characterizes black music as "the most original and beautiful expression of human life and longing yet born on American soil [and] *sprung from the African forests*," and religion as initially "*nature-worship*," also with roots in Africa (Baker Jr. 122; Du Bois 116, 118, emphasis added). According to Du Bois, blacks possess a uniquely "keen, delicate appreciation for Nature" that is historical and spiritual and, as such, is an important foundation for a positive formulation of African American culture in the modern present (120). Alain Locke's *The New Negro* continued and popularized this idea of natural culture by collecting a "panoply of folk sounds" and other "traditional artistic forms" that might be likened to the folk aesthetic of regionalists if it weren't for the fact that it situated Africa, rather than the United States, as this aesthetic's origin (122).[8]

For African American writers, the articulation of a more "natural" culture was a risky one, not least because of its implicit race essentialism. Managing this risk was fundamental to the Harlem Renaissance's project. Celebrating and carving out a unique black artistic culture—a goal that went hand-in-hand with debunking racial stereotypes—depended on maintaining notions of an essential African American race. Writers of the period struggled to negotiate the slippery category of race, which they needed, to some degree, as a site of coherence for their art, alongside the expectations and stereotypes held by white audiences, which they strove to defuse and dispel. Writers had to negotiate the "depth model" of race that dominated the hard sciences during this period. The idea that external and contingent racial markers, such as skin color, were understood as manifestations of an immutable interior (racial) nature corresponded to a shift toward internalizing—and further "naturalizing"—race in bodies.[9]

More liberal notions of race were beginning to emerge in the social sciences during the modern period. Most significantly, Chicago School sociologists established a set of assumptions and approaches that would guide social scientists for decades. Strategies like Robert E. Park's race-relations cycle—"a way of analyzing group relations and assessing a 'minority' group's progress along a fixed continuum"—along with theories like symbolic interactionism and Park's "marginal man" formulation served to "focus attention on racial dynamics as the irrational products of individual pathologies" (Omi and Winant 10). By contemporary standards, even their comparatively progressive attempts to connect race to culture and environment too often reinforced dominant technologies of race. For instance, in *Asian/American*, David Palumbo-Liu makes a strong case that, like more hegemonic models of race, Park's ultimately positions blackness as degenerative to white civilization. Interestingly, Park himself notes that in his contemporaneous United States, the census defined "a Negro" as "a person who passes for a Negro in the community where he lives" (293). Passing is but one indication of a long-standing insecurity about racial visibility, even as race continued to be naturalized and internalized in various ways. While one might view the twentieth century as a slow transition toward a general agreement that race is biologically insignificant, it is important to remember that race, like nature and Indianness, never fully makes this paradigm shift. Indeed, racial paradigms are themselves historically unstable.[10]

As a high-profile site where paradoxical notions of race, nature, and nation played out, Harlem was in many ways an unstable and incoherent space. Perhaps no one embodies the complicated politics of this modern city better than Claude McKay, a writer whose life and work offer revealing glimpses into a rich literary and historical period. "Jamaican by birth, British by nationality, and African American by cultural and political alignment," McKay embodies a diasporic subjectivity that was not unusual for Harlem in the 1920s, at which time approximately one-quarter of its residents were born outside the United States (Xavier 728; Osofsky 131). With his extensive and often politically motivated travels through Europe, the Soviet Union, and Africa, McKay's life mirrors the "literary cosmopolitanism" we find in his writing (Lowney 415). While he is often characterized as first and foremost a poet—his well-known sonnet "If We Must Die" has been called the "inaugural address" of the Harlem Renaissance[11]—his novels have begun to receive much-deserved attention in recent years.

Home to Harlem, McKay's first published novel,[12] was both popular and polarizing when it came out in 1928. Although it was a best seller, most black reviewers decried the book as "a black version of [Carl Van Vechten's] *Nigger Heaven*," which had been published two years earlier (Cooper 245). Hearty praises sung by white reviewers only fueled the controversy among black leaders. In his well-known review, Du Bois wrote that he felt "distinctly like taking a bath" after reading "the dirtier parts of its filth." He further accused McKay of "cater[ing] to that prurient demand on the part of white folk" to witness black "licentiousness," presumably for the money such catering would bring him (qtd. in Stoff 131). As part of an older generation of black leaders and artists, including Alain Locke, James Weldon Johnson, Jessie Fauset, and Charles S. Johnson, Du Bois worried about perpetuating stereotypes and instead "wanted to project a positive, even a heroic, image of blacks and black life" (Cooper 239). It is not surprising, then, that he would balk at a novel whose cast of characters includes "pimps and prostitutes, homosexuals and drug addicts, loan sharks and labor scabs, alcoholics, gamblers, sadomasochists, and corrupt cops" (Cooper 242). Of these early Harlem Renaissance leaders, only James Weldon Johnson was publicly supportive of *Home to Harlem*.

Even before this novel came out, the older generation of black writers and leaders found themselves in conflict with a new generation, including McKay, Langston Hughes, Countee Cullen, Jean Toomer, Zora Neale Hurston, Nella Larsen, Rudolph Fisher, Richard Bruce Nugent, and Wallace Thurman, who sought to represent *all* aspects of black culture, regardless of concern for white audience expectations. These writers made it "the artist's right and duty to discuss any aspect of black life that moved him to creative expression," even at the risk of courting stereotypes (Cooper 242). *Home to Harlem* can be read as a "militant assertion" of this belief (242). McKay was quite pleased with the novel's popularity. Following its publication, he "mischievously" told his publisher: "I see *Home to Harlem* like an impudent dog has [moved] right in among the best sellers in New York" (237). McKay also responded directly to Du Bois, saying in his own defense: "deep-sunk in depravity through he may be, the author of *Home to Harlem* prefers to remain unrepentant and unregenerate" (244). I can't help but point out that McKay's use of the word "unregenerate" echoes Ransom's. McKay's depiction of black culture is certainly at odds with Ransom's romanticization of a Southern culture based on slavery, but both authors meant to celebrate and, in a sense, defend a way of life through their writing.

In both cases this way of life was not, strictly speaking, "American." Indeed, like the complicated affiliations with nationality expressed by the Southern agrarians and other regionalists, not to mention those experienced personally by McKay, the relationship of the Harlem Renaissance to the nation was anything but transparent. Michelle Stephens identifies Caribbean Americans, including migrants from McKay's homeland of Jamaica, as having "no easily identifiable national homelands" (596). In her discussion of black transnationalism in the modern period, Stephens wonders if these colonial subjects might "be included in the new

European nationalisms emerging with the decline of empire? If not, could they turn to Africa as an originary homeland? Or should they locate home and nationalism in American citizenship" (597)? If Harlem is a geographic locus for a rebirth of culture, a reunion of diverse people, and a reinvention of past artistic forms, then it "owes its vitality to the very diaspora it recenters" (Fabre and Feith 3). In other words, if its "vitality" can be attributed, in part, to its diasporic composition, then Harlem's "renaissancism" was shaped by the historically different experiences of its residents. Literature like McKay's recognizes the tenuous and sometimes oppressive identity of the nation and instead "recenters" its own version of a "vitality" that refuses to be subsumed under American nationalism.

Written not long after the 1924 Immigration Act and the Marcus Garvey controversy, *Home to Harlem* was published in a tumultuous sociopolitical climate in which issues of national and transnational identity were on many people's radars. *The New Negro* emphasized the cultural pluralism of Harlem; in particular, several of its contributors had emigrated from the Caribbean. Although Haitians accounted for a small percentage of Caribbean immigrants, Haiti's revolutionary history and the American occupation of the country were issues that many Afro-American intellectuals were aware of. In fact, Du Bois's scathing review of McKay's first novel appeared in an issue of *The Crisis* devoted to challenging U.S. imperialism in Haiti.[13] McKay, who was living in Europe at the time of *Home to Harlem*'s publication, had become somewhat impatient with African American intellectual life, particularly its fickle attention to the situation in Haiti. In his essay on *Home to Harlem*, John Lowney claims that "McKay's exposure of the devastating impact of the American invasion of Haiti underscored the necessity for a renewed counterhegemonic pan-Africanist solidarity" (414). Indeed, the transnational perspective of this novel offers a helpful lens through which to read transracial relationships in Harlem and beyond its boundaries.

Lowney's article has been instrumental in "remapping" the novel in terms of its characters' diasporic migrations. Stephens, too, has identified McKay as one of several key figures in what she calls black transnational cultural formations in the United States, which tried to produce "*international* political and cultural conceptions of black collective identity" (597–98, emphasis in original). Carl Pedersen has moved to "resituate McKay as part of a Caribbean as well as a global African diasporic [literary] tradition" (260). And Dorothea Löbbermann reads Harlem as a place that "reaches out in many directions: spatially, into the international African diaspora (within the United States and outside it); temporally, into the African and American pasts, and—both with its utopian force and from our contemporary retrospective positions—into the future" (210). Along with more comprehensive studies of the Harlem Renaissance,[14] such as Baker Jr.'s, which have helped rescue the movement from its confinement to domestic borders and its mislabeling as a "failure," these scholars have revitalized conversations about *Home to Harlem*—conversations that have been limited by its rather negative initial reception in the black intellectual community and by the critical focus on the "primitive" characteristics of McKay's protagonist, Jake Brown.[15]

Attending closely to both the spatial and temporal dimensions of McKay's novel enhances understandings of Harlem as a simultaneously regional and transnational "home" and renders visible the complex politics of nostalgia in this era. *Home to Harlem*'s nostalgia differs from the Southern agrarians' pastoral nostalgia and from Roosevelt's nostalgia for the frontier, in that McKay invokes a more complex natural object: a natural *culture*—inspired by the African jungle but channeled through the Caribbean islands as well as the rural U.S. South—that exists on its own terms, irrespective of white culture or white nationalism. The civilization promoted by Roosevelt relied upon a constructed "savage" or "primitive" element against which to define itself. But McKay's primitivism declares its independence from these definitions, in the process "validating an autonomous racial identity" (Xavier 724). By re-rooting African American culture in its own historical terrain—and re-routing it across transnational geographies—McKay reclaims savagery as a healthy part of a precolonial black history and identifies "life" as something only blacks possess. McKay's counter-nostalgia thus does not simply invert but attempts to transform the dominant discourses of race, nature, and nation with which he was critically engaged. While the success of his attempt is debatable,[16] the effort is certainly bold. *Home to Harlem* can be read as another example of how dominant nostalgia was being contested by African American writers—who, like Indians, were often deemed "more natural" and so dismissed as "savage"—in their endeavor to "mov[e] Afro-Americans from subservience, low esteem, and dependency to the status of respected and boldly outspoken nation" (Baker Jr. 121).

McKay's addition of Caribbean migration stories to this endeavor is significant. If, as Lowney suggests, a "common experience of migration was crucial for the development of a pan-African consciousness among

Harlem intellectuals" (417), then the nostalgia accompanying these migrations should be addressed as part of any emergent multiracial, transnational consciousness that was forming during this time. This chapter examines in greater detail the process Ransom alludes to of being "snatched away from [one's] native land" and suggests that the nostalgia resulting from migrations that are, to some degree, forced may ignite a critique of the compulsory circumstances. Indeed, migration that is not entirely voluntary often carries with it counter-nostalgic impulses. McKay's black transnational nostalgia also complicates understandings of modern American literary regionalism as only interested in the local. Following the trajectories of his characters' nostalgias—locating them in historical and spatial terms—highlights Harlem as an intellectually and culturally rich "regional/national/global nexus" (Clifford 100). In crossing national boundaries, McKay's nostalgia decenters the American nation, complicates its dominant nostalgic metanarratives about race and nature, and allies his characters—and perhaps his readers—in a critique of racism.

* * *

McKay explains the value of nostalgia to his work in a letter to Max Eastman: "Whether poetry or prose, my writing is always most striking and true when it is a little reminiscent and nostalgic. The vividness of *Home to Harlem* was due to my being removed just the right distance from the scene" (qtd. in Melvin Dixon 53). Although the novel's nostalgia has not yet been analyzed in detail, critics have noted that "nostalgic, pastoral strains" were common in McKay's early poetic representations of his Jamaican childhood and of the Jamaican peasantry (Stoff 129). Poems like "The Tropics in New York" are fraught with "pangs of longing the poet feels for his homeland," which has been "lost to him forever" (Pedersen 259). McKay's nostalgia for Jamaica persisted throughout his life. This island of his birth was, for McKay, "an undefiled Eden where instinct and sensation reigned supreme"—a "paradise" (Stoff 130). Scholars most often treat nostalgia as an aspect of McKay's personal life rather than as something that might inform his political sensibilities. For instance, in his reading of McKay's primitivism, Michael B. Stoff treats McKay's nostalgia as distinct from his intellectual pursuits and renders it a mere side bar to his embrace of the primitive (142).

And yet, as McKay himself was aware, *Home to Harlem* is a nostalgic text, partly because he composed it while he was living abroad and so was tempted "to look back on Harlem with the same idealizing memory that he had of Jamaica after leaving there" (Russ 359). Nostalgic long-ing—for a "home" that is both natural and cultural—drives the book's protagonists and helps readers connect to his portrayal of Harlem life even as it highlights the injustices that persist in that space. The novel's various longings correspond to the journeys of the novel's two main characters—Jake and Ray—and to McKay himself. First, Jake's nostalgia for the rural South and his family there enables him to critique racism and the material inequalities that result from that racism within U.S. borders. Second, Ray's nostalgia for his homeland of Haiti prior to the American occupation contrasts with his situation as an exile in Harlem, causing him to generate a critique of the present that links foreign impe-rialism to domestic racism. Finally, McKay points to Africa as a nostalgic origin for African Americans and Caribbean Americans alike.

In describing this common origin, Stephens theorizes the power of a black transnationalism: it provides a shared sense of the exclusions of imperialism as it spurs "creative development of new international-ist alternatives to the nationalism of the imperial states" (604). A black transnational *nostalgia*, then, is homesickness that highlights the exclu-sions and exiles resulting from both imperialism and racism in order to reflect on these forces as historical processes. If imperialist nostalgia serves to unify a nation, then transnational nostalgia, with its boundary-blurring emotive force, disrupts nation formations. Such nostalgia also offers an "internationalist alternative" insofar as it unites non-whites through common longings for homes that bring into clear focus the negative repercussions of imperialism.

The idea of "home" demands careful consideration in a novel that takes the term as part of its title. Robert A. Russ suggests the novel should be read as "a desperate cry that there *is* no home to return to—it doesn't exist" (355, original emphasis), and he posits that "there is no true home for the displaced, alienated Blacks for whom race is always an issue to be confronted" (372). In this sense, neither Jake nor Ray has a "home"—at least, no home free of racial oppression. But Russ assumes that a home involves "peace, security, comfort, order" (358), and in these terms, McKay's Harlem is not a home at all. It is not a singular space, and it is certainly not a space of domesticity or conventional familial rela-tionships. It is a multiplicity of spaces—a collection of neighborhoods, each with its own constellations of relationships, stories, and lived-in places. The city is in flux; mobility and desire manifest in sex, music, dancing, and labor. Since Jake ultimately leaves Harlem for Chicago, Ray heads to Europe, and other characters float haphazardly around the various nooks and crannies of the city, it becomes tempting to classify these characters, along with Russ, as perpetually homeless.

Despite its appeal, though, the category of "homelessness" is limited in at least two ways. First, it threatens to negate agency for the transients and overlook the temporary communities they are able to form. As Melvin Dixon argues, "Afro-American writers, often considered homeless, alienated from mainstream culture, and segregated in negative environments, have used language to create alternative landscapes where black culture and identity can flourish apart from any marginal, prescribed 'place'" (2). Harlem might be considered one such "alternative landscape." Second, there are particular homes for which these characters long, and particular sets of social relations, histories, and politics that emerge when these longings are investigated more carefully. Rendering homecoming "only" imaginary forecloses that home's materiality along with the possibilities that open up when the "nature" of the home is examined.

Attention to the specific homes longed for by specific characters in McKay's novel generates a more nuanced conception of the transnationalism that characterizes the Harlem Renaissance. At the same time, such a way of reading rematerializes nostalgia: nostalgic longing becomes not about mere wistfulness for another time but about memory of another *place*—a place with a history. Outka's suggestion that a "negation of the present" is "inherent in nostalgia" is challenged by the homes in McKay's text (127). Homes that are located in the past—alternately Africa, Haiti, and the rural American South—are accessible to the characters as part of their present identities. Each of these homes is imported, in symbolic and narrative form, as a counterpoint to the present in such a way as to generate a critique of current circumstances and, in the process, extend the geographic possibilities for African American solidarity in multiple directions.

The novel's structure mirrors its transient characters, and a shifty chronology accentuates the sense that characters are moving in all directions at once. The plot is loose; the narrative movement is depicted through seasons, ending with springtime and a sense of "rebirth." The narrative begins with Jake's return home and ends with his departure, and Harlem serves as a kind of "switchyard" for the always-in-motion characters (Hutchinson, Introduction 6). In contrast to many mainstream regionalist texts, which tend toward a more realist notion of chronology and often follow a declensionist trajectory that corresponds to their nostalgic response to progress, McKay avoids linearity and instead asks readers to be flexible with our notions of time and space.

Jake is the character whose "routes" we follow most closely. We are never told exactly why Jake left his Southern home; however, his familiar "rural South–urban North geographical trajectory" identifies him with the Great Migration—a movement that is neither entirely forced nor entirely voluntary (Lowney 414). We might read Jake's mobility, then, in terms of a restricted agency. For instance, the railroad's presence in the novel taps into its role as a powerful historical symbol of, and engine for, mobility; however, Jake's railroad labor is hardly romantic (210). Jake's travels provide the novel's primary "trip tik," but they also ask us to reflect, along with him, on the injustices he encounters. While Jake is a cosmopolitan figure who crosses national boundaries from the novel's opening pages, his nostalgia is most often targeted at the U.S. South. As such, it intersects more with domestic narratives about the pastoral than with transnational discourse about migration and exile.

The novel begins with Jake's return home to Harlem after serving in France in World War I, deserting from the U.S. Army, and working temporarily in England. He is eager to get back to Harlem, full of longing for the city he knows best and for the "Brown girls" he imagines are waiting for him there (8). Of course, nostalgia is not the only thing propelling Jake back home. The military's racism prevented him from seeing combat in the war, and his frustrations with that racism led him to desert. Jake wonders, "Why did I want to mix mahself up in a white folks' war? It ain't ever was any of black folks' affair" (7–8). The war is no anomaly but rather part of "a transnational logic of racial and class hierarchy" to which Jake and others are "subjected" (Lowney 421). Jake is disillusioned with the racism he finds in Europe, which is masked as "friendly contempt," and he prefers the "white folks' hatred" in the United States, which is, at least, more direct and has the advantage of making him feel "strong and aggressive" (McKay 5). These sentiments set the stage for the rest of the novel and offer the first of many instances in which the longing to return home is conjoined with political critique.

An optimistic, forthright, "contented animal" who embraces life in Harlem (McKay 264), Jake embodies McKay's belief that "Afro-Americans, especially the rural Afro-Americans of Jamaica and the American South, were closer to the earth and more natural in their responses to life" (Cooper xiv). As his early longing for Harlem's "Brown girls" implies, nostalgia for Jake is often tied to sexual desire. For instance, in the chapter "Spring in Harlem," Jake is reminded of the "surging of desire in his boy's body and of his curious pure nectarine beginnings, without pain, without disgust, down home in Virginia. Of his adolescent breaking-through when the fever-and-pain of passion gave him a wonderful strange-sweet taste of love that he had never known again" (280–81). Although such description risks playing into stereotypes about oversexed black males, McKay makes Jake a likeable character—one who possesses a "core of decency under [his] primitivism" (Xavier 736). Here and in similar passages, nostalgia locates the "fruit" of black life in the past and so constructs the present as an ongoing effort to regain such moments of "passion." Jake's longing for his youthful "beginnings" resonates with Edward Said's theory of "return and repetition rather than simple linear accomplishment" (xiii). In this sense, Jake's childhood—like the African roots of Harlem's rhythms and, perhaps, like McKay's roots in Jamaica—is a beginning, not an origin.

Readers join Jake on several emotional "returns" to his Virginia home. But since the home for which Jake is nostalgic exists in the Jim Crow South, his nostalgia is necessarily fraught. As Dixon explains, "The South, the land of cane and ancestral territory for most American blacks, is both a hostile political field and an abundantly fertile cultural terrain. These tensions in nature and in geography match the 'warring ideals' of being black and American, which Du Bois called double consciousness" (34). And yet, what Michael Bennett calls an "anti-pastoral" is not at all what Jake's memories of the past convey—quite the contrary. His Southern home more closely exemplifies Leo Marx's complex pastoral in that it "manage[s] to qualify, or call into question, or bring irony to bear against the illusion of peace and harmony" associated with a more sentimental pastoral ideal (25).

Jake's fond memories are frequently disrupted, machine-in-the-garden style, by the harsh realities of his present. Through imagining a home that is natural and idealized, Jake is able to contrast that home with the "hostile political field" of the urban present, participating in a form of pastoral nostalgia that carries enormous political salience. When he gets sick with venereal disease and finds himself "doubled over" in pain in the corner of a bar, "[Jake] thought first of his mother. His sister. The little frame house in Petersburg. The backyard of bleached clothes on the line, the large lilac tree and the little forked lot that yielded red tomatoes and green peas in spring" (216). When his reverie is interrupted and his friends take him back to his lonely apartment to recover, he is greeted by the lackadaisical landlady who substitutes, inadequately, for his mother, who is "a loving memory only" (234). Jake's reflections exhibit nostalgia's literal meaning—a longing to return home—and he envisions particular natural objects as fundamental to that home. The lilac tree and the fruit and vegetable abundance, coupled with the sense of springtime's rebirth that emerges repeatedly in the novel, might capitalize on white readers' nostalgia for the pastoral. By invoking a peaceful memory and accentuating its contrast with his present situation, Jake's nostalgia draws attention to the continued oppression of blacks in the United States, manifested in poverty, alienation, and, for Jake, separation from family.

Jake's earlier memory of his sister points to a revisionary quality in his longings. Reminded of her by Ray's girlfriend, Agatha—a beautiful, educated black woman—Jake thinks wistfully of what his sister could have been like had she been given equivalent opportunities. She "might have turned out something lak this ef she'd 'a' had a chance to talk English like in books and wear class-top clothes" (209–10).[17] After encountering these lines, a new reading of the "little frame house in Petersburg" emerges. When paired with this other reference to home, the details of a rural, working-class existence stand out: the house is "little," and the "bleached clothes on the line" are "yielded" not by nature but by physical labor. Ransom's dream of a leisurely South is subtly dispelled by Jake's nostalgia for that region, which does not edit out labor. This nostalgic narrative is also honest about the limitations faced by Southern blacks no matter whether they migrated north or stayed put.

He looks backward, then, with "a sense of nostalgia that does not quite wish for a return" to that imperfect homeland (Outka 174). Jake is nostalgic not for the way the past actually was but for what it could have produced. He is nostalgic, in a sense, for a different *present* that could have evolved if conditions in the past had been better. As Svetlana Boym explains, it is common to yearn "not for the past the way it was, but for the past the way it could have been. It is this past perfect that one strives to realize in the future" (351). Even while he is nostalgic for his Southern home, Jake recognizes that if presented with different opportunities, his sister—and presumably he—could have had a different future. Nostalgia's "utopian force" comes through here: rather than functioning as a conservative, reactionary version of the past that justifies the present, nostalgia instead reimagines the future by contrasting it with the past. In the process, nostalgia causes the feeling subject—as well as, perhaps, the reading subject—to reflect on the conditions of possibility in the present that this particular past has generated.

* * *

Both Jake and his character double, Ray, think fond "home thoughts" in the novel, but the homelands they imagine are implicated in distinct political situations (152). Ray is an exile who was forced to leave home after the U.S. Marines occupied Haiti. For Ray, the "sudden upset of affairs in his home country had landed him into the quivering heart of a naked world whose reality was hitherto unimaginable" (McKay 224). His first mention of Haiti locates it in an ongoing geography of conquest as he informs Jake that it is an island "in the Caribbean—near the Panama Canal" (131). Jake is fascinated by Ray's recounting of Haitian history as a "romance of his race" and inspired by the tale of independence, "human wisdom[,] and nobility" under the leadership of Toussaint L'Ouverture. Most notably, the "revelation" Jake has upon hearing this history causes him to rethink his own racial stereotypes, which the reader has been aware of since his mention of the "dirty Arab crew" in the novel's second sentence (1). Second-guessing his own views on race, Jake "felt like a boy who stands with a map of the world in colors before him, and feels the wonder of the world" (134).

By connecting this history to the U.S. occupation of Haiti, Ray initiates a more extensive critique that includes imperialism and racism. Reflecting on his "home country" leads quickly to a consciousness of how U.S. imperialism abroad is enabled by the same race- and class-based distinctions that operate domestically. Just as important, Ray's focus on Haitian history decenters the United States nation and positions Haitian independence as the result of a genuine social revolution—a "more dramatic and picturesque" independence—contra an American past in which revolution generated only a very exclusive form of freedom (131). Jake's infatuation with Haitian history was not uncommon for African American intellectuals of the time, who saw in the Caribbean an opportunity to "better understand their own heritage" (Pamphile 129).[18] The conversation between Ray and Jake suggests a constructive potential for pan-African communities—a "common ground for cross-cultural dialogue among African American and Caribbean critics of American imperialism" (Lowney 426). Their shared awareness of the "transnational logic of racial and class hierarchy," and their longing to retrieve a heritage, and a home, that might subvert these hierarchies, unites them in a critique of their contemporary circumstances (Lowney 421).

Ray's political critique is underwritten by the nostalgia that results from his forced migration, after "Uncle Sam grabbed Hayti" (138). Here, as in other places where "home country" is referenced in the novel, Ray launches into an analysis of the Harlem "underworld" in which he has been, passively, "landed." Making essentially a Marxist argument, Ray foregrounds how the working class provides the labor for the leisure classes, arguing that "the people of this world, waiters, cooks, chauffeurs, sailors, porters, guides, ushers, hod-carriers, factory hands—all touched in a thousand ways the people of the other divisions. They worked over there and slept over here, divided by a street" (225). Ray's lengthiest and most intense "home thoughts" are meant to help him sleep during an uncomfortable layover in Pittsburgh, where he is plagued by annoying bedbugs and close sleeping quarters: "He flung himself, across void and water, back home. Home thoughts, if you can make them soft and sweet and misty-beautiful enough, can sometimes snare sleep. There was the quiet, chalky-dusty street and, jutting out over it, the front of the house that he had lived in. The high staircase built on the outside, and pots of begonias and ferns on the landing. . . . All the flowering things he loved" (152–53). Ray's nostalgia is like Jake's in that it evokes a pastoral setting: the familiar house, the "quiet" street, and the flora that encircle the home. Here, again, there is a sense of springtime, of "flowering things." Like Jake, who fluctuates between a painful, bodily condition and his nostalgia, Ray's physical discomfort interrupts the nostalgic thoughts that precede it. Both attempts to conjure nostalgia as an antidote instead promote further reflection on the (painful) present situation. What Ray intends as a catalyst for sleep instead becomes a catalyst for critique.

Immediately after this sketch of his peaceful, "tropic-warm" island birthplace—a loving description that perhaps betrays McKay's own nostalgia for Jamaica—Ray's attention returns to the current situation, in which his coworkers are "snoring with masticating noises of their fat lips, like animals eating" (153). With this unflattering image, Ray's thought process abruptly switches gears and he launches into some of the most provocative commentary of the novel: "These men claimed kinship with him. They were black like him. Man and nature had put them in the same race. He ought to love them and feel them (if they felt anything). He ought to if he had a shred of social morality in him. They were all chain-ganged together and he was counted as one link. Yet he loathed every soul in that great barrack-room, except Jake. Race . . . Why should he have and love a race?" (153). When Ray remarks that "man and nature had put [him] in the same race" as the Harlem "animals" he disavows, he implies that race categories are sanctioned by both culture *and* nature (153). Yet this seeming move toward naturalizing race in bodies is undermined by the passive context in which "they" are "put" in the same racial terms. If the sole reason for sharing a racial designation is skin color—"they were black like him"—then perhaps nature's distinction is as contingent and arbitrary as man's. The end of the paragraph likewise hints at the arbitrariness of race. The final question's implication is not only that Ray finds it difficult to justify "hav[ing] a race" but also that race is a quality superimposed from the outside. The question of why he should "have" a race reads like a rhetorical one, not a literal one, and challenges audiences to ponder whether Ray could simply decide not to have one, just as easily as he might decide not to love one.

Obviously, this is not an option. The black-skinned "kin" he considers in this passage are passive objects in nearly all the sentences here; they are "chain-ganged together" by the social category of their race. The notable exception to this passivity is in the first sentence: "These men claimed kinship with him." This "action," however, occurs within a narrow scope of possibilities. Essentially, blacks in Harlem have agency only to further "chain" themselves (and others) to racial designations that are not of their choosing. More hopefully, though, Ray's frustration with being "counted as one link" points the finger at the society that is doing the counting, thereby highlighting race's socially constructed "nature." A sense of duty emerges—what he here refers to as "social morality"— when Ray contemplates race, and his next line of thought delves further into race's social dimensions:

> Races and nations were things like skunks, whose smells poisoned the air of life. Yet civilized mankind reposed its faith and future in their ancient, silted channels. Great races and big nations! There must be something mighty inspiriting in being the citizen of a great strong nation. To be the white citizen of a nation that can say bold, challenging things like a strong man. Something very different from the keen ecstatic joy a man feels in the romance of being black. Something the black man could never feel nor quite understand.

> Ray felt that as he was conscious of being black and impotent, so, correspondingly, each marine down in Hayti must be conscious of being white and powerful. What a unique feeling of confidence about life the typical white youth of his age must have! Knowing that his skin-color was a passport to glory, making him one with ten thousands like himself. All perfect Occidentals and investors in that grand business called civilization. That grand business called

civilization. That grand business in whose pits sweated and snored, like the cooks, all the black and brown hybrids and mongrels, simple earth-loving animals, without aspirations toward national unity and racial arrogance. (153–55)

Such a rich passage must be cited in its entirety to fully appreciate its shifts in logic. In particular, Ray's slippage from race to nationalism and from nationalism to masculinity is an important one. Echoing Roosevelt's popular rhetoric, "white," "citizen," and "male" are conjoined as necessary traits constituting a "strong" American. Ray opposes white strength with black "romance" and seems to foreclose the possibility of the two categories collapsing. To be "black and impotent" is the apparently inevitable result of the power dynamics at work, especially in Ray's home country of Haiti. Ray's frustration about those specific politics and the way race-based distinctions operate in the United States comes through clearly here.

It seems, then, that Ray upholds a fundamental opposition between white and black, and that he identifies the former with civilization and the latter with the "ecstatic joy" resulting from "the romance of being black." But Ray emphasizes that this opposition results from the mutual constitution of social categories: blackness and whiteness are truth-effects that are "correspondingly" created. In other words, understanding what it means to be "white and powerful" depends upon a perception of others as "black and impotent." Rather than leaving it at that, Ray makes yet another rhetorical move: he pinpoints the cause of these power differentials. Once again calling into question the "naturalness" of racial categories, Ray posits instead that white racial unity—in which "the typical white youth" becomes "one with ten thousands like himself"—is based not upon natural attributes or even upon arbitrary social designations, but upon access to a capitalist system. Whites are "investors," and civilization is the "grand business." Ray's contemplations here and throughout the novel return to material realities: labor, inequity, and the economy of black bodies in transnational Harlem. If the novel reveals "a racist ideology that linked United States imperial foreign policy to domestic policies of segregation and discrimination," then McKay, via Ray, clarifies that this "link" is, at least in part, a socioeconomic as well as an ideological one (Lowney 426).

Finally, Ray's identification of non-whites as "without aspirations toward national unity and racial arrogance" deserves unpacking. The fact that these terms are linked with the conjunction "and" rather than "or" suggests their interconnection. Placing them in the context of the rest of the paragraph, it makes sense to read national unity and racial arrogance as central features of the civilization against which Ray is opposing "black and brown hybrids." These "hybrids" are striving for racial pride—not arrogance—by maintaining difference, experiencing only temporary unities and transient (inter)nationality. Specifically, blacks are not Americans. When McKay catches himself making this association, he quickly corrects himself: "Negroes, like all good Americans, love a bar. I should have said, Negroes under Anglo-Saxon civilization" (324). Races and nations are both identified as antithetical to "the air of life" the novel celebrates.

When Ray finally does fall asleep, he instantly finds himself "back home again" where his father's house is surrounded by "a vast forest full of blooming hibiscus and mimosas and giant evergreen trees" (157). Like the home of Ray's initial dreamy musings—and like Jake's garden of red tomatoes and green peas—home is again defined by its natural beauty and the blossoming fruits of springtime. This time, home is explicitly a "paradise," and the peaceful dream of an Edenic past is "arrested" by persistent bedbugs—"a thousand pins . . . pricking Ray's flesh"—that are the physically painful and all-too-present manifestations of his working conditions (158). In fact, Ray comments on the state of these conditions just before this passage, when he is angry and appalled at "the filthy fact of the quarters that the richest railroad in the world had provided for its black servitors" (156). Once again Ray makes a race- and class-based critique by exposing the economic subordination of blacks in the United States.

Ray's reflections expose what life "under Anglo-Saxon civilization" entails, and nostalgia is crucial to the development of this critique. It is precisely nostalgia's interruption by the harsh injustices of real life—and the contrast provided by nostalgia's romantic edge—that highlights those injustices for the reader. By taking as the object of his nostalgia a natural world where "civilization" has not yet invaded the region, Ray articulates a precolonial, preindustrial nostalgia that taps into broader nostalgic discourse. In particular, Ray's nostalgic reflections dance around a central dichotomy: that of the "magnificent monster of civilization" versus the "natural defenses of his island, where the steam-roller of progress could not reach him" (155). Through a preindustrial nostalgia that echoes that of mainstream regionalists, Ray is able to generate a critique of colonization and its aftermath(s) and unite "hybrids" of all nations in this critique. Significantly, it is "*because* Haiti is no longer a 'free nation'" (Lowney 424, my emphasis) that Ray is forced to access that homeland via nostalgia; his nostalgia, then, is a byproduct of imperialism, a backlash that generates critique. The "machine in the garden" turns out to be white imperialism—either military occupation, in Ray's homeland of Haiti, or the partially forced migrations and material inequities propagated by slavery and continued racial injustice, for Jake and other African Americans within the United States. Ultimately, Ray is able to conjoin a preindustrial with a precolonial nostalgia; the latter, especially, helps him connect with others of African descent.

* * *

The fact that both Ray and Jake long for pastoral homes where an aesthetic, fecund nature is prominent suggests that nostalgia for nature was a common ground upon which diverse residents of the United States in the 1920s could stand, even if they did so "without aspirations toward national unity" (McKay 155). En route to imagining a transnational collectivity, McKay's diasporic itineraries coalesce, however briefly, in Harlem. Of course, the Harlem Renaissance's transnationalism was "profoundly shaped by American racial culture and American power" (Hutchinson, Introduction 5). Thus, although "the 'nature' that Black 'primitives' are a part of is not American, but African" (Russ 372), McKay still must route his transnational stories through a domestic discursive context in which "nature" means specific things.

Through Ray, McKay suggests that, before the U.S. occupation, Haiti was a peaceful, pastoral society living out a symbiotic relationship with the natural environment. While it resonates with the dominant nostalgia characteristic of regionalist texts, McKay's idealization of the pastoral differs from other regionalist authors (like Cather) in important ways. Like Zitkala-Ša, McKay inverts the trajectory of frontier-to-pastoral evolution made famous by Turner. Rather than depicting nature as, originally, a battlefield—which is then glorified as a necessary stage on the way to a pastoral society—McKay situates the pastoral within a different history, in which it actually precedes frontier violence.

Nature rhetoric also helps McKay link Harlem and Haiti as romantic sites of black culture and relative independence. J. Michael Dash explains that Americans have tended to see Haiti as "the extreme case, whether it was virgin terrain, a garden of earthly delights where the black race could begin again or the closest and most histrionic example of Africa's continental darkness" (2–3). McKay conjoins these two "extreme" symbols of garden and wilderness in Harlem, making it a place where blacks can "begin again" by turning toward "Africa's continental darkness." Harlem is, in some ways, like the Haitian home Ray romanticizes, "an island of savage black people, who fought for collective liberty and was struggling to create a culture of their own" (McKay 134). Ray voices the connection when he leaves: "He had known happiness, too, in Harlem, joy that glowed gloriously upon him like the high-noon sunlight of his tropic island home" (267). Both are idealized, but in a way that forces the reader to reflect on the contrast between their Edenic, natural qualities (which exist primarily in memory) and the political realities that have damaged these environments.

Indeed, part of what connects Haiti to Harlem is their common origin in Africa—a complex origin that, for McKay, fuses frontier and pastoral discourse. Africa is Edenic but also wild, a virgin garden and an enclave for savages. In a sense, then, McKay brings together the two most prominent nature discourses of his time in support of cultural sovereignty for people of African descent. Africa is a real and a symbolic origin through which both race and culture are constructed in terms of roots. Nostalgia for nature—whether for a peaceful pastoral community, for the "wild" African jungle, or for some combination of the two—is instrumental to McKay's project of representing and celebrating a unique black culture. Transposing this culture into an urban space enables McKay to revise popular white associations of blackness with a "natural" primitivism and instead articulate a distinctive African American cultural tradition that is both historically grounded and performed every day within the urban environment of New York City.

Despite the risks of glorifying black connections to nature, McKay's larger project of chronicling a vibrant cultural "life" that is culled from a collective black history ultimately overshadows *Home to Harlem*'s intermittent race essentialism. By re-rooting African American culture, historically, in Africa—and tracing its routes across national geographies—McKay reclaims savagery as an integral part of a precolonial black history and identifies "life" as something only blacks possess. Nature imagery grounds this formulation, and natural metaphors abound in the text. For instance, whites are not only "strange to Harlem," but they look "like faded carnations among those burning orchids of a tropical race" (106). Blacks, by contrast, are "like trees. They wear all colors naturally" (320). And Ray, in whom life "burned . . . perhaps more intensely than in Jake," is described as "a tree with roots in the soil and sap flowing out and whispering leaves drinking in air," a description attributed to "that intense emotional energy so peculiar to his race" (265). These excerpts are representative of the ways that racial designations are sometimes reinforced in the novel, with nature helping to underscore racial difference.

Harlem itself is a colorful place, where "faded carnations" are inferior flora. McKay sorts characters on a color spectrum of "layers of brown, low-brown, high-brown, nut-brown, lemon, maroon, olive, mauve, [and] gold." No matter which of this range of colors describes them, McKay emphasizes that his characters share "ancient black life" and "the terribly sweet rhythm of black blood" at their "base," and he insists that this "black blood" inevitably overpowers and absorbs all other colors (57–58). In doing so, he revises associations of whiteness with purity and inserts blackness as the original, pure racial category—a radical move, and a common one in the novel. Within the context of the one-drop rule and sociologists' beliefs that miscegenation would "remove . . . all the characteristics of the black race" (Park 382), McKay's insistence on the dominance of black blood is a powerful form of "racial audacity" that posits blackness as a way of "assailing whiteness" (Xavier 715, 718). Even while it intermittently maintains essentialist racial categories, the novel also highlights the mutability of skin color: "Yellow balancing between black and white. Black reaching out beyond yellow. Almost-white on the brink of a change" (57). Clearly attuned to the anxieties surrounding racial passing, the novel's intermittent reminders that "you never can tell for sure about a person's race in Harlem" and "there's no sure telling white from high-yaller these days" (249, 252) trouble racial categories by noting that passing is a common occurrence.

It seems, then, that blackness is found not on the surface of the body—as skin color—but in the blood; it is the "juice o' life in [black] blood" that whites purportedly fear and envy (49). This rhetoric of blood sounds suspiciously like scientific discourses that were attempting to internalize race in bodies. However, it is the "juice o' *life*" the novel really showcases. "Life" is performed and experienced throughout the novel; it is mobile and transient, not fixed or internal. It is a creation of black culture in the face of oppression and racism, and as such, a powerful generative force as well as a source of fear, envy, and awe for whites. McKay speculates, "No wonder they hated them, when out of their melancholy environment the blacks could create mad, contagious music and high laughter" (267).

Harlem's cabarets are the space where characters "create" this culture in the present, though McKay reminds us of its African origins. The Congo—"a real throbbing little Africa in New York"—exemplifies the embrace of a black racial purity in tension with the demand to "cater to the fast trade" of offering up black culture as a spectacle for "ofay" tourists (29–30). Unlike other cabarets, where slumming has taken over and sacrificed the character of the places, the Congo endures "in spite of formidable opposition and foreign exploitation." McKay's use of such militaristic terms is telling; he makes a not-so-subtle critique of the slumming industry, which has compelled cabaret owners to become savvy "Harlem Negro manager[s]" and to "plunge deeper for the ofay trade" (29). The Congo, by contrast, is "African in spirit and color. No white persons [a]re admitted there" (30). If the Congo remains a "pure" space, it signifies a material purity at least as much as a racial one. That is, its freedom from financial and cultural "exploitation" is what most distinguishes it from other cabarets and what renders it uncorrupted. Thus, the Congo houses "life"—the working classes, with their "warm indigenous smells" that betray "the nature of their occupation[s]"—as opposed to the "veneer" of "Afro-Oriental garishness" found at cabarets where whites are allowed (30).

Music, and the dance that so often accompanies it, are central to the novel's representations of "life," and both occur frequently at Harlem's cabarets. Music encapsulates a fundamental contradiction that is so much a part of Harlem Renaissance art and literature: folk, blues, and jazz traditions were viewed as both "the primitive expression of an uncivilized people" and "the symbol of a freedom from restraint that many longed to achieve" (Fabre and Feith 18). Aware of this paradox, McKay takes charge of this symbol and writes into existence a version of primitivism he can then celebrate. The blues are both an important cultural tradition in their own right and an analogy for the black race and its ability to find joy within racist environments. As such, the blues are "the key to [Ray] and to his race" (McKay 266). McKay continually showcases the fact that "mad, contagious music and high laughter" are manifestations of an oppressed group's enduring vitality (McKay 267).

He repossesses this vitality and excludes whites from it, even as he tantalizes readers with its alluring "freedom from restraint." This scene, which takes place in a brothel in Philadelphia, is characteristic of the novel:

> The piano-player had wandered off into some dim, far-away, ances-
> tral source of music. Far, far away from music-hall syncopation
> and jazz, he was lost in some sensual dream of his own. No tor-
> tures, banal shrieks and agonies. Tum-tum . . . tum-tum . . . tum-
> tum . . . tum-tum. . . . The notes were naked acute alert. Like
> black youth burning naked in the bush. Love in the deep heart
> of the jungle. . . . The sharp spring of a leopard from a leafy limb,
> the snarl of a jackal, green lizards in amorous play, the flight of a

plumed bird, and the sudden laughter of mischievous monkeys in their green homes. Tum-tum . . . tum-tum . . . tum-tum . . . tum-tum. . . . Simple-clear and quivering. Like a primitive dance of war or love . . . the marshaling of spears or the sacred frenzy of a phallic celebration.

Black lovers of life caught up in their own free native rhythm, threaded to a remote scarce-remembered past, celebrating the midnight hours in themselves, for themselves, of themselves, in a house in Fifteenth Street, Philadelphia. (196–97)

This passage harkens back to a precolonial African past now reemerging in the "free native rhythm" being played out by the "tum-tums" and interspersed with Ray's conscious reflections on the scene. McKay attempts to make readers feel and experience the rhythm by repeating the onomatopoetic syllables. Yet even as he tempts his largely white audience with the hypnotic rhythm of this music, his prose insists whites can never understand it, since "the instinct of comprehension had been cultivated out of them" (267). Although music and dance are geographically transferable—the location of this event "in a house in Fifteenth Street, Philadelphia" indicates that black "lovers of life" can enjoy such moments in cities other than New York—such culture is not easily transferable to white Americans, whose histories, material conditions, and privileged racial status distance them from Harlem's black residents.

Here as elsewhere in the novel, nature rhetoric lends an "ancestral" and authentic quality to African American culture, and this culture's performance in urban space prevents any easy stereotyping of savagery, typically associated with rural nature. Just as the kind of "life" experienced at the Congo is linked to nature—the blues there are "fresh and green as grass"—this passage traces the roots of the blues to Africa's nature, to the "green home" of the African jungle, whose animal residents bear witness to the origin of this musical experience (36). This "ancestral source" precedes and transcends white culture, and McKay excavates this distinctive African root for present-day use by blacks in Harlem.

Perhaps most significantly, both the music itself and the experience of the dancers are identified with freedom on several levels. In addition to the overarching tone of raw sensuality, fostered by words like "naked" and the reverberating resonances of freedom-through-love, there is a distinct sense of agency in producing and owning this music. As Russ points out, the phrase "in themselves, for themselves, of themselves" mimics the rhetoric of the Gettysburg Address—a "repetition with a difference" that articulates a claim of self-government for Harlem's residents (365). While the piano player may be "lost in some sensual dream of his own," he is also a conduit between past and present—an interpreter of, and a vessel for, African American culture. He speaks to his audience in a common language, rooted in nature and representative of a transnational black history and culture.

The creation of a vital African American culture, manifested in music and dance, becomes a weapon with which to combat the poverty, harsh working conditions, and racism that plague the characters. In order to accentuate these conditions, many of the book's most intense excursions into Harlem's cultural "life" are cut short by these realities. Like so many of the more idyllic scenes in the novel—whether they exist in characters' minds or on the urban stage—this cathartic experience is interrupted, by a scream: "Raided!" (197). Unlike an earlier raid at the Baltimore hotel, this one is a false alarm. The police officer who enters unexpectedly is actually a customer of the brothel. Still, with his presence the dream of self-government dissolves into the reality of state control—in this case, control via capital rather than by overt force. The "free" music that precedes this interruption draws readers' attention to the freedom that has yet to be gained by Harlem's blacks. The fact that the officer—part of "the Moral Arm of the city"—frequents the brothel complicates any impulse white readers may have to condemn the behavior there (111).

The fact that the police can enter the brothel at will exposes the power dynamics at stake in Harlem. In his description of the Baltimore raid, McKay explains that undercover white cops "had posed as good fellows, regular guys, looking for a good time only in the Black Belt" (109). The consequences of such an incident reflect the struggles of African Americans to maintain control of their culture as well as uncertainty about racial categories. This raid prompts a backlash: "For a long time Negro proprietors would not admit white customers into their cabarets and near-white members of the black race, whose features were unfamiliar in Harlem, had a difficult time proving their identity" (111). Still, even though police and other whites might be present in Harlem, they can only buy or bully their way into black culture; they will never really have access to it.

Through a celebration of the primitive in scenes like this one, McKay is able to "establish [urban] place as a stage for performance" for Harlem's "life" and the vivacious characters he creates (Melvin Dixon 5). Harlem, a spatial metonym for (only) its black inhabitants, *is* life. If its environment is a frontier of sorts, it is one where black residents have been able to retain the best parts of a peculiarly black "savagery" in the face of (a far more savage, and far less moral) civilization. For McKay, primitivism is not a bodily essence or an intrinsic trait; rather, it is a way of life, a social practice engaged in by blacks in Harlem—a performance of sorts. By highlighting its performative quality, McKay conjures primitivism anachronistically, removing it from its position as the precursor to civilization on a teleological timeline of "progress," where white America was intent on placing it. Linked only loosely to a "scarce-remembered past," the primitive is unmoored from its temporal baggage and reborn in present-day movements—the "life" found in work, music, dance, or sex (McKay 197).

* * *

Of course, this sort of "life" was precisely what whites hoped to find in Harlem. A "Harlem Vogue, and more broadly a Negro Vogue of international dimensions" had reached its apex by the late 1920s (Hutchinson, Introduction 3). As Kevin Mumford explains, new sociological studies like those of the Chicago School, travel guides, and literature, which frequently represented urban space as a highly sexualized and racialized "interzone," contributed to the popularity of slumming. Mumford explains how "social reformers, intellectuals, sociologists, bohemians, white urban sophisticates—all can be understood as modern-day slummers," especially as each produced various "travel narratives" that reified problematic stereotypes without a corresponding intervention in the asymmetrical material relations governing urban space (135). In a similar way, reading literature by or about black urban residents was perceived by many white readers as a window into this "other" culture. Van Vechten's popular novel, for instance, was received and utilized as a sort of "literary guidebook, first for bohemians and later for mainstream urbanites" (Mumford 143).

Predicated on the belief that authentic black experience was there for the taking, slumming clearly involves a titillating aspect, perhaps related to the act of crossing social and racial boundaries and enabling the slummer to feel simultaneously superior and transgressive. Like all tourism—of nature, culture, or anything in between—slumming also depends upon and perpetuates nostalgia. Slumming involves the temporary fulfillment of a nostalgic impulse to return to a primitive nature—represented by a highly sexualized African American urban culture—from which bourgeois white Americans perceived themselves as alienated. In McKay's words, white Americans "were wearied of the pleasures of the big white world, [and] wanted something new—the primitive joy of Harlem" (109). Like the white tourists who visited the Indian Field Days and consumed the "authentic" Native American culture on display, whites took similar "nature tours" of Harlem. Following the closing of the frontier and the rise of the national parks, tourism had become a popular way of "knowing" nature in America for elite groups, for whom a voluntary experience in nature is always both available and temporary. Touring Harlem offered a way of appropriating and objectifying non-white people and their cultures, rendering the city itself a frontier of sorts: a land of opportunity, an environment conducive to "moral vacation," and a site of adventure (Mumford 150).

As Harlem became more and more "a zone of asymmetrical cultural appropriation" that relegated black residents to the forgotten margins (Mumford 155), McKay's challenge was to depict "life" in ways that would highlight but not reinforce these asymmetries. To this end, the novel's stories and characters often function to reveal the ways in which material conditions delimit the options for urban blacks. To the degree that blacks are "savages" in the sense of behaving immorally, McKay implies that they have been conditioned by the very "civilization" that keeps them oppressed rather than by any "natural" human traits. Harlem is a distinctive environment that must be assessed in terms of its unique political ecology. A minor character, Billy Biasse, explains to Jake, "Wese too thick together in Harlem. Wese all just lumped together without a chanst to choose and so we nacherally hate one another" (285). Billy's statement posits a causal connection between environment and behavior. What seems to come "nacherally" (in this case, hate) is an effect of poverty and crowded living conditions rather than any intrinsic racial characteristics. Billy's claim dovetails with an earlier conversation in which Jake tells Ray how material realities dictate the conditions of possibility within which people are given "a chanst to choose" their behavior: "Sometimes it's the people make the difference and sometimes it's the place" (202). In McKay's Harlem, the possibility that "it's the place" demands serious consideration.

Although Jake admits "rotten" people exist everywhere, the particularities of any place must be accounted for when judging the "difference" between people (202). McKay's fragmented, spatially mobile narrative and complex formulation of race make a "moral map" of the sort implied by sociological studies of the time difficult to draw (Mumford 139).

Indeed, if McKay set out "to survey the wilderness of black alienation and displacement" (Melvin Dixon 52), then his characters in *Home to Harlem* certainly appear to find a degree of pleasure within the mobility and culture such displacement spurned. Speaking from the perspective of Ransom's "transplants," McKay reveals that the black community in Harlem is anything but "deracinated." To the contrary, its roots deepen through movements across nations and communication across cultures. As McKay foregrounds the "natures" of Africa, Haiti, and the rural South, along with the diverse histories of these geopolitical regions, it becomes clear that "home" is not a static end in itself. Rather, it is an object of nostalgia whereby a shared history of colonialism might inspire transnational alliances to form and face the common enemies of racism and imperialism.

In his foreword to Ansel Adams's 1944 photodocumentation of the internment camp at Manzanar, *Born Free and Equal: The Story of Loyal Japanese-Americans*, then Secretary of the Interior Harold L. Ickes confidently proclaims that "Americanism is not, and never was, a matter of race or ancestry" (7). To the Japanese interned in the camp, whose very detainment belied Ickes's claim, this declaration would surely have struck a wrong note. Adams's goal of rendering the internees "loyal" American citizens—a goal predicated on the fact that they were not being treated as such—also challenges Ickes's assertion. Adams directly acknowledges ongoing racial, economic, and social tensions when he claims that "the spirit of Jim Crow walks in almost every section of our land" (101).

This tension regarding who counts as American gestures toward key questions raised by Adams's project. What qualities signified "Americanism" during this era? What does national loyalty entail, according to this text? Adams sometimes hints at answers, for instance when he says he hopes his book "will suggest that the broad concepts of American citizenship, and of liberal, democratic life the world over, must be protected," both in wartime and in times of peace (9). As *Born Free and Equal* makes clear, many of Roosevelt's ideals about "true" Americanness still held sway, and not only in the explicitly racist sense that Adams recognizes. More broadly, a notion of Americanness in which the American West functions as the proving ground for American identity finds its way into Adams's text and images.

As Adams chronicles the effects of landscape on the internees and constructs Japanese American identity in relationship to the challenges posed by an unforgiving natural world, he relies on the same nostalgic stories about the frontier that Turner and Roosevelt popularized earlier in the century. In his text and photographs, Adams strategically invokes such narratives, capitalizing on readers' nostalgia for the frontier in order to secure our allegiance to the detainees. At the same time, in attempting to prove that Japanese Americans possess the pioneer attributes that warrant inclusion in the nation, the text's nostalgia reinscribes racialized versions of national identity. Showing how, fifty years after the frontier's closing, it could still carry powerful political resonance, Adams draws upon familiar frontier rhetoric and imagery in ways that illustrate the injustice of the camps even as they uphold American ideals of exceptionalism, democracy, assimilation, and the opportunity to improve oneself through hard work.

The first image in the book, a dramatic photo of an internee gazing intently at the Sierra Nevada mountain range (Fig. 3), is a telling one in regard to this frontier nostalgia. The range rises gradually from the left to the right of the frame, inviting viewers to "read" the mountains and the man as we follow his gaze into the distance. His jaw is set, his chin is raised, his eyebrows form a sharp, straight line, which accents the intensity of his vision. His eyes are focused on the larger peaks, which must lie just beyond the photo's frame. A few pages later, Adams provides a narrative that could easily be a caption for this image by declaring that the "towering mountains" have "strengthened the spirit" of the internees (9). Some detainees have themselves recalled drawing strength from the peaks of the Sierras. As Jeanne Wakatsuki Houston recounts, Mt. Whitney reminded her father of Fujiyama, and the peaks "represented those powerful and inevitable forces [in nature] that cannot be resisted" (*Farewell* 88). Though the landscape could be "both stark and comforting," the mountains were "inspirational" to Houston and her family (92, 88).

Whatever stories Adams's camera wants to tell about them, the subjects in his portraits "gaze back and take control of the photograph," hinting at personal narratives and emotions like those chronicled by Wakatsuki Houston (Graulich 228). But the dramatic natural backdrops constantly threaten to tell a more nationalistic story, especially when combined with pioneer rhetoric. Proximity to Western nature has presumably taught the internees the skills to live as Americans. Adams writes: "From the harsh soil they have extracted fine crops; they have made gardens glow in the firebreaks and between the barracks. Out of the jostling, dusty

FIGURE 3. Ansel Adams, *Tom Kobayashi*, Manzanar Relocation Center, CA. (Library of Congress, Prints and Photographs Division, no. DIG ppprs 00243)

confusion of the first bleak days in raw barracks they have modulated to a democratic internal society and a praiseworthy personal adjustment to conditions beyond their control. The huge vistas and the stern realities of sun and wind and space symbolize the immensity and opportunity of America—perhaps a vital reassurance following the experiences of enforced exiles" (9). The language here echoes that used by Turner to describe his nineteenth-century pioneers, who exhibited "coarseness and strength," a "practical, inventive turn of mind," and were "quick to find expedients" to improve life on the frontier—an environment that was occasionally, if not ultimately, "beyond their control" (Turner 227–28). It is significant, too, that the detainees have created a "democratic" society, since only this type of social order would legitimize their identities as Americans within the narrative of frontier settlement.

Ironically, the history of Owens Valley is one of displacement, not democracy. Prior to the camp's creation at Manzanar in 1942, the region was home to Indians, who were displaced by prospectors and miners, who in turn gave way to cattle ranchers and farmers. The livelihood of these farmers and ranchers was "ruined" when the city of L.A. siphoned their water and destroyed the valley's fertility (Wakatsuki Houston, "Crossing Boundaries" 34). The very word "Manzanar," Spanish for "apple orchard," evokes the community of fruit growers who used to live in the area, even as the name masks the region's historical role of watching "enforced exiles" come and go. Of course, conditions in the camp were hardly pastoral. The once-green valley was largely desert by the time the camp was built, though detainees did plant gardens and find other ways to make their temporary homes more livable (Houston, *Farewell* 85).[1] Still, in *Born Free and Equal*, nonhuman nature provides "vital reassurance" of the ongoing "opportunity of America," even for those who have been denied its fruits. American identity is constructed in relation to nature's aesthetic sublimity as well as to its wildness—its "huge vistas" and its "stern realities." These narratives resonate with turn-of-the-century conceptions of national identity as sketched in Turner's frontier thesis as well as with the nostalgic touring of dramatic nature that had come to signify patriotic Americanness.

Much like Yosemite's Indians, the internees are on display in Adams's book, and we readers are invited to be visual tourists of life in the camp. As such, we are subject to the guidelines and rules that delimit the experiences of all visitors.[2] What we are most asked to witness are confrontations between the "stern realities" of the natural world and the internee-pioneers' perseverance, individualism, and hard work. Adams reiterates the ability of the internees to create "farms, gardens and the pleasure park" (20). He remarks on their "fortitude" and their "cheerful adaptation" to difficult circumstances (44). In Adams's text, the arid West stands in metonymically for America, and the inhabitants of this land are applauded for their ability to harvest food from such intractable country. In a statement that could hardly be more quintessentially American, Adams muses that there is "nothing in the world, perhaps, as poignant as the emergence of crops from harsh and barren land" (80, 84).

By noting the "poignancy" of this ability to make a living off the land, Adams alludes to the emotional level at which national identity is formed and at which his argument works. He expresses a commitment to personalizing the internees' stories so that readers can connect with them on a "human, emotional basis" (9). Readers are meant to *feel* for them, as well as to imagine what these human beings' own feelings might be concerning their imprisonment. Many of these "exiles" were likely homesick for the lives—homes, friends, businesses—they were compelled to leave behind and to which most could never return. Adams notes that the nostalgia many of the detainees may feel is also, at least potentially, a national one. He identifies a "homelessness" Japanese Americans were asked to adopt by responding to the loyalty questionnaires: if they forswore allegiance to the emperor of Japan, they would become "people without a country," since their alien status prohibited them from becoming U.S. citizens (39). Adams even speculates that nostalgia may be one of the reasons some internees retained their allegiance to Japan (40).[3]

Nostalgia thus invites readers to bridge the gap between ourselves (presumably already "loyal Americans") and the also-loyal, also-pioneering, internees. However, contra Turner and Roosevelt, Adams imagines that this shared frontier nostalgia might prompt a more inclusive conception of American identity, one that has space for pioneers of all kinds. This emotional appeal works in conjunction with the ideologically problematic appeal to readers to see Japanese Americans as "model minorities."[4] They are "law-abiding and industrious" (7). They keep their chins up, even in less-than-ideal circumstances. Education, professional training, and military service are high priorities for the internees, Adams assures readers; "everyone seems interested in some form of work, service, sport, or other activity" (52). But despite their work ethics and affirmations of loyalty, "America has not assimilated all who have assimilated America" (54).

Although Adams's argument seems politically progressive in its desire for a more inclusive nation, it reveals a problematic reliance on assimilation, which he suggests is the internees' common desire. Judith Fryer Davidov observes that Adams's focus on the Nisei, who were generally more "accommodationist" in their responses to the camps, is fitting for his "official" presentation of life there (233). One of the industrious farmers he showcases states frankly that he "would like to assimilate more" (85). Moreover, for Adams, the ideal post-internment policy would involve "scattering" the uprooted internees "throughout the country" where they can "prove their worth as individuals, free to move about the land" (102). It seems, then, that while Adams is savvy in his associations of the internees with nostalgic nature narratives, he maintains the liberal myth of the United States as a land of opportunity for all, where self-made men and women have the chance to begin again, provided they are willing to work hard—and assimilate.

Adams also embraces the ideal of the United States as a "melting pot," in which color-blindness is the implicit goal of assimilation. He writes of a choral group he features in the text: "When you see them and hear them you do not think of their being of any particular race or nationality; they are simply human beings—singing" (92). This idea that we are all "simply human beings" reflects a broader shift in the mid-century United States toward universal humanism in racial discourse. Donna Haraway characterizes the 1940s as a time of an emergent antiracist, liberal biological humanism that emphasized "flexibility, progress, cooperation, and universalism" (*Modest_Witness* 238). This new "flexibility" meant that racial designations were becoming less stable, and Adams's text reflects that instability by reconnecting race and nature in new ways, much like Claude McKay's *Home to Harlem* did a bit earlier.

By dramatizing racial conflict in the West, the quintessential home of American nature, Adams implicitly contests the historical whitewashing of those landscapes. That he did so at a time when the war was not yet over, and racial tensions in the United States were high, is to his credit. At the same time, his reinvention of the West as a place with room for all "loyal" Americans upholds the traditional links between nature and nation that have long bolstered American exceptionalism. Adams's faith in the enduring qualities of the United States is grounded, both metaphorically and materially, in nonhuman nature. After all, he proclaims, "America is as stable as the mountains, as severely eternal as the ocean and the sky!" (108).

A two-page photo spread near the end of the book once again asks readers for compassion by drawing on nature's "ancient" sense of justice. Dramatic, snow-covered peaks and wispy clouds hover above shadowy foothills and sunlit aspen trees. The caption informs us: "In the presence of the ancient mountains the people of Manzanar await their destiny" (106). This caption renders the detainees passive, as well as patient, victims—a rhetorical strategy Adams rarely invokes. But rather than undoing the work of constructing the Japanese Americans as hardy, self-reliant pioneers, this statement works alongside that construction, strengthening their association with the nation by affiliating them with an "ancient," and so, by implication, a timeless and reliably just, natural world.

Such dramatic shots are vintage Adams, the kind of photos that commonly appear on posters and postcards sold in national park visitor centers. Probably because of these sorts of images, Neil Campbell dubs Adams photography's "own 'Turner,'" likening him to U.S. history's monumental myth-maker (*Cultures* 15–16). Campbell explains that "in Adams's West the past is sacred, complete, and untouchable"; his images thus repress "the West as . . . a zone of contact and encounter" (*Rhizomatic West* 184). This may be the case for much of Adams's more popular landscape photography. But in *Born Free and Equal*, it is precisely the mythical character of his landscape photography—its "pull to authenticity, origins, and tradition" (*Rhizomatic West* 184)—that strengthens his case for social justice and highlights the West as the primary contact zone in which national identity is negotiated.

Adams's photography does often depict a "monologic, monumental vision of a preserved wilderness devoid of humanity" (*Rhizomatic West* 183), but, as this book shows, these monumental representations of nature can potentially have a range of impacts when humans are present. Even when they promote the problematic myth of nature as an unpopulated, pure, or authentic space, his images are a part of a visual history of nature preservation in the United States in which powerful images have helped inspire support for nature management agencies like the National Park Service and, occasionally, helped preserve wilderness areas more directly, as Subhankar Banerjee's photography has done recently for the Arctic National Wildlife Preserve. As part of this established visual history, Adams's images in *Born Free and Equal* do something more complex: by including humans, they enlist mythical nature in order to build a case against a particular social injustice.

At a time in American history when the human-nature binary was on the brink of collapse, *Born Free and Equal* not only shows the lingering power of the American frontier but also anticipates new ways frontier rhetoric might function. The fact that Adams can portray Japanese Americans as pioneers gestures toward a trend in frontier rhetoric. As Patricia Limerick observes, the word "pioneer" has become unmoored from its anchor in whiteness: "The American frontiering spirit, sometime in the last century, picked itself up and made a definitive relocation— from territorial expansion to technological and commercial expansion" ("Adventures" 88). Rhetorically speaking, even yesterday's "savages" might be deemed pioneers, provided they can lay claim to uncharted intellectual, artistic, technological, commercial, or other "territory." As Limerick shows in her discussion of African Americans headlining as pioneers in civil rights, it can be jarring when a designation historically associated with the taming of nature and the civilizing of people of color is used to connote success for those very people.

Odd though it may seem, this rhetorical shift mirrors a broader ideological unmooring of associations between race and nature—a destabilization of meaning that enables creative recombining of categories. John F. Kennedy's "New Frontier" is perhaps the best-known example of an American president deploying frontier rhetoric, though his attention to "unconquered pockets of ignorance and prejudice" as well as "poverty" suggests a more justice-oriented and racially aware use of the rhetoric than, say, Roosevelt's (qtd. in Limerick, "Adventures" 81). The "frontiers" of Alaska, outer space, and cyberspace also suggest the flexibility of frontier rhetoric. At the same time, many frontier narratives still invoke traditional binaries, celebrate competitive capitalism, and bolster U.S. power abroad. Chapter 6 and its corresponding interchapter return to a discussion of the complicated shifts in how Americans understand the frontier.

As it anticipates these shifts, Adams's text both resonates with older, nostalgic nature rhetoric and foreshadows fresh ways of understanding our complex engagement with nonhuman nature. Some of these fresh ways began to emerge in mid-century nature writing and environmentalism. Chapter 3 situates texts by Aldo Leopold and Rachel Carson on the cusp of a more sophisticated understanding of human-nature relations, albeit without a pronounced racial awareness. Their pivotal texts illustrate a shift from understanding nature as material and distinct from human cultures to seeing the two as necessarily and complexly intertwined. Just as Adams does in his defense of the internees, these writers draw upon familiar American nature narratives as they sound alarm bells for another marginalized entity: the more-than-human world. Unlike Adams, though, Carson and Leopold simultaneously question some of the very nature narratives they draw on, especially the frontier and its damaging legacies. Indeed, for these authors, *all* humans and many environments have become victims of frontier ideology, not just people of color who found themselves on the wrong end of the civilization-savagery continuum.

Pastoral nature, by contrast, still serves for both Carson and Leopold as an ideal that might be revived in the present—or at least invoked as a rhetorical strategy for environmentalism. For these two preeminent nature writers, nostalgia for the more harmonious human-nature relations represented by a pastoral ideal serves as an affective check—an emotional second-guessing of so-called progress in the face of its negative impacts on humans and environments. This "check" would perhaps become most widespread with the "end of nature" rhetoric of the 1980s, when environmental activists and writers chronicled growing fears of having crossed a line into a postnatural world. By mid-century, though, nostalgia for a lost, or potentially lost, natural world was already shaping the American environmental imagination.

1980s
end of nature
nostalgia

3 / Nostalgia's Caring Capacity: Rachel Carson's *Silent Spring,* Aldo Leopold's *A Sand County Almanac,* and the "Last Call" for Nature

The years immediately following the Second World War, particularly the 1950s, are usually represented as a time of wealth and optimism, when the country looked forward instead of backward—an era to feel nostalgic *for,* but hardly a nostalgic time itself. Americans like to recollect the decade as one of blanket prosperity characterized by increased wages, the growth of suburbia, better buying power for the United States in the wake of the war, and new imagined communities created on—and by—television.[1] The "fifties"[2] supposedly consisted of white, patriotic, middle-class, nuclear, suburban families, for whom things like poverty, racial tension, premarital and adulterous sex, abortion, infidelity, divorce, and murder simply did not register—the Norman Rockwell families depicted in popular television shows like *Leave It to Beaver* and *Ozzie and Harriet.* Of course, nostalgic versions of the period gloss over uncomfortable facts. For instance, roughly a quarter of Americans were living below the poverty level, with no food stamps or housing programs to assist them (Coontz, *The Way We Never Were* 29). Contrary to the whitewashed visions of the fifties promoted by pop culture, "real life was not so white [or so simple] as it was on television" (30).

Why, then, are Americans so often nostalgic for the fifties? Stephanie Coontz suggests that what we really miss about this decade is its optimism, particularly when compared to the depression of the 1930s and the war of the 1940s. In his brief history of the environmental movement, Hal Rothman echoes Coontz in observing that, during this time of relative stability, few people were nostalgic for the prewar period (1).

Still, this optimism was the result of complex forces—not all of them democratic or progressive. As Coontz explains, "The social stability of the 1950s . . . was a response to the stick of racism, sexism, and repression as well as the carrot of economic opportunity and government aid" (*The Way We Really Are* 44). One need look no further than the example of the Japanese American internees, many of whom had lost jobs, businesses, and homes during the war, to see how racism and other forces ensured the unequal distribution of the nation's postwar wealth.

Despite the social and economic limitations of the postwar era, the general health of the American economy helped spotlight the suffering of one demographic: the natural world. It was during the relatively prosperous post-WWII era that the alarming impacts of humanity on our environment began to catch the easily distracted eye of the American public. As Rothman points out, "the paradox" of the environmental movement consists in the fact that Americans are most concerned about the environment when they have the luxury to be (5). Historically speaking, "Americans have shown a tendency to be 'green' when it is inexpensive—economically, socially, and culturally—but a reluctance to collectively sacrifice convenience and even the smallest of material advantages to assure a 'cleaner' future" (5). This paradoxical pattern still holds true, and today's activists struggle to make environmentally friendly lifestyle choices more affordable, or at least not excessively costly.[3] Fortunately for nonhuman nature—and for humans who value things like clean air and water—the fifties and sixties were decades in which going green was a luxury Americans could afford.

Earlier environmental writers and activists like Henry David Thoreau and John Muir had written eloquently about the value of preserving the natural world—often, at least in part, foregrounding personal pleasure and self-improvement. A conservation ethic, guided by a sustainable but anthropocentric and economically motivated land use philosophy, dominated American nature management in the late nineteenth and early twentieth centuries. By 1945, however, development was encroaching on more and more remote places, and people were beginning to second-guess their rapacious resource consumption. Rothman argues that, by mid-century, conservation had lost its political power; "its embrace of orderly progress [seemed] paradoxical, and many of its concerns [seemed] archaic" (3). Building on earlier preservationist efforts, a new and improved version of environmentalism, based on protection rather than multiple use of resources, was slowly emerging. Of course, "wise use" never fully went away; indeed, as I will note in later chapters, a neo-conservationist ethic would reemerge later in the century. Still, a new environmentalism, which contained the seeds of its grass-roots counterpart, the environmental justice movement, was slowly building momentum. Nostalgia was central to environmentalism from its mid-century beginnings, and it became, for better and for worse, increasingly entrenched as the movement went mainstream.

The publication of Rachel Carson's *Silent Spring* in 1962 has been claimed as an origin of both mainstream environmentalism and environmental justice. *Silent Spring* was instrumental in sounding alarm bells and exposing the mounting costs of the "impetuous and heedless pace" of "progress," some of which, like smog and polluted waterways, were becoming increasingly visible to the American public (Carson 17). In this brave exposé, Carson carefully documents the negative impacts of pesticide use on animals, humans and our environments. While it drew criticism even before its publication—including from some in the scientific community who dismissed her warnings as "feminine hysteria" (Lytle 7)—this seminal environmental work reflected a growing knowledge that "a separation of a pristine natural world from a somehow fouled and human-created world" was an "anachronistic" way of thinking (Rothman 19).[4] Indeed, Carson was on the cutting edge of a broader shift toward seeing nonhuman nature not as culture's opposite but as inextricably connected to the "human-created world."

Her book warned readers about the destruction and pollution of not just the environment but also our own bodies, and it did so in a way that was both accessible and affective. *Silent Spring* combines testimonies from everyday Americans—the bearers of local knowledge who founded and continue to drive the environmental justice movement—with data from experts in the scientific community to make its historic case. Far from being clinical, though, Carson's rhetoric strategically "convey[s] ... both emotion and analysis" (Foote 744); she sought to reach readers' hearts as well as their minds. Her epigraph from Keats's poem "La Belle Dame Sans Merci" sets up the mood of loss that informs her narrative. As Bonnie Foote puts it, "the poignant elegance and tragic imagery" of the romantic tradition guide her story from the beginning (742). Carson's is an example of what William Cronon calls a "declensionist narrative": one in which "the tragic flaws of a self-deluding people finally yield crisis and decline" ("Place for Stories" 1361). Although environmental narratives are, arguably, too often declensionist (a point I will return to at the end of this chapter), Carson and other environmentalists know as well as historians do that "a good story makes us *care* about its subject" in a way that simply chronicling information does not (Cronon 1374, original emphasis).

This "caring capacity" marks Carson's text from its opening pages. Her "fable for tomorrow" sets up the rest of the book by imagining a world in decline, symbolized by a small town where "no birds sing." Carson describes a pastoral environment, situated "in the heart of America," that has been destroyed from within by humans' use of DDT and other forms of chemical control. Her first two paragraphs sketch an Edenic community, full of new life, vibrant sounds, active animals, and even tourists who come to enjoy bountiful nature. The "abundance" and "beauty" of the town, she assures her readers, have deep roots; it has been this way "from the days many years ago when the first settlers raised their houses, sank their wells, and built their barns." After invoking this bucolic environment, Carson quickly clouds our pleasant vision in an abrupt narrative turn. Without warning, a "strange blight crept over the area" and transformed its abundant life into "stillness" and death. Carson does not name the "shadow of death," but instead uses the fable to entice us to read the rest of the book, in which she will "attempt to explain." She also clarifies that, although this town does not exist, "every one of these disasters has actually happened somewhere," and some communities have experienced "a substantial number of them." The death she only fictionalizes here has the potential to become "a stark reality we shall all know" (13–15).

Carson's fable is significant in that it both generates and capitalizes on nostalgia for a natural world that has been destroyed. As Lawrence Buell notes, its "pastoral oppositionalism" prevents the fable from being "a simple nostalgia piece" (*Environmental Imagination* 44). Indeed, the not-so-simple nostalgia Buell alludes to is key to the effectiveness of her book. By assuring us that towns like this one have existed since the "first settlers raised their houses," Carson draws obliquely on the widespread American nostalgia for our pioneer ancestors (who, so the story goes, paved the way for the kind of pastoral scene described here) and identifies this fictional town with nature's longevity—a move that underscores the moral "rightness" of the town. The small town is a nostalgic site in its own right, especially given the demographic shifts of the early part of the century (toward cities) and those Carson's contemporaries were seeing (toward suburbs). In addition to invoking both pastoral and frontier nostalgia, Carson also takes advantage of imperialist nostalgia: the longing of first-world countries for the very thing—either a culture or an environment—they have destroyed. Locating destruction in our own backyards, she warns that the homes of all Americans—not just those of marginalized or oppressed groups—are at stake. With this warning, Carson gives imperialist nostalgia a specific target: everyday environments.

Carson is clever enough to both invite our nostalgia for the environments we are damaging and criticize the ideologies that enable imperialistic behaviors. Like many authors before and since, she draws on the civilization-savagery binary in her critique. Sometimes her rhetoric is subtle—for instance, when she calls our assumption that "nature exists for the convenience of man" a holdover from a more "primitive" scientific era (261–62). She is more directly critical on other occasions, for example, when she wonders whether "any civilization can wage relentless war on life without . . . losing the right to be called civilized" (99). Carson is particularly adept at connecting the human domination of nature to the domination of other humans. For instance, she notes the "ironic significance" of the use of similar chemicals for insecticides and for "new and devastating weapons in man's war against his own kind" (35). As Cheryll Glotfelty has shown, Carson "employs Cold War rhetoric . . . to mobilize support for a protracted war on despoilers of the environment" ("Cold War" 159). When she ends the book with the observation that we have turned our "most modern and terrible weapons" against the insects and the earth, we can't help but add one more victim to this list: ourselves (Carson 262).

Silent Spring spoke to barely suppressed anxieties during the Cold War era and exposed the country's postwar confidence as, at least partly, delusional. The book also tapped into the seemingly perpetual American nostalgia for nature, especially its pastoral mode. Nostalgia does not govern Carson's text; she is not writing in the grips of it, or of any emotion. Rather, she uses nostalgia as an emotional tool in her argument. She deploys it, in the same way she does her war rhetoric. Even while Carson identifies the many problems of her present and elicits her readers' nostalgia in order to inspire them to address those problems, she also locates nostalgia in the future in a unique way. In a sense, she threatens us with it. This desperate longing is what we will feel if we don't take action, she implies, and once such nostalgia sets in, it may be too late to change course. Ultimately, nostalgia has a catalytic potential for Carson's argument. If, as she asserts, "man has forgotten his origins," then nostalgia might help us recover them and move toward a more responsible future (44).

* * *

While *Silent Spring* is frequently heralded as one of contemporary environmentalism's literary and political origins, many scholars and activists locate an earlier origin in Aldo Leopold's *A Sand County Almanac*, which was published posthumously in 1949 after being declined by numerous presses.[5] At first the text was underestimated as "just another collection of charming nature essays," and its profound thesis was overlooked; however, the *Almanac* enjoyed a surge in popularity in the late 1960s (Nash 83). Rothman credits Leopold with instigating a "protoecological side of the [conservation] movement," marking him as primarily a conservationist but one who helped define the terms of modern environmentalism (33). Roderick Nash presents a useful perspective on these new terms: "When ecology helped Americans think of other species and the biophysical world as an oppressed and exploited minority within the extended moral community, the contemporary environmental movement received its most characteristic insignia. Old-style conservation, plugged into American liberalism, became the new environmentalism" (64). Bringing a career in conservation to bear on delineating a more ecocentric perspective—and perhaps, depicting "his own ecological redemption from past conservationist sins" (Dorman 316)—Leopold's work bridges the perceived divide between conservation and preservation, as represented in most historical accounts by the seemingly antithetical perspectives of Gifford Pinchot and John Muir.[6]

Although the *Almanac* upholds some traditional conservationist priorities, like hunting, it revises those priorities by extending moral consideration to the more-than-human world, treating nonhuman nature as an "oppressed and exploited minority" and pushing its audience to reconsider long-standing economic attitudes toward land and species. Leopold's influential text marked the beginnings of a new environmentalism that entailed a renewed skepticism about certain American nature narratives, especially frontier rhetoric and its role in enabling the human domination of nature. Still, this environmentalism was not wary of all nature narratives: it tended to hold on to a lost pastoral past as an ideal we might strive for in the present.

Scholars disagree about whether the text is more anthropocentric than biocentric, or whether Leopold's deep ecology is tainted by rugged individualism, but everyone agrees that the *Almanac* is important.[7] A must-read for anyone with even a glimmer of interest in environmentalism, ecology, or environmental ethics, the book is sold in most National

Park Service visitor centers, usually in its mass-market form. The cover of this edition touts its role as "the classic statement of the joy and beauty found in a style of life that protects the environment." This sense of affirmation and optimism distinguishes it from Carson's: while Leopold does chastise humanity for its harmful effects on the natural world, and he does warn us about the potential consequences of ignoring those effects, his *Almanac* also celebrates the human capacity to live "in harmony with [our] surroundings." After all, the life he chronicles—his own—is an example of just that.

By the late '60s, radical counterculture movements, guided in part by an "antitechnocratic, pastoral mentality," were eager to celebrate such a life (Marx, "Pastoralism in America" 38–39). But in 1949 the *Almanac* reached readers who most likely did not see anything wrong with the status quo and who, for the most part, would have seen "progress" as bringing big pay-offs. A "development-oriented ethos" governed the years immediately following the war, and, by the late 1940s, conservation "as an ancillary form of progress" was just beginning to fall out of vogue (Rothman 26, 19). As Wallace Stegner notes, Leopold's optimistic contemporaries would, by and large, have found his ideas "heretical," especially with their "socialistic" underpinnings and their vocal distaste for progress ("Legacy" 237). Leopold surely knew he was facing a tough crowd. If his argument is, on occasion, anthropocentric, it might be because, as he admits, "man brings all things to the test of himself" (8). Or, if we give him more credit as a political strategist, we might conclude along with Nash that he deemed it "prudent to be ethical with regard to the natural order that sustains the human one," especially in the wake of "conservation policy wars," and so deployed a more tactical anthropocentrism (81). It wasn't until the 1960s, at which point the *Almanac* and essays from *Round River* were combined into a single text, that his audience would become more receptive to the idea of "intrinsic rights to existence of nonhuman life forms and of life communities or ecosystems," the insight Nash and others credit as the "intellectual dynamite" of the text (81).[8]

There is surely "dynamite" in his ideas, but Leopold's rhetoric is rarely explosive. He is gentle in his reminder that progress imposes a "cost in things natural, wild, and free" (xvii). Employing the rhetoric of marginalization, Leopold designates himself as part of a "minority" who sees "a law of diminishing returns in progress" (xvii). He describes his sand farm in Wisconsin as a "refuge from too much modernity" and "a backwash of the River of Progress" (xviii, 50). By embracing this outlier perspective, Leopold treads cautiously as he asks his readers to identify with one person's somewhat renegade experience. Combining an often playful autobiographical chronicle with quite serious critique, the *Almanac* culminates in its famous articulation of an American land ethic, usually summarized by the well-known statement that "a thing is right when it tends to preserve the integrity, stability, and beauty of the biotic community. It is wrong when it tends otherwise" (262). His ethic is groundbreaking not for its warning of the "spiritual dangers" wrought by our increasing disconnection from the nonhuman world, but rather for proposing a solution that merges science and morality (6).

If his land ethic is, as J. Baird Callicott concludes, "an affective-cognitive posture of genuine love, respect, admiration, obligation, self-sacrifice, conscience, duty, and the ascription of intrinsic value and biotic rights," then nostalgia deserves credit for its role in inspiring this "posture" ("Conceptual Foundations" 214). In particular, part of Leopold's affective success derives from his ability to draw on post-frontier concerns about overcivilization and invoke a familiar pastoral nostalgia that is largely opposed to progress—an "affective-cognitive" narrative that may have fallen on deaf ears in the late '40s but sounded far more compelling to readers two decades later. Through both sincere and anticipatory nostalgia—his own and that which he hopes to elicit in readers—Leopold invokes nostalgia as an affective indicator of excess progress and as a useful emotion in connecting humans to our environments, to other species, and to each other in healthier, more sustainable ways.

Leopold enlists a range of rhetorical strategies to make his critique and to outline a land ethic that his audiences might move toward. His representations of nonhuman nature are the scaffolding for this construction. On many occasions, he describes nature as a "kind of literature" that lies open for us to read (27)—a strategy Carson, too, employs when she characterizes nature as an "open book" that has been too-long "unread" (65). For Leopold, nature's residents are owners of a vast "historical library," an "accession of new books" that contain "allegories" for historians, naturalists, and laypeople to interpret (Leopold 32, 27, 17). Occasionally, nature is positioned as a "comic-moral instructor or commentator on the human world" (Sayre 118). Humans are, from this perspective, merely "dull pupils" (Leopold 68). Now and then, nature is a dramatic "show" for spectators to observe (35–36). As Robert F. Sayre notes, nature is even figured as a painter (118). These descriptions are, of course, anthropomorphic, and they implicitly uphold a human-nature binary; yet Leopold does render human and nonhuman animals equal coinhabitants of a world that is, itself, intrinsically valuable.

Moreover, by personifying nature, Leopold takes advantage of a strategy Sayre identifies as a feature of the sentimental tradition—a literary tradition that typically promotes beneficence, sincerity, refinement, and self-discipline. Within nineteenth-century American sentimental literature, Sayre explains, nature offered a prime setting for fostering these values. Sayre points out that sentimentalism has a history of fighting for the underdog. Leopold—and many writers and environmentalists who followed him—were able to draw on this tradition to effectively "make nature the weak, 'endangered species,' and so evoke sympathy for it" (Sayre 117). This strategy could work in the twentieth century in a way it could not have in the nineteenth because only since the closing of the frontier had American nature become a "weaker side" that needed protection. Indeed, it worked especially well in the late '60s, when high-profile civil rights battles were demanding protection for marginalized people. In this context, an also-marginalized wilderness, an endangered species, or a polluted river could more readily be cast as an object of sympathy and a cause around which to rally.

Sayre's contribution to Leopold studies acknowledges that the *Almanac* has "extended the range of human sentiments" readers can feel about nature, and I suspect he would agree that emotion is more than just an intermittent rhetorical strategy for Leopold (119). The book is a call to grieve, to mourn the loss of the more-than-human world that we have destroyed. It is, at a fundamental level, a nostalgic text, both in the sense that it describes nostalgia and attempts to elicit it in its readers. Although Sayre rightly notes that "Leopold saw human superiority to animals not in our science or invention but in our nostalgia and grief," he does not investigate that nostalgia in any depth (119). As we saw with Zitkala-Ša's stories, sentimentalism and nostalgia can work together in the service of an author's interests. But it is important to see how nostalgia functions as a narrative strategy that is part of a long national history with the emotion, as well as the history of environmental rhetoric.

Although my analysis focuses mainly on Leopold's essays, since this is where nostalgia shows itself most prominently, it helps to consider, first, nostalgia's function in the *Almanac* as a whole—that is, the nostalgia promoted by its structure. Scholars have traced the increasing generalization and abstraction that occur as readers move from the evocative descriptions and "embodied dialogue" of part 1 to the expository essays of the fourth part of the book.[9] William Barillas gives a helpful overview:

"By moving from the local to the universal, from natural history through autobiography to ecological theory, the structure of Leopold's book creates, as John Tallmadge comments, 'a climate of belief that will make us receptive to Leopold's doctrine of land citizenship.' If Leopold changes his reader's outlook, he does so by first providing entertainment and instruction regarding ecological issues as they affect particular places and people. Like all good nature writing, *A Sand County Almanac* succeeds as both polemic and poetry, as science and literary pastoral" (90). I agree that the structure of the book encourages a "climate of belief" that is prompted in part by the threat of loss. Perhaps, then, the organizational strategy of the text is to "hook" us with loving descriptions of nature—to make us see and feel for the particular environment Leopold has come to love—then remove these details and engender a sense of loss. Coming into a reading of "The Land Ethic" with a strong sense of both beauty and loss might encourage readers to listen more closely to Leopold's recommendations.

As poetry gives way to polemic, nostalgia increases. But Leopold does not just document currently existing nostalgia; he goes beyond that to anticipate the loss of our ability to grieve and the loss of our desire to wonder what used to be. In effect, he worries about the absence of nostalgia. He warns the reader that, if we continue to fail to grieve, we will continue down the path of decline that we call progress, to the point where we may no longer even know what we have lost. Indeed, the anticipatory nostalgia Leopold conjures sounds a lot like what Scott Slovic, working from Janet Landman's book *Regret: The Persistence of the Possible*, calls "'anticipated regret'—nostalgia for what was or could have been." Slovic describes this emotion as "a nostalgia experienced, paradoxically, before actual loss" (*Going Away* 38). Environmentalists today often draw on this kind of nostalgia for political purposes, but Leopold and Carson may have been among the first to deploy it as a prominent feature of an environmentalist manifesto. If Leopold, as Carson does in her fable, helps "readers see a vanished world, and he hopes, love it" (Sayre 121), then this love is contingent on our willingness to anticipate that disappearance and the nostalgia it would bring.

The most overt invocations of nostalgia occur in Leopold's essays, but there are nostalgic moments in the month-by-month descriptions as well. In "July," Leopold muses that "what a thousand acres of Silphiums looked like when they tickled the bellies of the buffalo is a question never again to be answered, and perhaps not even asked" (49). A few pages later, he admonishes humans for a historical absence of emotion in the face of species loss: "Few grieved when the last buffalo left Wisconsin, and few will grieve when the last Silphium follows him to the lush prairies of the never-never land" (54). Leopold continues to situate himself in the minority—he represents the "few" who *will* grieve—and he asks us to join this minority by acquiring a stronger sense of history and an ability to read the landscape, to care about it, and to love it.

For those readers who are not cognizant of environmental loss, Leopold provides a detailed record. His text is declensionist in tone but evolutionary in content; he admonishes us to learn humility from Darwin and remember that "men are only fellow-voyagers with other creatures in the odyssey of evolution" (117). In a Darwinian sense, Leopold's nature registers change but not value-based gains or losses. If nature makes no value judgments, though, changes can and should be measured by humans, especially if we are to learn to "read" nature as a historical text. Leopold models this approach for us in "Good Oak." In this oft-cited section of the *Almanac*, Leopold tells a "tree-based history" of the region by sawing through the trunk of a dead oak tree, working slowly back in time, ring by ring, to the end of the Civil War (Rogers 62). Leopold catalogs multiple environmental losses, which neither people nor the tree seems to have noticed. It is not a nostalgic history that the tree yields. The past is fraught with excessive hunting, extreme weather, species extinction, and the commodification of nature. Although his history contains some "gropings toward" ecological awareness—for instance, the proclamation of Arbor Day in 1889—it mostly lists casualties of the "march of empire" (Leopold 17, 16). We may not want to return to a past peppered with bitter winters, record-breaking fire seasons, or Civil Wars, but we may long for the days and years just before the last pigeon flew, just before "Wisconsin parted with its last cougar," or just before "the last wild Wisconsin turkey was killed" (12, 16). These losses should inspire our nostalgia in the present, even though we cannot return to the past.

The "pith-year" of the oak is 1865. Most significantly for national history, of course, this year marks the end of the Civil War. For Leopold, the war resolved the question of whether the "the man-man community" was "lightly to be dismembered"; however, he points out, we have failed to ask the same question of the "man-land community" (16–17). The year is an important one in regional history as well, since it "stands in Wisconsin history as the birthyear of mercy for things natural, wild, and free" (17). John Muir offered to buy his brother's farm that year, and, according to Leopold, the idea of wilderness preservation was presumably born. Sounding a bit like the NPS origin story, with its benevolent vision of stewardship and "mercy" toward "wild" nature, this environmental origin myth situates Muir as a founding father. Leopold suggests that the "core" of the history nature tells contains the roots of environmentalism, which we might uncover with the proper tools (17). Indeed, tools are prominent characters in the story, helping Leopold carve out a complicated "allegory" for environmental historians (17). He suggests that a "good history" depends on "the diverse functions of saw, wedge, and axe" (19, 17). Only with these three perspectives—which offer year-by-year, collective, and "diagonal" views of the past—can we make some sense of the "hodge-podge called history" (18–19). The "Good Oak" story reminds us that origins are never simple and must be broached from multiple perspectives in order to get a more accurate sense of the past. More obviously, the anecdote illustrates that nature contains our collective past, and when we destroy it, we destroy, in a very real sense, our nation's history.

Though it gestures toward the nation's past, the *Almanac* is more explicitly concerned with a regional environmental history. On this particular sand farm, the passage of time is marked, cyclically, by seasonal occurrences: the return of geese and familiar flowers in springtime, or the chopping of wood and the banding of chickadees in early winter (84, 103). By inviting us to witness a complete annual cycle—the "cycle of beginnings and ceasings which we call a year"—Leopold holds up a different version of time than the one promoted by national metanarratives of the past, like Turner's (3). He counters the notion of progress by his *Almanac*'s very form, through its cyclical chronicle of the seasons, which are always (to invoke Said) "beginning again." Nature provides the "theater of evolution" through which we might browse the "historical library" of our local environments (32).

With his affectionate descriptions of nonhuman nature, organized by month, the overall impression of the *Almanac* is of a man who knows, and loves, his home environment. Picking up on Thoreau and anticipating Stegner, Wendell Berry, and other successive environmental writers who champion a "sense of place," Leopold advocates local knowledge and a rooted life. He poses "the important question, who is the more thoroughly acquainted with the world in which he lives," himself or the other "wild things" with whom he shares a neighborhood, and he challenges us to ask the same question of ourselves (83). Leopold may be in the minority—indeed, his agrarian existence might appear antiquated to some contemporary readers—but his idyllic life is one that many American readers have historically found enviable. Above all, Leopold's

Almanac makes readers experience, vicariously, the emotions he feels for the place. Prominent among these emotions is nostalgia.

* * *

After subtly introducing nostalgia in the *Almanac,* Leopold becomes more heavy-handed in the essays. At times, he directly theorizes the emotion. "On a Monument to the Pigeon" is perhaps Leopold's most explicit exploration of nostalgia. He begins by describing a monument erected to "commemorate the funeral of a species" that now lives only in museums and books: the passenger pigeon. He elicits our nostalgia with dramatic language, reminding us of the sad reality that "no living man will see again" these fine birds, and that "book-pigeons," ironically, "live forever by not living at all." He even anticipates the failure of the monument to effectively memorialize the birds when he speculates that "a decade hence only the oldest oaks will remember [pigeons], and at long last only the hills will know" (116).

Leopold makes concessions to readers who might be champions of progress when he admits to certain general gains in creature comforts. However, he fosters doubts as to whether the loss of this particular creature is worth those gains: "Our grandfathers were less well-housed, well-fed, well-clothed than we are. The strivings by which they bettered their lot are also those which deprived us of pigeons. Perhaps we now grieve because we are not sure, in our hearts, that we have gained by the exchange. The gadgets of industry bring us more comforts than the pigeons did, but do they add as much to the glory of the spring?" After urging us to evaluate the "the glory of the spring," to feel the loss of the pigeon "in our hearts," and to consider whether this loss might be of some significance, Leopold defends himself from the accusation of "economic moralists" that "to mourn the pigeon is mere nostalgia" (118). Since he just spent two full pages eliciting our nostalgia (not to mention the many other nostalgic evocations leading up to this section), it is apparent that Leopold does not see this emotion as "mere" escapism or romanticism. Instead, it is a key emotion in connecting humans to our environments and to other species in ways that make us want to care for them and, as such, an integral part of Leopold's rhetorical strategy.

Our ability to feel nostalgia is also, for Leopold, one thing that distinguishes humans from other animals.[10] In two paired paragraphs—which are repeated nearly verbatim in the "Monument" section—he offers two speculations about "objective evidence of our superiority over the beasts." In both paragraphs, it is not our technology or consumer products that set us apart—not "Mr. Bush's bombs and Mr. DuPont's nylons" (117, 119). In the second of the symmetrical paragraphs, it is our sense of history—or, rather, our ability to "see America as history," which is not exactly the same thing—that distinguishes us. Seeing America "as" history involves journeys through the past that use the landscape as time machine and historical subject, the kind of historical vision Leopold models for us in "Good Oak."

In the first of the paired paragraphs, we discover another ability that makes humanity unique: our ability to grieve. Leopold explains that "the Cro-Magnon who slew the last mammoth thought only of steaks. The sportsman who shot the last pigeon thought only of his prowess. The sailor who clubbed the last auk thought of nothing at all. But we, who have lost our pigeons, mourn the loss. Had the funeral been ours, the pigeons would hardly have mourned us" (117). As he indicates elsewhere, there remain far too many sportsmen and sailors among us. "We" are asked to move beyond their thoughtlessness and recover an ability to mourn that is presumably innate but underdeveloped. His crucial point is that, as humans, we have the potential to feel as well as to survive. To make this point, he associates mourning with we Americans who, having surpassed the Cro-Magnons in some aspects, at least, have evolved the capacity to think of more than just food and basic necessities. We also have the incentive to do so, now that modern humanity is destroying nonhuman nature at an accelerated pace.

The beginnings of these two paragraphs are equally worthy of comparison. In the first, Leopold informs us in a gently worded admonition that we are to blame for the relatively new phenomenon of species extinction, that "for one species to mourn the death of another is a new thing under the sun" (117). Two pages later, he changes the wording just slightly to read: "To love what *was* is a new thing under the sun, unknown to most people and to all pigeons" (119, original emphasis). Here Leopold seems to want us to recognize nostalgia as, in some sense, a recently evolved emotional phenomenon—a backlash against environmental destruction and, in that sense, both a "new" and a positive development. Buell stresses that Leopold is "careful to keep sentiment under control" in these paragraphs; indeed, he does seem to "qualify" his "elegy with astringent afterbite" when he notes that the pigeons "would hardly have mourned us" if the tables were turned (*Writing* 195). However, this reading underestimates the importance of human emotions in the "Monument" section. Leopold assumes that we mourn, and that we love, and he asserts that to fail to do these things is, in some sense, unnatural.

While Sayre designates the affective response Leopold expects from us "sympathy," I believe it is more appropriately called nostalgia (122). Indeed, the two main emotional phenomena Sayre (I think, rightly) identifies in Leopold's text, "grief for the dead and sympathy for the endangered," are nostalgic as well as sentimental ones (120). The first, grief for what has been lost, is classic nostalgia. It is the longing to return to a time and place that once was—or, a variation of this, the longing to return what was, a lost animal, plant species, or environment, to us. Either way, the nostalgic object is a prelapsarian world in which all species exist intact. The second, sympathy for that which is endangered, functions as a form of anticipatory nostalgia, much like the warning Carson gives to her readers in her "fable for tomorrow." If we are to have this sort of sympathy, we must acknowledge the reality of that first emotion—grief for what has been destroyed. This grief is both already occurring, for those of us who mourn the pigeons, and expected to increase as more endangered species and landscapes are irrecoverably lost.

No emotional ground is off-limits for Leopold, and on several occasions he capitalizes on the nostalgia many people feel for childhood to entice us to heed his warnings. He invites us to connect the sense of loss associated with childhood to the broader sense of environmental loss his book describes; if we can feel the former, then perhaps we can also feel the latter. For instance, when pausing to regard some initials carved into an aspen tree Leopold speculates that: "The old man was dead now; in his later years his heart had thrilled only to his bank account and to the tally of his flocks and herds, but the aspen revealed that in his youth he too had felt the glory of the mountain spring" (135). Leopold repeatedly asserts that we are most inclined to connect with nature when we are young. He even wonders whether "growing up is not actually a process of growing down," since his earliest impressions of nature "retain a vivid sharpness of form, color, and atmosphere that half a century of professional wildlife experience has failed to obliterate or to improve upon" (128). In another allusion to childhood environments, he writes, "When the last corner lot is covered with tenements we can still make a playground by tearing them down, but when the last antelope goes by the board, not all the playground associations in Christendom can do aught to replace the loss" (227). By eliciting nostalgia for childhood, during which all environments are potential playgrounds, this passage reminds us that some losses are irreplaceable.

It is these irreplaceable losses that Leopold describes with the greatest sense of urgency. In his powerful "Marshland Elegy," the first essay after the *Almanac*, he voices his fears about species extinction most poignantly. He worries that the "high priests of progress," unable to apprehend the value in an undrained marsh, nearly destroyed crane populations in Wisconsin; for these birds, "the song of the power shovel came near being an elegy" (106–7). Contrasting the tragedy of the ruined marsh with the near miss of the cranes, Leopold offers a reminder that writing elegies is a rhetorical strategy that concerns both actual and potential loss. In this elegy, Leopold nostalgically invokes the "Arcadian age" of this ecosystem, during which "man and beast, plant and soil lived on and with each other in mutual toleration, to the mutual benefit of all" (106). Unhappily, this situation was altered by "new overlords," who, guided by an exclusivist notion of community and an economic relationship to the natural world, "did not include soil, plants, or birds in their ideas of mutuality" (106–7). Invoking a narrative of interruption, not unlike the tactics used by Claude McKay, Leopold references a lost Arcadia and fingers us—nature's "overlords"—as the machines in our own gardens.

In a passage that resonates remarkably with Carson's fable, Leopold ends the essay with a warning: "Some day, perhaps in the very process of our benefactions, perhaps in the fullness of geologic time, the last crane will trumpet his farewell and spiral skyward from the great marsh. High out of the clouds will fall the sound of hunting horns, the baying of the phantom pack, the tinkle of little bells, and then a silence never to be broken, unless perchance in some far pasture of the Milky Way" (108). In this passage, where no cranes sing, we are haunted by the noise of the hunting horns and the predatory baying of "phantom" hounds. Gesturing, perhaps, toward a post-apocalyptic world, Leopold imagines that these noises, too, will cease, replaced by an endless silence. Leopold asks us to measure our actions against ecological standards: "geologic time" and the "far pasture of the Milky Way." If the end result is "a silence never to be broken," then clearly we have failed to meet nature's standards. As indicated by this and other concrete examples, it is more than just a general sense of loss that Leopold writes about; it is the loss of particular species and particular environments that he suggests should warrant our nostalgia. Thus, his nostalgia is "replaced"—tied to landscapes, animals, histories, and ecological communities. He constantly channels and roots our longings, giving us specific objects toward which we should direct our emotional energies.

At the same time, though, the text resonates with more abstract nostalgic nature narratives that have shaped the nation's self-image. Like the "checkerboard of prosperous farms" Carson writes about in her fable (13), Leopold conjures a pastoral ideal only to represent it as threatened by humanity's reckless (and economically driven) utilitarianism. Barillas situates Leopold in the Jeffersonian tradition insofar as he celebrates the yeoman farmer, chooses to settle in and educate himself about a single place, and writes in "colloquial, commonsensical language" (92). His analysis situates Leopold in a line of Midwestern pastoralists who show how "Jeffersonian, utilitarian, and Romantic values may be modified" and contextualized in order to formulate "a progressive land stewardship" (6). Although Jeffersonian ideologies bolstered U.S. expansionism and the destruction of ecosystems to make way for agrarian practices, Jefferson himself adhered to the pastoral belief in "the allegedly superior moral integrity of people who live closer to the soil" (Marx, "Pastoralism" 50).[11] It is this morality that Leopold seeks to recover in echoing Jefferson's ideals; his nostalgic pastoralism is designed to expand our moral horizons.

One step in doing so, Leopold claims, is enlarging our notion of the beautiful. In romanticizing his own daily life in the American Midwest, Leopold suggests that the "commodification and abuse of the midwestern landscape result, in part, from an inadequate sense of the beautiful in nature" (Barillas 96). By valuing a less dramatic ecosystem than that typically preserved in the United States at that time, Leopold draws our attention to the importance of protecting even places that aren't widely considered beautiful.[12] He also picks up the mantle of earlier nature writers, such as Thoreau and Muir, who similarly championed nature's underdogs.

As the "Good Oak" anecdote reveals, Muir was a key figure in Wisconsin's history and a key predecessor for Leopold. Muir was not the only important figure to share a neighborhood with Leopold. Frederick Jackson Turner also spent his boyhood in the area, quite close to Leopold's farm, in fact, and the two were acquaintances. They were inspired by the same landscape and its history; Turner's "famous 'frontier thesis' originated in research into land-tenure patterns around his home town" (Barillas 89). The historical coexistence of these figures suggests the complicated overlap between pastoral and frontier ideologies that occurs in Leopold's text, among many others.[13]

While his pastoralism is apparent, Leopold's language does, at times, also resonate with frontier imagery—primarily the yeoman farmer of the Turnerian tradition. Occasionally he even sounds a bit like an apologist for the progressive hunter-hero of the Rooseveltian adaptation. For instance, he identifies hunting as an "instinct" that is "bred into the very fiber of the race" and chastises "supercivilized" humans who are unmoved by nature's offerings (227). In naturalizing hunting as an "instinct" and accusing Americans of becoming too civilized, he seems to maintain the early-century fears of overcivilization popularized by Roosevelt. Much like Zitkala-Ša did, Leopold takes advantage of ongoing American anxieties about overcivilization to, in effect, alarm his readers into agreement. We might excuse these Rooseveltian moments by recalling Sayre's insights about the sentimental tradition, specifically the point that, within this tradition, it is considered a sign of refinement to recreate in nature (227). Here and elsewhere—for instance, when he defines a conservationist in terms of how he uses an axe—Leopold reveals his lingering conservationist priorities and aligns himself with that historical position (72–77). Indeed, as Buell points out, Leopold opposed trophy hunting—Roosevelt's favorite way of rediscovering manhood in nature. As a "hunter-turned-environmentalist," Leopold believed the ideal hunting experience was one that "gave way to nature appreciation" (*Writing* 183).

And yet, Leopold does demonstrate what seem to be sincere traces of frontier nostalgia when he harkens back to the pioneers to recover a tradition that values "self-reliance, hardihood, woodcraft and marksmanship" (213). Explaining how this tradition plays a role in the contemporary moment, Leopold suggests it is a return to these values that prepares such a young man "to face the dark and bloody realities of the present" (211). It is no surprise to hear Leopold laud Roosevelt as a "great sportsman" who "expressed this intangible American tradition" (214). It is also no surprise to hear Leopold repeat the now-discredited idea that "ontogeny repeats phylogeny in society as well as in the individual," an idea sometimes used to bolster white supremacy (212). However much Leopold sounds like an advocate for "regeneration-through-regression," the past he wishes to return to is at times more Turner's than Roosevelt's (Slotkin, *Gunfighter* 38). In particular, he is Turnerian in his desire to invoke a pioneer past that shapes national identity via an agrarian, democratic collective, "a kind of Whitmanian hero *en masse*" (34).

The rhetoric of civilization that comes along with this ideal has its drawbacks, though, not the least of which is that it requires a "savage" counterpoint. Leopold cannot avoid tapping into both poles of the familiar civilization-savagery binary. In "Wildlife in American

Culture," Leopold begins with a romanticization of Native Americans based on a distinction between their "primitive" behaviors and their "civilized" ones (211). Here, he describes Indians as "wild roots" to which non-Natives might return. Sounding remarkably like Turner, Leopold defines proximity to nature as part of "our distinctive national origins and evolution." When a boy scout "has tanned a coonskin cap, and goes Daniel-Booneing in the willow thicket below the tracks," he is "reenacting American history" (211). Although certainly not invoking the heroic "Indian-fighter" of Roosevelt's myth, Leopold's history does not include Indians as actual participants; rather, they are merely symbolic counterpoints to "our" civilization—part of the regenerative "proximity" that has added exceptional character to American identity (Slotkin, *Gunfighter* 34). Moments like this must be identified as, at best, exclusive and, at worst, racist.

That said, there are times when Leopold's embrace of rugged individualism seems far more tactical. A case in point is his story of two boys canoeing the Flambeau River. For these young men, the canoe trip serves as an "interlude" between the "two regimentations" of college and the military. Leopold argues that it is not "novelty" or "healthful exercise" that are valuable in this trip; rather, it is the opportunity for the canoeing "adventurers" to taste "freedom" (119–20). Leopold is specific about the sort of freedom at stake. It comes from being free of civilization's trappings—free of things like watches, servants, police officers, and roofs over heads. More than that, though, it is the "elemental simplicities of wilderness travel" that are traditionally valued as part of the American pioneer experience: the "complete freedom to make mistakes," as well as a "taste of those rewards and penalties for wise and foolish acts . . . against which civilization has built a thousand buffers" (120).

This rhetoric implies a certain Rooseveltian emphasis on regeneration. But in a one-sentence paragraph that caps off this section, Leopold makes an interesting move: he anticipates and laments the absence of nostalgia in future generations who, "having never seen a wild river, will never miss the chance to set a canoe in singing waters" (124). In language that resonates with today's environmental warnings—for instance, the often-voiced fear that our grandchildren may never see a glacier, or know what a polar bear was, due to global warming's impacts—Leopold once again hypothesizes an inability to feel the kind of longing he values, a future in which nostalgia is absent. Slovic expresses ongoing worries about this kind of a future when he asks, "Is the 'worst' the end of something or the feeling of loss after something ends or disappears? Or is it *complacency*—the lack of feeling or engagement, the suffering pain-lessness of enervation—that is the worst that can happen to us?" ("Be Prepared," 42, original emphasis). For Leopold, the answer was clear long ago: emotional complacency is the most frightening fate. The idea of never lamenting the opportunity to take a canoe trip down a river, never missing the chance to experience this wild freedom, is perhaps the worst of all futures, for it implies both the irrecoverable destruction of wilderness and the loss of our ability to engage emotionally with the more-than-human world.

In passages like this, we can see what Robert Gottlieb has in mind when he characterizes Leopold as both "deeply entrenched in the tradi-tion of rugged individualism" and the country's "first deep ecologist" (35). Indeed, Leopold does walk a fine line between conservation and preservation. Returning to his celebration of sportsmanship, it is notable that Leopold ends by suggesting that wildlife research might be under-stood as a new "sport" in which even amateurs can realize the "fun" that "lies in seeing and studying the unknown" (220). With this sly move from eliciting nostalgia for the frontier to suggesting the pleasures of developing an ecological conscience, Leopold demonstrates his ability to use familiar, even troubling, narratives in the service of promoting environmentally progressive ones.

Although he is nostalgic for certain components of pioneer experi-ence, Leopold occasionally makes an unmistakable critique of the fron-tier, at least insofar as it is equated with the quest for unchecked progress. When he tells the story of the killing of a sole grizzly bear in Arizona by a government trapper, Leopold avows that it is, ironically, our pioneer her-itage that has caused us to destroy nature. He reminds us that the "con-gressmen who voted money to clear the ranges of bears were the sons of pioneers. They acclaimed the superior virtues of the frontiersman, but they strove with might and main to make an end of the frontier" (145). Ultimately, Leopold draws attention to the negative effects of frontier values by informing us that "we, too, [a]re the captains of an invasion too sure of its own righteousness." A bit later, he is even more blunt about how our pioneering behaviors have served us: "Man always kills the thing he loves, and so we the pioneers have killed our wilderness" (157). In a subtle linkage of human-nature domination to imperialism, Leopold admits that he and his fellow forest officers "acquiesced" in the bear's death, even while they lamented the Native Americans who were "needlessly extinguished" by the Spaniards (145). While this sentiment risks romanticizing Indians as themselves a kind of "wilderness," it does ask readers to examine the hypocrisy in permitting some kinds of conquest while ignoring or sanctioning others. It also indicates an effort to redirect imperialist nostalgia—much like Carson does—toward a more careful consideration of exactly how we destroy our own environments.

He ends his discussion of Escudilla—now free of bears and "safe for cows"—as he so often ends his stories, on a note of nostalgia (144). Giving us yet another example of a nonhuman animal that we have destroyed, Leopold sadly concludes that "Escudilla still hangs on the horizon, but when you see it you no longer think of bear. It's only a mountain now" (145). Whether anticipating a marsh that lies "forgotten under the wheat," lamenting that the "feathered lightning" of the passenger pigeon "is no more," or wondering what he will do with his three sons when there are "no more deer in the hills, and no more quail in the coverts," Leopold frequently ends his descriptive stories with the expectation, or the reality, of loss (173, 118, 233). By the time we get to "The Upshot," we have been subjected to countless moments of nostalgia, both his own, personal, and heartfelt nostalgia, and the kind he anticipates—even wishes—for all Americans who are affected by ecological destruction. Leopold's final words to us before "The Land Ethic" are representative of the latter kind: "No more snipe whistling in the meadow, no more piping of widgeons and chattering of teal as darkness covers the marshes; no more whistling of swift wings when the morning star pales in the east? And when the dawn-wind stirs through the ancient cottonwoods, and the gray light steals down from the hills over the old river sliding softly past its wide brown sandbars—what if there be no more goose music?" (233). Adequately primed to hear his message in the final section of essays, readers exit part 3 with both "a taste for country" and the threat of that country's loss, a threat conveyed by the final image of a silent marsh.

* * *

I would be remiss if, in dwelling on Leopold's nostalgia, I reduced him to an emotional strategist. As the last excerpt makes clear, there is sheer beauty in his language as he shares with his readers the joy he finds in the natural world. In the words of John Tallmadge: "His essays on wild geese, for instance, convey as much yearning, exultations, and praise as the most strenuous poem of Shelley. Leopold's sense of beauty is complex but it is romantic and involving rather than abstract and contemplative. Thus, it contributes to our sense of him as a warm and engaging person:

we admire and are drawn to thinking people who can also be deeply moved" (128). I can't help but point out that Tallmadge's laudatory description gestures toward the sorts of nostalgic passages I have been highlighting, particularly in its mention of "yearning." Complementing Sayre's observations about sentimentality, Tallmadge offers a reading of this environmental masterpiece that shows how Leopold foregrounds his own sentimental refinement and asks us to join him in becoming a "thinking person" who also has the capacity to care for nature.

It is perhaps the book's biggest strength that it uses both lyrical description and fervent pleas to "deeply move" its readers; it shows us how and why to care, it models such caring, and it urges us in no uncertain terms to do so—or else. His writing is clearly an attempt at inspiring us to "feel, understand[, and] love" nonhuman nature (251). Ultimately, though, as Tallmadge notes, "The price of his ecological wisdom is loneliness, isolation, and an aching sense of loss. If we wish to emulate him, we have to accept those terms" (129). It is this "aching sense of loss" that permeates *A Sand County Almanac* and that, perhaps, contributes to its lasting appeal. Indeed, once nostalgia was demedicalized, it did begin to describe, in some circles, an individual who was "sensitive and imaginative, devoted and loyal" (Ritivoi 25). Following the sociologist Fred Davis, Ritivoi explains that, by the 1950s, nostalgia had "lost completely its pathological connotations" and instead could signify "an effort to discover meaning in one's life, to understand oneself better by making comparisons between the past and the present, and thus integrating experiences into a larger scheme of meaning" (29). Knowingly or not, Leopold demonstrates how nostalgia might move us toward just such meaningful, comparative, and integrative purposes. He also personally embodies such nostalgic sensitivity and dares his readers to feel it too. If the alternative to "knowing [the value of wilderness] in your bones" is being an "ineducable tyro" or one who is "very, very old," then many readers will be inclined to learn to "think like a mountain," even with the aches this brings (138, 271).

While these invitations were less likely to be accepted by readers in the 1940s and '50s, the 1966 preface to the *Almanac*, written by Leopold's son, Luna, and Carolyn Clugston Leopold, confidently addressed a much more receptive generation of readers—a generation already "demonstrating and working for social causes" (xv). The preface identifies nature as a cause that should be a top priority: "Of all the causes that attract the attention of these young people, the plight of nature is one which may be truly a last call. Things wild and free are being destroyed by the impersonality of our attitude toward the land" (xv). The preface also suggests that aestheticized nature—Barry Lopez's false geographies— has replaced actual "harmony between man and land" in this period. Speaking to a generation that was beginning to place new value on "getting back to nature," this "powerful plea" was well received. As Leopold's *Almanac* became a sort of Bible for burgeoning environmentalists, its elegiac tone served as a model for an environmentalism that combined nostalgia and a sense of crisis in an effort to spur people to action.

Leopold's "last call" was, of course, nothing of the sort.[14] Countless writers after him have chronicled nature's "plight," often by demonizing humans as callous, materialistic destroyers of our world. Carson, in particular, anticipates the "end of nature" rhetoric that Bill McKibben would popularize nearly thirty years later. For instance, she acknowledges that history consists of "interaction between living things and their surroundings"; however, she asserts that in the twentieth century "one species—man—acquired significant power to alter the nature of his world" (16). The fear that humans have irreversibly altered first nature was part of what inspired both Carson and Leopold to plead for the protection of unspoiled nature, if for nothing else, then "as a standard against which we can measure the changes our own activities bring about" (Carson 78). Leopold makes a similar point in his essay on wilderness preservation, suggesting that "each biotic province needs its own wilderness for comparative studies of used and unused land" (275). There is a sense of urgency, a sense that even these "samples" are diminishing far too quickly, but also hope that we might still intervene.

Not long after the publication of *Silent Spring*, another noteworthy "elegy" emerged on the scene: Edward Abbey's *Desert Solitaire*. Abbey's plea for nature relies on similar strategies and often sounds even more desperate. He begins the book with this warning: "This is not a travel guide but an elegy. A memorial" (xiv). His elegy, which Peter Wild labels sentimental, "indulges in the literary luxury of celebrating a romantic land that has just slipped through his fingers" (Wild 140). For instance, Abbey describes his beloved Glen Canyon, before it was "drowned" to create Lake Powell, as "an Eden, a portion of the earth's original paradise" that humans destroyed (152). Scholars debate the degree to which Abbey reenacts a sort of regenerative frontier narrative,[15] but there is little doubt that nostalgia contributes to his environmental message. Slovic credits Abbey with bringing together "apocalyptic social critique, sweet nostalgia for an edenic era of personal and societal innocence, and almost giddy sensualism" (Afterword 258).

In *Desert Solitaire*, Abbey comments explicitly on the connection between nature, specifically wilderness, and nostalgia:

> Suppose we say that wilderness invokes nostalgia, a justified not merely sentimental nostalgia for the lost America our forefathers knew. The word suggests the past and the unknown, the womb of the earth from which we all emerged. It means something lost and something still present, something remote and at the same time intimate, something buried in our blood and nerves, something beyond us and without limit. Romance—but not to be dismissed on that account. The romantic view, while not the whole of truth, is a necessary part of the whole truth. (167)

The idea of wilderness surely does not elicit nostalgia for everyone, and the genderedness of his words (forefathers? womb of the earth?) will no doubt alienate some readers. But Abbey deserves credit for identifying nature's complexity—it is always both "something lost and something still present," something "remote" and something "intimate"—and for connecting nature with loss. His implicit advice, that we should sort the "justified" nostalgia from the "merely sentimental" and use both to ascertain the "whole truth" about our histories and ourselves, suggests nostalgia's role in assessing political and environmental changes. This advice is more pertinent than ever.

To sympathetic readers, Leopold, Carson, and Abbey showed how nostalgia is one "justified" response to environmental degradation, a response that might help inspire, among other things, wilderness preservation. Like Abbey, who knew that being too successful with his loving descriptions of the desert would draw more tourists and spoil the very area he worked to protect, Leopold recognized the ironies of wilderness preservation. For instance, he remarks somewhat despairingly that "all conservation of wildness is self-defeating, for to cherish we must see and fondle, and when enough have seen and fondled, there is no wilderness left to cherish" (Leopold 108). Even as he argues for more preservation, he suggests the best we can do is to keep aside some "tag-ends of wilderness, as museum pieces" for those of us who might want access to the "origins of [our] cultural inheritance" (265).

Understanding Leopold's *Almanac* as a precursor to the elegies by Carson and Abbey helps us begin to sketch a genealogy of environmental rhetoric that leads to the present day. It also helps us rethink the movement's origins and, perhaps, consider new ways of using affective language to foster environmental ethics. As Leopold's text suggests, nostalgia can have productive consequences for readers and activists alike. To his mid-century audience, many of whom would have had the luxury to think ecologically instead of just economically, nostalgia for unspoiled nature may have been a catalyst for new ecocentric perspectives. As Stegner points out, Leopold's nostalgia aligns him with his forerunners—Cooper, Thoreau, Emerson, Muir, and Whitman among them—in that there was often "the dark bass of warning, nostalgia, loss, and somewhat bewildered guilt" in their writing as well (Stegner, "Legacy" 235). If the novelty in Leopold's text lay in its troubling assertion that "science corroborates our concern, not our optimism," then the deep resonance of these "dark bass" notes help cement that message (235).

Leopold, Carson, and, more controversially, Abbey, deserve credit for inspiring more people to value "intangible assets—scenery, solitude, and other similar values" in addition to, or even instead of, so-called progress (Rothman 31). As the 1950s and '60s marched on, environmentalism became a more prominent item on the national agenda. With this newfound centrality, nostalgic longings of all kinds—for the frontier, for pastoral communities, for pristine wilderness, for nature as a site of adventure—continued to proliferate in sometimes startling combinations. In much the same way that Leopold's Indians were occasionally reduced to romantic symbols in the development of his environmental ethic, this emergent American environmentalism often promoted its agendas at the expense of more comprehensive forms of social justice.

Iron Eyes Cody—a.k.a. the "Crying Indian"—is perhaps best known for his role in a public service announcement (PSA) that aired for the first time on Earth Day 1971 as part of the "Keep America Beautiful" campaign. The PSA begins with Cody—wearing braids, feathers, and "traditional" garb—paddling a canoe along what appears to be a pristine stream. Loud drum beats accent his steady, deliberate strokes. Suddenly, the camera zooms in on a scrap of newspaper adrift in the water and the tone darkens, as ominous music in a minor key casts doubt on the idyllic scene. The camera pans out and our Edenic stream is revealed as illusory: it is, in fact, a canal in an urban landscape, marred by smog, smokestacks, highways, and more pollution strewn about the water's edge. A deep-toned voiceover warns, "Some people have a deep, abiding respect for the natural beauty that was once this country. And some people don't." The camera zooms in on Cody as he steps ashore, and the voiceover works with a close-up shot to identify him as among the "some people" who do have this "abiding respect." The rebuke that "some people don't" is punctuated by a careless driver tossing the remains of a fast-food meal at Cody's feet. As he looks down at the trash, then slowly back up at the audience, a single tear runs down his cheek, signifying his profound emotional witness to the wreckage of the natural world. That final, poignant look is an iconic one for many Americans.

Cody, the son of Italian American immigrants who adopted an American Indian identity by claiming Cherokee and Cree parentage, "played

The natural beauty that was once this country...

The natural beauty of clear, blue skies. Mighty flowing rivers. Tranquil lakes and unspoiled valleys and hillsides. The natural beauty of America is ours to protect. It starts with things you can do. Like not littering the sidewalks. By actively supporting programs to clean up our rivers, lakes and streams. Or planting trees to help purify the air. We can make America beautiful again.

People start pollution.
People can stop it.

Keep America Beautiful
advertising contributed
for the public good

HELP FIGHT POLLUTION CAMPAIGN
MAGAZINE AD NO. HFP—1789-72——7" x 10" (110 Screen)   B-50
Volunteer Agency: Marsteller Inc., Volunteer Coordinator: W. Howard Chase, American Can Company

FIGURE 4. Iron Eyes Cody (a.k.a. the "Crying Indian") paddles a canoe in support of the "Keep America Beautiful" campaign, 1972. (Courtesy of the Advertising Council Archives, University of Illinois University Archives, RS 13/2/207)

Indian" in his day-to-day life as well as on the big screen. A high-profile advocate for both environmental protections and Native American causes throughout his life, Cody also starred in several Western films alongside former president Ronald Reagan.[1] But his most influential act was certainly this award-winning PSA. His emotional performance combined with the PSA's central message—that "people start pollution; people can stop it"—helped launch a successful anti-pollution campaign and energize the emerging environmental movement.[2] The PSA reflects key insights sparked by earlier environmentalist texts like Rachel Carson's—most importantly, that nature is part of everyday life, that urban spaces are as worthy of protection as rural ones, and "that public health and the environment, human and natural environments, [a]re inseparable" (Gottlieb 84). By embracing and reenacting American Indian iconography, Cody helped introduce the American public to some of the environmental movement's main goals: to challenge unchecked capitalism and to begin a fight for "quality of life" for (at least some) Americans.

At one level, then, we might read the PSA as an instance of counter-nostalgia. It begins by tapping into the dominant nostalgia for a "lost" Edenic nature (which, of course, would only appeal to certain viewers) through the image of the Indian paddling down a bucolic stream, then disrupts that nostalgia with the striking components of its anti-pollution message. Viewers are instructed to look to the past—to what "was once this country"—to find natural beauty and to use that ideal as motivation for present-day preservation efforts. The opening shot of Cody paddling down the seemingly secluded stream marks the original Eden from which modern Americans have fallen. Counter-nostalgically, the disruption highlights the disjuncture between past and present, invoking a pre-lapsarian world that might serve as a vision for the future. The PSA accuses non-Natives of neglecting their responsibilities as stewards of the land and generates an affective response that could, and did, fuel political action.

However, whether the PSA generates a desirable environmentalist ethic is questionable, at best. Ginger Strand's essay in *Orion Magazine* raises some legitimate concerns as it brings a finely tuned greenwashing radar to bear on this now-classic visual text. She points out that the Ad Council, who helped with the ad's creation, was simultaneously promoting the very disposable food products and packaging the ad condemns. Moreover, the PSA promotes the liberal ideology of the mainstream environmental movement through which individuals—the "people" who can and should take action to stop pollution—are too often encouraged to take small-scale, personal actions rather than advocate for broader change by addressing systemic problems. Strand concludes that the ad is "greenwash gold," explaining that Cody's tear is "a rebuke to individuals rather than a rejection of the ideology of waste." If we agree with Strand's reading, which I do, then even the PSA's benefits to environmentalism are severely limited.

As significant—and as unfortunate—is the way the PSA capitalizes on dominant stereotypes about Indians as uber-environmentalists to achieve its goals. In this nostalgic tale, Indians are visually and symbolically conjoined with the nature for which their "deep, abiding respect" is famous. In his much-discussed book, *The Ecological Indian: Myth and History*, Shepard Krech III opens with a discussion of the Crying Indian campaign as playing into the too-simple myth of Indians as "noble ecologists" whose sustainable way of life was destroyed by an invasive white culture (15).³ While this is certainly true, it is also the case that, by constructing a direct connection between Indians and nature, the PSA upholds a human-nature binary that affiliates Indians with the latter. With its polarizing rhetoric and corresponding imagery, the PSA creates an opposition between Native Americans and the rest of America: the "some people" of its initial proclamations who do respect nature are held up as models for those people who do not. However successful its anti-pollution message, then, the PSA perpetuates the myth of the disappearing Indian as spokesperson for an also disappearing natural world, and its success at raising environmental awareness comes at the expense of Native American interests. Moreover, although the PSA pins responsibility for environmental problems and solutions on consumer-oriented Americans, there is no corresponding sense of responsibility pertaining to ethical problems (or ethical solutions) regarding human beings. There is no suggestion that "people started colonialism; people can stop it." At best, the PSA implies a kind of social alchemy by which, if Americans care for the environment (presumably through the simple act of throwing away garbage properly), their efforts might mysteriously dry the tears of this nation's native residents.

While Cody himself worked for both environmental and Indian causes, this PSA subsumes the interests of American Indians to those of nature. The appeal to protect the environment is achieved by concealing the ongoing marginalization of indigenous people. Cody's tear may represent "a tear for the fate of America," but it is an America whose budding interest in protecting the environment overshadows an even greater cause for shedding tears: the racism and domestic colonization that are embedded in this nation's history and continue to this day. The result is a substitution of an interest in nature's "fate" for a concern for the fate of Indians—indeed, for all Americans who are unable to achieve the "quality of life" sought by early environmentalists.

* * *

A follow-up to the original PSA aired in 1998. This second version also features Cody's famous tear—this time trickling down a two-dimensional portrait of his larger-than-life face, which is displayed on the inside of a bus stop shelter. As it does in the original, litter dropped by careless consumers falls at the feet of the Crying Indian. This PSA opens with honking horns and other noisy street sounds; distracted commuters eat snacks and drink from to-go cups while waiting for their bus. Although they are, to their credit, riding public transit, these Americans have clearly not learned their lesson about pollution. One man sets his Styrofoam cup down on the sidewalk, another crushes a cigarette butt under his heel, and a third aims his newspaper toward a trash can but misses. It flutters to the ground next to the other litter, and a slight breeze lifts the trash in lazy circles. An eerie, almost post-apocalyptic emptiness ensues once all the people have boarded the bus, and the camera brings us from the ground level up to Cody and his tear. Finally, simple, lowercase, white letters on a black screen caution us that the issue of pollution is "back by popular neglect."

This urban space is even further removed from "nature" than in the 1971 PSA; there is no idyllic stream from which "progress" has distanced us. Obviously designed to capitalize on the nostalgia generated by Cody's famous tear as well as his popularity (after all, his image is also "back by popular neglect"), this PSA replicates the problems of its precursor: displacing Indians from real communities and environments, and collapsing Native Americanness into a vague realm of anti-consumerist "authenticity" in ways that dehumanize them and dehistoricize their present-day concerns.

There is one important difference between the first- and second-generation PSAs, though. The iconic nature of this particular Indian, and perhaps of American Indians more generally, is oddly foregrounded here. The superficial image of the Crying Indian at the bus stop just might provoke questions about where the "real" Indians are in this slice of everyday life. While the tear itself is brought to life (it falls in real space and time, even on the flattened-out face of Cody), one can't help but wonder how this simulated Indian's relegation to a mere image—a sort of floating signifier of environmental concern—affects the new PSA's message. Is the transformation of the Crying Indian into an image (albeit, an image marked by some evidence of reality) merely a move to update the message for today's media-savvy audience? Or does it reflect a further marginalization of Native Americans by rendering them an easily commodifiable image detached from its past?

Although the answers to these questions are, of course, debatable, it is safe to say that, as a symbol of critique, the Crying Indian works precisely because of his pastness. Cody's face and tear are meant to signify capitalism's opposites: nature, authenticity, and an anti-progress ethic. Even though the second PSA has been updated for a late-capitalist audience, his face and tear are identical to the 1971 version, and so the two-dimensional Indian remains "irremediably mired in the past" (Huhndorf 196). Nostalgia operates at two levels now: the first, at which the generalized Indian stereotype is "mired in the past" for many Americans, and the second, at which Iron Eyes Cody functions as a particular nostalgic image, gesturing back to the 1970s and the birth of mainstream environmentalism. The latter operates through the former, in fact, as Americans are reminded (via nostalgia) of the golden days of the environmental movement, whose mission we've purportedly "neglected." This nostalgia depends upon the stereotyped image of Indians as both "past" and "natural"—stereotypes that have functioned throughout the history of European colonization but were especially powerful during this period.

The discovery that Iron Eyes Cody is not an Indian at all but, in fact, an Italian American from Louisiana further highlights that the popular Cody is an image, not a real person.[4] The PSAs are effective because he appears to uphold the stereotype of the noble savage. His ancestry does not, in a sense, matter. This perceived substitutability of Indian identity was common to countercultural movements in this period, which anticipated a shift toward a trendy multiculturalism that, together with postmodernism, "emphasized the openness of meaning" (Deloria 172). Indianness, like other identity positions and cultural signifiers, "could mean whatever one wanted it to mean. On the other hand, and almost alone among a shifting vocabulary of images, Indianness could also be a sign of something unchanging, a first principle" (167). Put another way, "mainstream Americans began to imagine Indianness as a set of individual qualities" that could be appropriated, rather than a historically specific set of identities (Huhndorf 160). As hippies played Indian to perform rebel identities, the more powerful image of the Indian as "first principle" became central to mainstream environmentalism's nostalgic plea to save the earth. Unfortunately, saving the earth did not necessarily entail paying attention to all of earth's inhabitants, and the "neglect" of certain human cultures remained under the radar of a largely white, middle-class environmental movement.

Likening nature to marginalized humans was becoming a successful method of arguing for nature's protection. However, in the incipient environmental movement this tactic rarely worked the other way; that is, even if the call for nature's protection was effective, arguments for social justice were often neglected by early environmentalist agendas. Leopold's and Carson's work anticipate a new trend, though, and it has since become more common to depict human cultures themselves as "endangered." Countercultural movements sometimes seized on this language.[5] The environmental justice movement has also deployed this rhetorical tactic, defending some humans as "endangered species" (di Chiro 316). Recently, Richard Louv, the author of the influential *Last Child in the Woods* and the inspiration for the "Leave No Child Inside" campaigns, cites the notion that "the child in nature is an endangered species" as a "fundamental idea" of the children and nature movement.[6]

Initially, though, environmentalism was heavily influenced by deep ecology's central tenets, including a perceived separation between humans and nature, a bias toward protecting pristine nature, and an individualization of responsibility for environmental problems. If somewhat progressive in their urban, everyday locations, the PSAs nevertheless exemplify a blind spot of mainstream environmentalism during the 1970s: namely, its tendency to dwell on the human domination of *nature* without connecting that relationship to the human domination of other *humans*. Although accusing white Europeans of destroying nature was commonplace in the environmentalism of this period, damages to human cultures did not yet receive similar acknowledgement.

American Indian writers, however, have long since known that human-nature and human-human relationships are complexly intertwined. Leslie Marmon Silko's widely anthologized essay "Landscape, History, and the Pueblo Imagination" defuses the idea that human beings are "somehow *outside* or *separate from* the territory" they experience (1005, emphasis in original). She highlights the positive implications of this worldview— not just "survival" but "harmony and cooperation"—by noting that for ancient Pueblos "survival depended upon harmony and cooperation not only among human beings, but among all things—the animate and the less animate" (1006). Similarly, Linda Hogan introduces her collection of essays *Dwellings* with the reminder that "humankind is not separate from nature" (12). N. Scott Momaday's nonfiction clearly shares these views. He prioritizes human-nature interconnectivity when he locates the origin of American literature with "the first expression of man in the American landscape"—an expression that "certainly antedates writing"—and thus identifies Indians as the first American authors (3).

In the following chapter, I consider Momaday's *House Made of Dawn* alongside his own nonfiction and within its sociohistorical context, including the stereotypes about Native Americans that were in vogue when it was published in 1968. This novel's Pulitzer Prize marked "a beginning for the political awakening and cultural revival that was to characterize the era of Red Power," and some critics have credited it with kicking off a Native American literary "renaissance" (Teuton 45). Of course the idea of a "renaissance" seems to undermine Momaday's assertion about American Indian literature as an ancient, even foundational, storytelling tradition. Simon Ortiz is among those who take issue with the term "renaissance" since, as he rightly observes, "the literature has always been there; it just hasn't been written" (Coltelli 6).

With awareness of this long-standing literary tradition, situating Momaday's *House Made of Dawn* as part of a broader "political awakening and cultural revival" helps illuminate its engagement with the volatile social and political landscape of its particular time period, including its burgeoning environmental sensibilities and progressive movements for social equality as well as its more problematic political realities, like the Relocation Program. Because of this engagement, the novel has a great deal to teach readers about the reconfiguration of nonhuman nature in the national imaginary, about shifting perceptions of American Indians, and about relationships between Euro-American and Native American literatures more generally, especially in terms of articulating a land ethic that contains nostalgia at its core.

4 / Remembering the Earth: N. Scott Momaday's Nostalgic American Land Ethic

While political radicals of the 1960s and '70s invoked symbolic Indians to protest the Vietnam War and fuel their "revolutionary identities," the Red Power movement focused its political energies on issues pertinent to real Indians (Deloria 165). Termination and the Relocation Program of the 1950s and '60s, which sought to end federal responsibility for tribes and encourage movement to cities, became the latest in a long line of federal legislation that may have been, within a certain assimilationist logic, well-intentioned but that produced negative effects for Native people. Termination meant the loss of tribal sovereignty and, for some tribes, the end of federal recognition and the federally funded services that came with it. Termination targeted tribes like the Menominees and the Klamaths, who were thought to have sufficient resources to sustain themselves without help from the federal government. However, their experiences proved largely negative, and termination was ended by the mid-1960s.[1]

Meanwhile, the Relocation Program moved as many as 100,000 Indians to urban areas but did not generally provide sufficient support for those individuals to face the cultural, geographic and economic challenges involved in the transition. One effect of relocation was the fragmentation of Indian cultures in the name of assimilation. More positively, the greater concentration of Indians in cities facilitated pan-Indian communities and contributed to the period's rise in political activism.[2] Partly in response to these new policies, a host of new organizations, including the widely known American Indian Movement (AIM), emerged to fight for self-determination. High-profile protests marked the decades: the nine-teen–month occupation of Alcatraz Island, "fish-ins" in the Northwest, protests at Mt. Rushmore and Plymouth Rock, the "Trail of Broken Trea-ties" and the occupation of the Bureau of Indian Affairs (BIA) building, and the notorious "Wounded Knee II" protest at the Pine Ridge Reserva-tion, which culminated in the unfortunate deaths of several activists and two FBI agents, as well as the controversial imprisonment of Leonard Peltier.

The tumultuous civil rights era proved an opportune time for Native Americans to make political strides.[3] In addition to garnering greater vis-ibility for Indian issues and renewing interest in "the recovery of Indian cultural identity and homelands," the Red Power movement had a hand in ending termination policies, prompting the passage of new legislation during the Nixon administration to support self-determination, and helping secure increases to BIA budgets as well as funding for scholar-ships, drug and alcohol recovery, health care, and other programs (Teu-ton 4).[4] Even with these gains, the popularization of reductive Indian imagery by the counterculture and the environmental movement threat-ened to obscure both the histories and the ongoing political concerns of Indians. In particular, the environmental movement's exploitation of the image of Native Americans as uber-environmentalists was usually invoked in connection with a nostalgic, Edenic past that valued nature most when it was unoccupied by any humans, including the country's indigenous inhabitants.

If the environmental movement saw Indians as the quintessential environmentalists, the counterculture was more interested in their "rebel" image, often embracing Indians as symbolic antidotes to an American nation they saw as excessively militant and consumerist. Growing out of both the Beat movement of the late 1950s and the 1960s New Left political organizations, the counterculture was, in Robert Gottlieb's words, "a disparate collection of social movements, new forms of cultural expression, and semireligious groups and ideas [that] con-nected the New Left critique of the consumer society and quality-of-life concerns with a desire to go 'back to the land,' or at least back to a simpler, more communal, more natural form of social life" (98).[5] Like regionalist writers of the 1920s and '30s, counterculturists were motivated in largely reactionary ways, defining themselves by what they were not, espous-ing anti-nationalist rhetoric, and sometimes preferring to "drop out" of American society. The counterculture did not fully articulate a cohesive "oppositional politics" but rather offered, at most, "an often unfocused search for new values" (Gottlieb 100). In keeping with both postmodern trends and the broad, often vaguely formulated goals of the counterculture movement, "[Indian] identities had power only as the symbols crunched together around an ill-defined, culturally centered notion of rebellion" (Deloria 165). Though not all counterculturists were environmentalists,[6] both groups valued simplicity, often expressed by the idea of getting "back to nature." Indians were the perfect symbol of a "more natural form of social life," especially for those who conjoined a critique of progress with an invocation of the pastoral ideal. Nature, one of the nation's time-honored counterpoints to technological advancement and unchecked capitalism, legitimated the counterculture's experiments with new ideological positions and provided the geographical spaces— communes—in which these experiments could be conducted.

By Earth Day 1970, nature had become a rallying cause for many Americans. Earth Day organizers strove to reconcile "anti-establishment and consensus-seeking impulses," and media representations of the event emphasized the need to curb pollution and develop new technologies, but both stopped short of calling for systemic change. The result was a broadly liberal political event that even the Nixon administration could embrace (Gottlieb 113). Although some New Left and counterculture participants walked away feeling betrayed by environmentalism's quest for consensus, concerns about the "environmental crisis" had become integrated into mainstream politics—for better and for worse (Rothman 85). Professionalization, institutionalization, and the kind of consensus seeking exhibited at the first Earth Day meant that more radical voices were frequently drowned out by moderate bureaucrats, especially after Ronald Reagan took office (Gottlieb 113). By the end of the 1980s, Gottlieb explains, mainstream environmentalism had defined itself "less as a movement and more directly as an adjunct to the policy process" (124). Critics today continue to note the disadvantages of this policy-oriented approach.[7] In addition to these limitations, environmentalism remained relatively elitist and anthropocentric throughout its formative years, and it failed to contend with "the intractable problems of race and class in society" (Gottlieb 113).[8] It would be at least a decade after the first Earth Day[9] before the environmental justice movement would begin to articulate a different agenda by foregrounding environmental racism, drawing attention to everyday environments, and problematizing mainstream environmentalism's white, middle-class perspective.

For the most part, the early mainstream environmental movement did not operate according to the ethics and warnings laid out by Aldo

Leopold and Rachel Carson. Despite Carson's concerns about the power of industry "experts" to shape political realities, most environmental organizations continued to court expertise at the expense of local knowledge. Leopold's famous proposal that "a land ethic changes the role of *Homo sapiens* from conqueror of the land-community to plain member and citizen of it" remained largely unheeded, as he himself had predicted in the years leading up to his death (204). His land ethic may have influenced many individuals, especially those concerned with deep ecology, and deep ecological tenets did, in turn, shape early environmentalism's decisions, priorities and rhetoric. However, in "The Legacy of Aldo Leopold," Wallace Stegner calculates that the environmental movement has been far more successful at enacting essential legislation than it has been at "spreading a real environmental conscience" (241). In terms of an ethical attitude toward nonhuman nature, the American public remains "a long way yet from where Leopold hoped we might one day arrive" (244).

Meanwhile, American Indians have long embraced and articulated land ethics of their own. As Lee Schweninger points out—and the Crying Indian PSA illustrates—the idea of a Native American land ethic often involves stereotyping that represents Indians as "keepers of the earth" or worshippers of a "Mother Earth goddess" ("American Indians and Environmentalism"). These generalizations are possible, in part, because of the tendency to assume a *single* "Native American" belief system and a single indigenous land ethic.[10] Still, many Indians do proclaim unique relationships to nonhuman nature, and oftentimes there is overlap between their articulations of these relationships and the dehistoricized stereotypes that circulate. Within this matrix of representations, it can be difficult to distinguish the true from the false, the authentic from the ersatz. Schweninger does so by way of Louis Owens, who asserts that Native writers embrace "a holistic, ecological perspective, one that places essential value upon the totality of existence, making humanity equal to all elements but superior to none and giving humankind crucial responsibility for the care of the world we inhabit" (qtd. in Schweninger, *Listening to the Land* 1). This rhetoric may sound like the facile labeling of Indians as the ultimate environmental stewards. But Schweninger explains why Owens's account is different: "Owens writes of himself and his contemporaries, not of nineteenth-century ideals; he places himself within a specific, complex, and vital context" ("American Indians"). In other words, the most accurate American Indian land ethic is one that is suitably complex, continually reevaluated and adequately contextualized.

It is in this spirit that I consider Momaday's land ethic. Momaday outlines this ethic in his nonfiction, most notably in the essay "An American Land Ethic," which he published in 1971—the same year the Crying Indian PSA first aired. In the essay he warns that we are at a critical juncture in our relationship with the nonhuman world: "We Americans need now more than ever before—and indeed more than we know—to imagine who and what we are with respect to the earth and sky. I am talking about an act of imagination, essentially, and the concept of an American land ethic" (47). Momaday explains, urgently, that our very humanity is at stake; a land ethic *must* emerge "if we are to realize and maintain our humanity, for our humanity must consist in part in the ethical as well as in the practical ideal of preservation" (47). Americans have tended to focus on the pragmatic aspects of preservation, but the ethical component is "alien to, or at least dormant in, most Americans" (48). Although he claims that "the American Indian has a unique investment in the American landscape," Momaday clearly hopes for a more universal ethic in the future, one that is rooted in a Native perspective but ultimately involves all people (33). To cite just one example of his inclusive rhetoric, Momaday counts himself as an "American" as well as a Native American when he writes "we Americans." This rhetorical move helps break down the Native/non-Native binary and invite all readers to hear his message. Momaday's land ethic grows out of a "racial memory" that American Indians once had—a concept I will return to shortly. Yet his "remembered past" is one that anyone might return to by way of imagination, language, and a re-conception of nonhuman nature as sacred.

Even though the ethic is open to all, Momaday does privilege an Indian perspective as his model. He compares his understanding of Native conceptions of earth as possessed of "spirit" with "modern society in general," which he accuses of seeing the earth as "dead matter" (Isernhagen 31). Such a conception informs modern practices of private land ownership, an idea Momaday claims is "alien" to Indians, whose "cultural intelligence" does not perceive such a thing ("Land Ethic" 40). He describes Native relationships to nonhuman nature in terms of what he calls "reciprocity": "Reciprocity is required by the fact that the powers of the natural world are distributed throughout all of its forms. The ideal relationship is expressed narratively through images of mutuality and interdependence, preeminently in the image of kin or 'family ties' between humans and other species" (Bol 26). An understanding of nature as "dead matter" enables its exploitation and reifies a separation between "live" humans and their environments. By contrast, the idea of reciprocity fosters a sense of "interdependence" between humans and environments—a moral rather than a utilitarian relationship.

Like Leopold, Momaday yearns for an "investment" that is not primarily economic, but ethical. Also like Leopold, Momaday draws on pastoral nostalgia to lament the effects of so-called progress, claiming that "our whole experience as a nation in this century has been the repudiation of the pastoral ideal," and the result has been a "psychic dislocation of ourselves in time and space" (47). Momaday's ethic is rooted in a relocation, a rediscovery of our place in the landscape. As Schweninger explains in *Listening to the Land: Native American Literary Responses to the Landscape*, for Momaday, this "rediscovery" might take place "through the imagination insofar as it is through imagination and the power of words that one captures, recaptures, or recognizes the sacredness of the land" and finds the sense of reciprocity Momaday advocates (138).

What is striking about Momaday's land ethic is the extent to which it must be recollected. It is first and foremost a *remembered* past we must try to access. Momaday elaborates: "Once in his life, a man ought to concentrate his mind upon the remembered earth, I believe. He ought to give himself up to a particular landscape in his experience, to look at it from as many angles as he can, to wonder about it, to dwell upon it. He ought to imagine that he touches it with his hands at every season and listens to the sounds that are made upon it. He ought to imagine the creatures there and all the faintest motions of the wind. He ought to recollect the glare of noon and all the colors of the dawn and dusk" (45). This passage, which Momaday initially included in *The Way to Rainy Mountain*, is notable in that it situates the remembered earth not just as a physical entity but also, even primarily, as something "to concentrate [one's] mind upon." Indeed, the infinitives Momaday uses to describe this process of remembering conflate inhabiting with imagining: "to wonder" is followed up with "to dwell"—a verb with both mental and physical connotations—and both are compounded by repeated requests "to imagine." The section ends with the charge "to recollect," reminding us once more that this imagined earth is in the past and must be recovered.

When Momaday concludes the essay with the insistent assertion that "Americans must come again to a moral comprehension of the earth and air," the phrase "come again" denotes a return, a recovery, a circling back to an earlier land ethic (49). Since Momaday defines his land ethic, in part, through an "act of imagination," readers are able to gain limited but valuable knowledge of tribal cultures through Momaday's fictional accounts (Su 97). I will revisit the politics of this recollection—in particular, how non-Native readers are invited to participate in the process—in my discussion of *House Made of Dawn*. For now, let me stress that it is more than imagination, language, and a sense of sanctity that are required to access Momaday's remembered earth. Emotion, specifically a nostalgic longing to return to what Momaday might call an "appropriate" way of life, is also essential. Because an investment in the land has been lost over time, a subtle, backward-looking perspective shapes his conception of what a land ethic should mean. As Schweninger observes, the "ethical regard" Momaday theorizes in his essays is not always precisely formulated; his fiction helps clarify what the ethic entails. A closer look at the role of nostalgia in Momaday's best-known novel rounds out prior accounts of his land ethic, offers new insights into this important text and contributes to discussions of ethical environmentalism that are more important than ever.

* * *

As a Stanford-educated Wallace Stegner fellow, a student of the modernist writer and critic Yvor Winters, and a scholar of Emily Dickinson and Frederick Goddard Tuckerman, Momaday was certainly shaped by non-Native as well as Native American cultural traditions. His experience confirms that "any simplistic oppositional approach to Native American literature must be replaced by a more complex dynamic" that recognizes Native and non-Native traditions as "sometimes in conflict, sometimes cooperative, but always interactive and mutually transformative" (Toy 28).[11] Within American Indian Studies, there is often an "imagined divide" between those who, like Craig Womack, advocate Native nationalist perspectives, and those who, like Phyllis Toy, urge more cosmopolitan or "interactive" perspectives (Tatonetti 279). I agree with Lisa Tatonetti that there is more common ground between the perspectives than is sometimes granted, and I do not wish to reinforce this divide. I hope to treat Native American literatures as distinct artistic and social endeavors that Paula Gunn Allen (1996) has characterized as moving toward increased sovereignty and self-definition. At the same time, I believe Native literatures can best be understood as always in dialogue with non-Native cultures and traditions—a dialogue that occurs in the face of unequal power dynamics, which demand recognition.

With this sense of dialogue in mind, I suggest that *House Made of Dawn* engages and challenges the most prevalent stereotypes of its historical period concerning Indians and nature. Momaday describes his approach to stereotypes as "turning the tables": "I'm using the stereotypes against the perpetrators of the crime as they've used them against me and have for generations succeeded. They fail to see the Indian, they see him in their own terms, and of course it's a false view. So I take the false view and throw it back" (Isernhagen 45). In *House Made of Dawn*, Momaday does this by redefining the kinds of stereotypes revealed in the Crying Indian PSA: the "false view" that depicts Indians as political rebels, as authentic "natural" humans (and so, spokespersons for nature), and as always disappearing into the past. In his seminal first novel, Momaday reappropriates these stereotypes of Indianness for different, oppositional, ends.

House Made of Dawn has been read, convincingly, as a critique of colonialism and its corresponding religious, modernist, and assimilationist projects.[12] Indeed, Father Olguin's failed attempt to restore "an order of industry and repose" through religious mentoring is clearly mocked in the book; his literally blind eye, and his desperate claim ("*I understand!*") at the novel's end, render him a parody of Christian tolerance (53, 210, original emphasis).[13] Similarly, the novel's albino character might easily be read as a symbol of white imperialism, whether understood as "Western modernity, colonialism, Christianity, or some combination of those three Euro-American forces" (Douglas 11).[14]

However, most critics of the novel have overlooked the ways in which its critiques are fueled, in large part, by nostalgia. Phyllis Toy notes "the elegiac emphasis . . . many readers have attributed to the novel" but does not attend to the content or the effects of these elegies (33). Indeed, she assumes that nostalgia is antithetical to her critical project of reclaiming sovereignty for the indigenous cultural traditions in the text. Jason Stevens assesses the novel's move to "magnify both the nostalgia for lost origins and the incertitude of identity" (605). Yet Stevens, too, dismisses nostalgia's potential when he concludes that "the tragic and elegiac chords of [Momaday's] work subdue the sense of victory he elsewhere sounds when describing the heroic conquest of his ancestors' imagination or the ancestral storyteller's agility before his audience" (624). Stevens misidentifies frontier nostalgia in a text that is much more rooted in a pastoral tradition when he equates nostalgia with what he sees as Momaday's failed attempt at participating in "the return-to-wilderness motif" (605). Since the idea of nature as a "proving ground" for identity is a highly Westernized one, very unlike the understandings of nature Momaday expresses in his interviews and his nonfiction, this reading measures Momaday's work by white European conceptions of wilderness (623). More promisingly, Sarah Schiff acknowledges that nostalgia becomes, for Momaday, "a strategic act, one that counterbalances a romantic thirst for origins with a violent quest for redress" (100).

For John Su, Momaday's nostalgia is without question a political ally. Su's book *Ethics and Nostalgia in the Contemporary Novel* focuses on how nostalgia intersects with concerns in the 1960s and '70s within ethnic studies, particularly in regard to writing alternative cultural histories. He traces how nostalgia functions in very different ways for two of the book's characters—Tosamah, a Kiowa preacher living in Los Angeles, and Abel, Momaday's mixed-blood protagonist, who has just returned to his home in New Mexico after fighting in WWII (90). For Momaday, Su explains, nostalgia "opens up the possibility of 'recalling' individuals and places that would otherwise be lost even as it foregrounds their loss" (*Ethics* 97). While Tosamah's nostalgic memories foster continuity between his Native past and his urban present—in effect, keeping alive a cultural history that is threatened with extinction—Su believes that Abel fails to heal himself because his nostalgia "only increases his sense of alienation" even if he successfully "inspires the recollections of others" (99, 105).

Although my reading of Abel is more hopeful, I share some of Su's premises, including the idea that nostalgia does not necessarily "subdue" an author's political agenda but rather "can enable characters and readers alike to acquire, in certain instances, a kind of historical knowledge that recasts past events in the light of unfulfilled possibilities" (89). As compelling as Su's analysis is, though, it does not foreground how Momaday's nostalgia for nature is in dialogue with the dominant nostalgic narratives about both nature and American Indians that were in circulation at the time of the novel's publication. With this context in mind, it becomes possible to understand Abel as inspiring sympathy and enabling Momaday to capitalize on the popular back-to-the-land stories that predominated in this period. The novel is not just nostalgic for a lost tribal heritage that is grounded in a particular place; it is also playing into the prevalent pastoral nostalgia that governed mainstream conceptions of nature in this period in a way that elicits readers' nostalgia and, so, enlists them in its political project.

In other words, Momaday's exploitation of dominant, nostalgic conceptions of the natural world and of American Indians is what grounds his critique. Pastoral nostalgia can sometimes obscure imperialistic histories and their legacies, but it can also highlight them. *House Made of Dawn* reveals the overlap between the pastoral nostalgia embraced by the countercultural and environmental movements and the imperialist nostalgia many Americans feel. To cite Su again, "Precisely because [nostalgic] narratives focus on what could have been, readers can perceive more clearly what circumstances or forces prevent individuals from realizing the relationships for which they long" (90). Momaday's novel probes readers' imperialist nostalgia in his related critiques of colonialism, racism, and the Relocation Program—the circumstances and forces that prevent Abel and many nonfictional individuals from finding (or recovering) healthy relationships. At the same time, the text also constructs an ethical relationship to nonhuman nature, an American land ethic that begins with a nostalgic return to an imagined pastoral past—a community that was not necessarily "real," but "could have been." Although many readers would be situated as outsiders to the pastoral community Abel remembers, the novel's nostalgia invites all readers to consider the positive alternatives that might emerge from a return to the remembered earth.

A conflicted and sympathetic protagonist, Abel embodies the nostalgic dimensions of Momaday's text. After a ceremonial prologue and a detailed description of the desert landscape and the town of Walatowa, we are introduced to a deeply troubled (and stumbling drunk) Abel, who has come home from fighting in WWII to live with his grandfather, Francisco, on the Jemez Pueblo reservation. The novel traces Abel's unsuccessful attempts to reintegrate into his home community, his murder of "the white man" Juan Reyes, his ensuing trial, his release and relocation to Los Angeles, and—after failing to hold a job, relapsing into repeated drinking binges, and suffering a serious beating—his second return home. During this return, his grandfather dies, and Abel participates in the Jemez ritual of the dawn runners, the same ritual that opens the novel.

Abel's story is a timely one. By 1960, approximately 35,000 Indians had relocated to urban areas; in Los Angeles, where Abel lives temporarily, the Indian population grew from 5,000 to 50,000 by the year 1980 (Porter 57). An attempt to further the nation's assimilationist project, relocation was also informed by an ideology of uplift that has long infused liberal ideas about race, which tend to either erase specific cultural histories altogether or appropriate them in ahistorical ways as part of a vaguely defined multiculturalism. Yet the character of Abel resists both assimilation and this uninformed brand of multiculturalism in several ways. His personal history reflects the combined influences of Christianity and Kiowa, Navajo, and Jemez Pueblo cultures. The origins to which Abel returns are "endlessly hybridized" (Toy 28). He has never quite fit in on the reservation; the fact that his unknown father was "an outsider" makes Abel himself "foreign and strange" (Momaday 11). The suggestion that Fray Nicolas, a Catholic priest who had worked on the reservation, "sired" Francisco, Abel's grandfather, complicates Abel's own origins and emphasizes the multicultural component of the novel (205). By making Abel's lineage uncertain, Momaday highlights the cultural hybridity of many Native people, refusing to collapse them into a single "Indian" identity.

Moreover, Abel's difficulties starting over in L.A. reveal the flawed logic of relocation as well as the racism that continued to plague American Indians after WWII, despite their disproportionate service in the U.S. Armed Forces. The expectations of "the Relocation people" and the various characters' attempts to "help" Abel adjust to life in L.A. reinforce the novel's sense of a tension between two worlds: Abel's home, linked with the past and with nature, and L.A., associated with the future and with capitalism. Indeed, the book jacket of the Perennial Library edition (1989) describes Abel as "a young American Indian . . . [who] lives in two worlds. One was that of his fathers, wedding him to the rhythm of the seasons, the harsh beauty of the land, the ecstasy of the drug called *peyote*. The other was the world of the twentieth century, goading him into a compulsive cycle of sexual exploits, dissipation, and disgust." Of course, this description simplifies and misreads Abel's experience. The significance of peyote and "sexual exploits" is exaggerated and sensationalized here; he is not "goaded" or tempted by a new world so much as he is nearly destroyed by it. Still, the jacket description sketches a dichotomy that would be accessible to audiences, especially those who might share the counterculture's distaste for consumerism and other "twentieth century" priorities.

More than just clever marketing, the description echoes a subtle geographic and temporal binary that Momaday does, at times, play into. The "rhythm of the seasons" is implicitly identified as both Native and past compared to its alternative, "the world of the twentieth century." This new "world," exemplified by the city of L.A., presumably does not respect "the harsh beauty of the land," and instead has corrupted itself and its residents by encouraging "disgusting" behavior. This binary is important to understanding Momaday's novel, but not only because of the ways in which it structures the character development of this "young American Indian." The novel exploits the opposition by depicting Momaday's ideal of reciprocity and simultaneously positioning non-Native readers as alienated from it—much like Claude McKay did with his depictions of Harlem life. Momaday's vision of environmental interdependence—a land ethic in practice—surely would have been attractive to an audience of increasingly savvy environmentally minded readers. By representing the "rhythm of the seasons" and "the harsh beauty of the land" in nostalgic terms, the novel capitalizes on the broader American nostalgia for an idealized pastoral community—the primary nostalgia that informed mainstream environmentalism as well as the counterculture. Yet readers are situated in a position of unfulfilled longing for the realization of these reciprocal relations.

In the process of generating this nostalgia, the narrative compels readers to identify with Abel's longing and so, with the book's political critique. Attentive readers must question what has propelled Abel into this state of liminality. Or, put another way, why is Abel homesick even after he has returned home? The answer that he "lives in two worlds," while perhaps a starting point for inquiry, is not entirely satisfying. A more sustained look at the ways in which the novel represents the spatio-temporal-cultural rift, and the nostalgic longing this rift precipitates, is in order. Abel's closest friend and roommate in L.A., Ben, who is from a Navajo reservation and relates to Abel because of this, describes very clearly the differences between urban and reservation life:

> [L.A. is] a good place to live. There's always a lot going on, a lot of things to do and see once you find your way around. Once you find your way around and get used to everything, you wonder how you ever got along out there where you came from. There's nothing there, you know, just the land, and the land is empty and dead. Everything is here, everything you could ever want. You never have to be alone. You go downtown and there are a lot of people around, and they're having a good time. You see how it is with them, how they get along and have money and nice things, radios and cars and clothes and big houses. And you want those things; you'd be crazy not to want them. (181)

Several key points emerge in this rich description. First, conspicuous consumption is both identified and identified *with* in this passage. "You see how it is with them," and this seeing generates desire. Ben goes on to elaborate that "you can buy anything you want" in "those stores" (181).

Ben's observation that "you'd be crazy" not to buy into consumerism is quite true; Abel's failure to connect with L.A., even at the basic level of capitalist desire, renders him "crazy" in the eyes of those who encourage his assimilation. Second, this consumer culture is identified as a community, a space of belonging. Ben claims that "you never have to be alone" if you successfully complete the urban assimilationist project. And finally, the process of acclimating to this new environment is very much a spatialized one. This geographic and cultural formulation is significant in its construction of urban space as the new site of community. Here, "downtown," where "there are a lot of people around," is diametrically opposed to the reservation, where there is "nothing" but land that is "empty and dead."

Ben also claims to believe that a "man with a good job can do just about anything he wants" (178). However, this simplistic meritocratic perspective is unconvincing and comes across as self-justification. When he says "I could find some place with a private bathroom if I wanted to, easy," it sounds childish and untrue. His own life disproves these hopeful statements. The experience of poverty is a key facet of life in L.A., and class brings together characters across ethnic and tribal boundaries in the novel. Sean Teuton argues, in fact, that "more than any other feature of urban living, it is poverty and not contact with Western culture that damages the lives of American Indian people" (72). Despite his claims to the contrary, Ben seems to be intuitively aware that the racism embedded in American culture perpetuates the cycle of poverty and effectively prevents assimilation from ever being "successful," even if he still embraces it as an ideal.

If Ben is situated as a hinge between the past and the future—in touch with both, even if he is inclined toward assimilation—Angela St. John, a wealthy white woman who has come to Walatowa to take advantage of its mineral springs, embodies the temptations and flaws in the consumerist "world of the twentieth century." When we first meet Angela, she is negotiating an economic exchange by appealing to the local priest, Father Olguin, for a laborer who can help her cut wood to heat her home. She tells him she "shall be happy to pay whatever," and that she hopes "one of the Indians" might be available (30). Her approach highlights the colonial relationship, in which "the Indians" are substitutable labor sources rather than individuals with lives and histories. Her generalized reference to "the Indians" also aligns her with relocation and its tendency to negate tribal and cultural distinctions. From the moment Abel comes to work for Angela, she is "offended" by his ambivalence about economic exchange; he "did not care one way or the other" when she paid him, and he "would not buy and sell" his labor in ways that are familiar or comfortable to her (33).

To Angela, Abel is a "dark," natural Other; watching him chop wood, she objectifies and sexualizes his body. When they make love not long after he begins working for her, Abel is described as "dark and massive above her," and she notes his "dark skin" (64). "What will you do to me?" she wonders aloud, and she silently likens him to animals: "the badger at the water, and the great bear" (64). While Momaday seems to verge on reinforcing stereotypes about oversexed Indian men, it is important to remember that this is Angela's perspective. As Su points out, "The question of legitimate and ethical narratives comes to the fore through [her character]" (102). Arguably readers are supposed to be troubled by her perspective, especially since she espouses common stereotypes about Native Americans. For instance, Angela likens Abel to "a wooden Indian—his face cold and expressionless" and characterizes a Jemez Pueblo ritual she witnesses as "beautiful and strange," "grave and mysterious," and above all, "serious" (36). She admits the Pueblo people are "intent upon something that she could not see," and she classifies "the trick" to perceiving this "something" as "see[ing] beyond the landscape" (36). Given the prominence of landscape in the text, her proposal accentuates her inability to grasp Indian culture except through the lens of her own cultural imaginary (36). Angela's lack of vision sharpens the reader's; we are able to see how interconnected stereotypes of nature and Indians are conjoined in the non-Native imagination in ways that romanticize and simplify both.[15]

One never feels further away from understanding either Abel or his home than when the narrative is told through Angela's outsider perspective. She is a tourist of both nature and culture, and her tendency to romanticize both prevents her from understanding either. When she watches Abel and the albino participate in the Feast of Santiago ritual, she finds it "empty of meaning" (43). A bit later, when Angela visits Abel in an L.A. hospital after he has been beaten almost to death, she recounts a story she tells her son Peter (who, she says, "always ask[s] her about the Indians") featuring a woman who mates with a bear. Ben, Abel's friend and roommate in L.A., seems impressed that she knows this story—that she apparently "made it up out of her own mind"; however, he corrects her version with the Navajo one, which his grandfather passed along to him (187). When Abel and Ben see Angela on the streets of L.A. walking out of a shop, she looks "like one of those women you see in the magazines" (176–77). This characterization functions as a counterpoint to the earlier description of Abel as "a wooden Indian," since now we see Angela through Abel's gaze. She is described in bourgeois terms: she is "neat," "clean-looking," and "rich-looking" in her "plain white dress and little white shoes and gloves" (177). A representative of the wealthy consumer culture of L.A., she belongs to a world far removed from Abel's reservation life and unavailable to him in the city, a world positioned as the future.

The novel subverts any positive identification with Angela and L.A., and instead creates sympathy with Abel and the reservation, through its abundant descriptions of landscape and its nostalgia for community. First, the novel's many beautiful descriptions of the reservation landscape complicate any easy dismissal of that land as "empty and dead." The fact that Angela goes to Walatowa for healing and then returns to her home in L.A. signifies the alienation that results from seeing nature as "dead matter." Though similar attempts to recover a lost connection to nature were common during this time period, Momaday's readers would hardly want to be identified with Angela and her superficial connections to the land and its inhabitants. For her, nature is a temporary escape from reality, a space for individual regeneration but not an essential part of everyday life.

If Angela's character upholds an ideological separation between "civilization" and "nature," Momaday's descriptions of the town present us with an understanding of nature as home and of human cultures as inherently "placed." From the opening pages, it is clear that Momaday's descriptions of culture begin and end with nature. Invoking phrases and images from the Navajo Night Chant, including the novel's title, the prologue is infused with natural imagery—vibrant colors, multicolored clay and sand, a "dark wilderness on the mountains," and "beautiful" land that is "very old and everlasting" (1). Our first glimpse of Abel locates him in the landscape, where he is so small he seems "almost to be standing still, very little and alone" (2). Immediately afterward, Momaday describes Abel's home from a more intimate perspective, beginning with the river, the valley, the canyon floor, and finally the town itself, with its "intricate patchwork of arbors and gardens" where the townspeople work (5). In contrast to the nostalgic prologue, where nature is described using the past tense, Momaday uses the present tense to tell us about the town. The implication is that this human community is firmly anchored in a "very old and everlasting" landscape, but the culture itself is not disappearing. This town is alive and well. Its inhabitants know the land, work the land, and celebrate the land through ceremonies.

The townspeople's relationship to land is contrasted with non-Native understandings of nature in such a way as to expose the violence of colonization and assimilation. In one of the most striking instances of such exposure, Momaday sets up a powerful dichotomy—more complex than the reductive one on the book jacket—between those with "tenure in the land" and those who have become "estranged" from it (57). Specifically, those with "tenure" have been invaded by a colonial power, "latecoming" invaders with "an alien and inferior aspect, a poverty of vision and instinct, by which they are estranged from the wild land, and made tentative" (57). Again, estrangement, or alienation, from "the wild land" is posited as the key distinction between native "creatures" and the "latecoming things" that are threatening to displace them. Although this tale begins with animals as its protagonists—the "beasts of burden and of trade" are the aliens, contrasted with "the innumerable meaner creatures" whose presence predates theirs—it soon becomes clear that the story applies to human "creatures" as well. Interestingly, Momaday utilizes the language of "poverty" to describe the imperialists and so inverts the likely expectation that it is the reservation's residents who are poor. On the contrary, Indians are rich in "vision and instinct," since they remain connected to the land in ways that sustain their culture in spite of colonization.

A significant part of this connection is nostalgic, and Momaday's descriptions work to generate longing for a harmonious life prior to colonization. For instance, the mesas suggest that "the prehistoric civilization has gone out among the hills for a little while and would return; and then everything would be restored to an older age, and time would have returned upon itself and a bad dream of invasion and change would have been dissolved in an hour before the dawn" (57–58). For the townspeople, who "do not hanker after progress and have never changed their essential way of life," this kind of nostalgia becomes "a resistance and an overcoming, a long outwaiting" in the face of colonization (58).[16] In this important passage, which Schweninger calls "uniquely political," Momaday clearly suggests that (as Abel's case shows) "dislocation from the land results in the evils, the effects of the 'bad dream,' of colonization" (Schweninger, Listening 141).

This passage does stand out for its overt politics, but to call it "unique" is to ignore the powerful politics of nostalgia that permeate the text. As Su notes, the "nostalgia for the lost 'older age' establishes a promise for the future: the hope for restoration becomes marked in the landscape itself" (Ethics 105). In the same way that the Relocation Program enabled pan-Indian connections by bringing together individuals from disparate backgrounds, this passage suggests that a "nostalgic connection to the past substitutes for a common cultural heritage as the basis for shared experience and community among the living" (Su 106). A pan-Indian, even pan-ethnic, sense of community in the present might emerge via nostalgia, since that affective connection allows people to "identify with places not historically associated with their tribal identities" (Su 117). If Abel's initial return to town "had been a failure, for all his looking forward," then perhaps it is better to look backward (Momaday 58).

Representing Abel as backward-looking (not to mention an alcoholic) puts Momaday at risk of unintentionally reinforcing stereotypes.[17] But as others have noted, he steers clear of stereotypes; specifically, he "refuses any easy attribution of Indian as environmentalist" by developing in his characters more "nuanced" connections to landscape (Schweninger 141). Abel's flaws make him human. He is not a political rebel or a spokesperson for nature. He has to work to determine who he is; like Momaday's land ethic, his identity must be recovered via a deliberate process. Here, too, Momaday avoids stereotypes and essentialism. As Teuton argues, Abel "heals his attachment to home not by satisfying the essential spiritual demands of his own Indianness but by following a discernable process to compose a more substantive view of himself in relation to his ancestral place" (53). By linking Abel to "an idealized version of the past," Momaday aligns him with a certain kind of pastoral nostalgia that readers would likely pick up on (Su, *Ethics* 99). The sympathy he generates on behalf of Native Americans results from the novel's telling of "a tale of imperialism and resistance" (Douglas 4) that has fostered loss and alienation. Just as the wolves that "once" lived in the mountains of the Southwest are invoked with a nostalgia that castigates their exterminators, a sense of loss, and the frequent portrayal of Abel himself in sympathetic, even victimized, terms works to align the reader with him.

Momaday manipulates readers' imperialist nostalgia by portraying Abel's struggle to reclaim what has almost been irrevocably taken from him. From Abel's traumatic memories of the war to his cultural isolation during the courtroom scene, the disturbing events in the novel work to suture readers, emotionally, to him. When Abel is beaten nearly to death by a racist law enforcement officer, only the most hard-hearted reader would fail to take pity on him. Nearly all of the characters, Native and non-Native alike, offer him some degree of compassion, but Ben is particularly adept at evoking sympathy. His descriptions of Abel as "already sick inside" generate reflection about the causes of this sickness (166).

The war, in particular, was a turning point for Abel, and readers cannot ignore the fact that his service is rewarded with illness, misunderstanding, exclusion, violence, and continued racism.

Ben, who takes a survivalist approach to assimilation, explains Abel's "sickness" as a result of being unable to forget his life before relocation: "If you come from the reservation, you don't talk about it much; I don't know why. I guess you figure that it won't do you much good, so you just forget about it. You think about it sometimes; you can't help it, but then you just try to put it out of your mind. There's a whole lot more to think about, and it mixes you up sometimes if you don't just go along with it. I guess if we all came from the same place it would be different; we could talk about it, you know, and we could understand" (153). Even though he and Abel both grew up on reservations, they rarely talk about the past. If even Ben and Abel are only "kind of alike" (163), then what hope is there for those of us with radically different backgrounds to relate to one another?

Tosamah's character offers one answer to that question. Unlike Ben, who at times seems to believe that a clean break with the past is the only way to adjust to contemporary American culture, Tosamah turns to his Kiowa grandmother to recount a remembered past to which all individuals might return to discover an ethical relationship to nonhuman nature. In the same way that Momaday invokes his own tribal elder, Ko-sahn, in his "Land Ethic" essay, Tosamah's sermon "envisions Rainy Mountain [as] a Pan-Indian site of memory" (Su 98). The fact that the "old stories" are "timeless," "sacred," and "eternal" give them more credence and identifies them with a land ethic that is imaginative and linguistic, as Tosamah's celebration of "the Word" suggests (Momaday 95). Tosamah's sermon asks Abel, and readers, to connect to a Native past rather than distance ourselves from it or romanticize it. Although he mocks "the white man" for being "sated and insensitive" to the power of language and, so, to the power of a land ethic, he admits "it was not always so with him" (96). There is hope, then, that even non-Native readers might connect with Tosamah's history (95). Through Tosamah's character, Momaday suggests it might be useful to bring together disparate voices and histories in the service of promoting environmental and social justice.

Although Tosamah's might be an example of what Momaday controversially calls "racial memory," the preacher's recollections do not necessarily alienate non-Native readers. Various scholars have defended Momaday from charges of essentialism associated with this phrase,[18] and Schiff makes an especially strong case that racial memory draws on "separatist, racially specific claims to a mythic heritage while endorsing a fundamental, communal experience of it" (100). To return to "An American Land Ethic," we might recall that Momaday describes "Kosahn's racial memory as 'latent' in all Americans," and in doing so he "reaffirms the idea that anyone theoretically could possess her knowledge" (Su, "Ghosts" 376). Of course, there is a fine line between "possessing" knowledge and appropriating an unfamiliar culture. Su rightly notes that "identification" with Momaday's ancestors from a non-Native subject position would involve more than just learning the stories; it would entail "learning about the[ir] cultural and historical contexts" ("Ghosts" 376). The possibility that, as Ben says, "we could understand" one another involves sensitive bridging of cultural and geographic distances, not the "forgetting" of history mandated by assimilation, or the closing off of tribal cultures to the exclusion of those who genuinely want to understand, or the vague belief that getting "back to nature" will magically heal social maladies.

Tosamah's history might be accessible to "us, who have heard it for what it is," whose imaginations are engaged by his words, but we must approach his stories with ethical intent and careful attention (Momaday 98). Since he is such a charismatic character and speaker, Tosamah's tone can be hard to evaluate. For instance, he seems to echo Ben's sentiments when he accuses Abel of being too "primitive" to adapt to modern culture (149). But when Tosamah says Abel is "too damn dumb to be civilized" after being given "every advantage," his sarcasm is apparent. Using Tosamah as spokesperson, Momaday asks us to consider the material forces involved in assimilation and cultural loss. Tosamah suggests it is the government's goal to render Indians "harmless" through a process of assimilation, including "let[ting] him fight on their side" in WWII. He rattles off a list of expected behaviors for Indians: "He would get some fat little squaw all knocked up, and they would lie around all day and get drunk and raise a lot of little government wards. They would make some pottery, man, and boost the economy." By Tosamah's account, it is not Abel's murder of the albino but his violation of "the Jesus scheme" that results in his being "put away" in prison. Abel's is not a case of one broken law; he is a challenge to an entire assimilationist project. Tosamah's reference to Abel as "that poor cat" shows his sympathy for Abel in the face of a process of assimilation that is always foreclosed: "They've got the right idea. They put us away before we're born" (148–49).

Constantly reminding readers of the cultural rift in which Abel lives—the sense of being always already "put away"—the word "longing" resounds throughout the novel. Nostalgic longing targets several objects in addition to landscape, including childhood, community, ritual, and story. It also functions at several registers in the novel, in addition to the basic longing to return home. At the most obvious, Abel's home-coming—a physical return home that is incomplete, and so, fraught with longing, until the final pages of the book—propels the novel's plot. As I suggested earlier, the novel's nostalgia often invokes a harmonious life before colonialism, and Abel's prewar memories give us a glimpse of what this life might have been like. These memories help facilitate his "re-placement in his homeland by remembering a former, whole self in relation to family and place," a process that mirrors a broader longing for a tribal past prior to colonialism (Teuton 59–60).[19]

As part of this "re-placement" process, Abel often longs for "move-ment on the land," a moral and aesthetic "right motion" that integrates him and other creatures with their ancestral landscape (Teuton 58, 60). For instance, before attending the Eagle Watchers Society's hunting rit-ual, Abel "brooded for a time, full of a strange longing" (Momaday 19). This longing marks the intensity of his earlier vision of two eagles flying in "perfect motion" (Teuton 64), a vision that allows him to participate in the Society's ceremony. During the ceremony, Abel witnesses a cap-tured-then-freed eagle flying away—another vision that "fill[s] him with longing" (Momaday 22). Longing thus facilitates Abel's quest to "re-place himself" (Teuton 60) by recovering physical and cultural connections to wild nature.

At this point in the novel Abel is struggling in that quest. His longing inspires him to set free the "bound and helpless" eagle the Society had opted to keep by killing it (Momaday 22)—a decision Teuton explains "flout[s] the consent of the Society" and constitutes a "grave crime" (64). Significantly, killing the eagle anticipates Abel's killing of the albino—a figure that might be read as "unnatural" or, at least, as a rarity within the natural world. Understood as a symbol of colonialism, as he often is, the albino character underscores the unnaturalness of colonial violence and contributes to the novel's political critique. Together, Abel's killing of the eagle and the albino teaches him that he should "consult negative forces within the interpretive context of the tribal community," not attempt to eradicate evil from the world (Teuton 67).

This "interpretive context" is transmitted through memory, and much of Abel's longing is particular to his tribal context. But some of it is directed at more commonplace events, which are not unique to his childhood or his tribe's past. For example, the wistful story of a young girlfriend of Abel's begins: "*There was a girl at Cornfields one summer, and she laughed, and you never saw her again*" (166, emphasis in original). Abel had returned home from his first time away at school, during which he was "homesick." His return is marked by an ecstatic sense that "*the land was going on forever and nothing had changed*" (166–67). His romantic encounter with a laughing girl named Pony at a dance fuels nostalgic longing in the present, when Ben recounts the narrative. The narrative ends the way it begins—*And you never saw her again*—leaving the reader with a sense of lost innocence and playing on a classic form of nostalgia: nostalgia for childhood (173). A similar memory finds the young Abel accompanying his grandfather herding sheep. After lengthy descriptions of the new snow, the cold, and Abel's youthful excitement, the memory concludes: "And you were little and right there in the center of everything, the sacred mountains, the snow-covered mountains and the hills, and gullies and the flats, the sundown and the night, every-thing—where you were little, where you were and had to be" (157). Tosa-mah's sermon romanticizes childhood in a similar way, since "a child can listen and learn. The Word is sacred to a child" (94). Connecting with readers on this broad affective level, the novel asks for empathy and poses the implicit question: What is unique about Abel's childhood, and about his lost innocence? The answer seems to be that, for Abel, being "in the center of everything" means being connected to landscape, family and culture.

A similar instance of nostalgia occurs toward the end of the novel, when Ben tells Abel a story that reaches into the past in order to imagine a more hopeful future. Like the image of Pony laughing by the fire and the image of a young, small Abel surrounded by snow-covered peaks, this story connects nature, ritual, and interpersonal relationships. Ben says:

> I prayed. He was going home, and I wanted to pray. Look out for me, I said; look out each day and listen for me. And we were going together on horses to the hills. We were going to ride out in the first light to the hills. We were going to see how it was, and always was, how the sun came up with a little wind and the light ran out upon the land. We were going to get drunk, I said. We were going to be all alone, and we were going to get drunk and sing. We were going to sing about the way it always was. And it was going to be right and beautiful. It was going to be the last time. And he was going home. (189–90)

The temporal fluctuations in this vision are remarkably shifty. Ben's story resonates with earlier scenes in the novel where the two friends stood on a hill overlooking L.A. and drank and sang with their urban Indian community,[20] and it anticipates a similar experience in Abel's hometown. Even as Ben identifies this future homecoming, he also marks its end: "It was going to be the last time." And yet conjoining "the way it always was" with the prediction that "it was going to be right and beautiful" suggests a certain continuity. Situated as it is before Abel's second return home and his participation in the dawn running ritual, this passage sets up what Abel's homecoming will look like and prepares the reader for the book's final scene.

As Teuton explains, Abel's goal has been to "relearn a lost attachment to his place of origin," and his participation in the Navajo ritual in the closing pages of the book is one example of a "social practice that perpetually reintegrates bodies with the world" (51, 53). In the end, when "the light [runs] out upon the land," Abel is running in the dawn ceremony, in a scene that synthesizes home, nature, and ancient ritual in order to generate hope for the future. As Toy explains, and William Bevis before her, homecoming is central in much Native American literature: "If one does not know one's relationship to others, or if one does not 'come home' to one's place within tribal tradition, there can be no personal or spiritual 'identity' at all" (Toy 29).[21] Unlike most Euro-American conceptions of identity, the one she describes is collective, based on "one's relationship to others," rather than strictly personal. This final scene illustrates the book's broader view of "going home," in which home is linked with a communal past—"how it was, and always was"—as well as with landscape.

While an indigenous conception of land and identity is certainly central to the novel, Momaday's descriptions of Abel's home also resonate with the broader American tradition of the pastoral. Abel's is a community where the sun directs behavior and "the town seem[s] to disappear into the earth" (30). The boundaries between town and earth frequently collapse in the novel, and many descriptions of the town begin with the landscape. Abel's idea of home is closely tied to landscape and labor, as in the following passage: "When the first breeze of the evening rose up in the shadow that fell across the hills, he sat down and looked out over the green and yellow blocks of farmland. He could see his grandfather, others, working below in the sunlit fields. The breeze was very faint, and it bore the scent of earth and grain; and for a moment everything was all right with him. He was at home" (30). Here and in similar passages, being "at home" involves a transitory, multisensory experience of the natural world (visual, olfactory, and tactile) as well as a physical relationship to it, through labor and ritual. In this pastoral setting, there is no assumption that nature mysteriously provides for humanity. Successful harvesting is contingent on nature's cooperation, "gift[s] of God," *and* human labor (6). The juxtaposition of this passage alongside Angela's request for assistance from "one of the Indians" foregrounds the different conceptions of work, nature, and identity at stake in the text. Angela's attitude toward Indian labor highlights her empiricist approach to nature and to people: both are instruments she uses to her advantage. Hers is a utilitarian attitude, which contrasts with the kind of land ethic Momaday's work recommends.

Likewise, Father Olguin's attempt to return to the past, which is conducted primarily through reading the journals of his predecessor, Fray Nicolas, also serves as a counterpoint to Abel's nostalgic longing. Father Olguin's "return" does not imagine hope for the future but, rather, justification for the present. For him, tradition is rooted in the journals of a selfish priest who alienates himself from the "dark customs" of the people he is supposed to "help." In reading this text, Father Olguin is "consoled" by this "glimpse of his own ghost" (48, 53). Nostalgia fosters consolation and self-assurance for Father Olguin, a self-assurance that is largely delusional, given his outsider status in the Jemez Pueblo community. By the novel's end, Father Olguin has come to accept his limited role. He resigns himself to "certain exclusion, the whole and subtle politics of estrangement" even as he tries to convince himself that this estrangement "had been brought about by his own design, *his* act of renunciation, not the town's" (194, emphasis in original). The final image of Father Olguin is a pathetic one. When Abel comes to him in the pre-dawn hours to inform him of Francisco's death, Father Olguin greets him with irritation: "Do you know what *time* it is? I can understand how you must feel but—" (210). When Abel deserts the sleepy priest mid-sentence, Father Olguin makes a final attempt at compassion, shouting "I understand! *Oh God! I understand—I understand!*" as he looks out "into the darkness" (210). The reader is left with little hope that whatever dim understanding there is will translate into action, and Father Olguin remains a stranger in the town.

Unlike Angela and Father Olguin, who relate to the reservation as a resource for inspiration or self-justification in the present, Abel's relationship to his home is rooted in tribal heritage and a collective cultural past. Though readers do not get the satisfaction of seeing Abel fully live out this land ethic, we do get glimpses of him finding spiritual renewal in the landscape. When he recovers from the drinking binge that accompanies his initial homecoming, for instance, Abel is in a bad state. "He had not eaten in two days, and his mouth tasted of sickness. But the morning was cold and deep, and he rubbed his hands together and felt the blood rise and flow" (26). Abel's interactions with his native landscape often suggest intimacy, not distance. He is not simply a spectator gazing out over the landscape. Abel's experiences with nature exemplify Momaday's notion of "reciprocal appropriation," which entails humans "invest[ing]" ourselves in the landscape and "incorporat[ing] the landscape into [our] own most fundamental experience" (Bol 3), and with Teuton's definition of a "Native sense of place," in which "the materiality of the land itself often determines the realm of possibilities for a homeland" and for its residents (49).

Abel's nostalgia shows that the geographic dimensions of his home are inseparable from its cultural significance. As both metaphor and reality, this text's landscape is integral to an ethical ecological worldview in which connection and belonging are central. This understanding of nature is rooted in Native American spiritual and ceremonial traditions, which Paula Gunn Allen describes as embracing a "permanent, ineradicable connection to All-that-is" (165). Unlike the Euro-American nature narratives of the frontier or the sublime, which typically emphasize an individual's transient, self-serving encounter with a natural other, Momaday's representation of the human relationship to nature celebrates enduring connection and community. In contrast to the liberal conception of identity in the United States as autonomous and sovereign, identity for Momaday is interpersonal, reciprocal, and collective. Likewise, the Native sense of place that is central to identity formation emerges from a relationship to nonhuman nature that is developed through "a comparative, evaluative process," not a binary or static one (Teuton 71).

Abel's return to his natural home and eventual "connection to All-that-is"—his grandfather, his cultural heritage, and the landscape of his hometown—provide a dramatic contrast to the alienation many non-Native Americans have created by separating themselves from nature. This notion of alienation is key to the novel's critique of colonialism, and again nostalgia plays a key part in facilitating the critique. Even though Abel is alienated from his own home for much of the novel—especially during his post-relocation life in L.A., in which he is physically as well as spiritually exiled—his home is eventually accessible to him through ritual. By having Abel return to the reservation, Momaday frustrates the goals of relocation and its proponents. He also represents the many relocated

Indians who did eventually return home.[22] Moreover, by participating in the ritual of the dawn running, Abel enacts a return that is the first step on a longer journey toward recovery. I am not alone in reading the novel as a return to ritual.[23] It is tempting to misunderstand Abel's return as a replenishment of his identity that is final and permanent. However, to read the ending this way would be to misrepresent the ritual.

The final section begins with focused aesthetic detail: "The river was dark and swift, and there were jagged panes of ice along the banks, encrusted with snow" (193). From this starting point, the perspective pans out, sketching the valley, the mountains, the fields, and finally the town, which "lay huddled" within this blanketing environment. Unlike L.A., which "smells pretty bad" and is checkered with alleys that are "dark and empty," the pastoral beauty of Abel's hometown is comforting (173). The multi-perspectival, almost cinematographic, representation of the village adds to its appeal. It is a familiar scene, with elements of the American pastoral, but it is made particular, and so more enticing, through Abel's personal history there. In contrast to the opening ritual, Abel can "see at last," and what he sees are "the mountains and the sky . . . the rains and the river and the fields beyond . . . the dark hills at dawn" (212). He is still running alone, but he seems to have gained a renewed attachment to place, an attachment Su claims "is the precondition for community" (Su 117).

Simon Ortiz concludes something similar when he reads the ending as an "affirmation that dawn will always come and renewal of life will be possible through resistance against forces which would destroy life" (11). I would extend Ortiz's analysis by emphasizing that *House Made of Dawn* presents origins as hybrid sites to return to repeatedly, sometimes physically, sometimes through story or memory, in order to reassess and update them. As Su puts it, "Abel's story draws attention to the fact that nostalgic recoveries occur against a backdrop of fragmentation, displacement, and loss that is not erased" (*Ethics* 104). This understanding of origins as fragmented resonates with Edward Said's notion of "beginnings" as something from which one departs, then returns, in a kind of ongoing journey Momaday describes as "not linear and permanent . . . but circular and, in interesting ways, continuous" (Woodard 48). Abel's return illustrates the value in revisiting the past as a dynamic process, not one that could, or should, ever be closed or finalized.

Perhaps as part of his critical engagement with the "simple" past idealized by the counterculture and environmental movements, *House Made of Dawn* invokes a simplistic nostalgic origin at times. Its nostalgia functions like Claude McKay's and Zitkala-Ša's in that it reaches back to a harmonious time and place that precedes the violent history of colonization. Tosamah longs for the Native life, ritual, landscape, and culture that existed prior to the processes of modernization set in play by Euro-American colonization. Even if he himself never actually experienced it, the harmonious community imagined by the novel did exist, at least insofar as the kinds of reciprocal, ethical relationships to landscape were a part of the tribal culture he describes. It is the disjuncture between this origin and the realities of colonialism—realities that began in the past but continue to shape the present—that lies at the heart of the book's political critique.

At the same time, Momaday formulates origins of disharmony that are complex enough to trouble the American progress myth. Abel's mixed heritage and his difficulty accessing his past are examples of this historical impurity. We all access our pasts as a series of fragmented "nostalgic recoveries," the novel suggests. If Momaday's land ethic is an imaginative one, then so, for instance, is Leopold's. The purportedly collective American history he gestures toward is recovered in much the same way that Momaday accesses his ancestors' stories: through oral and written stories, through traces of culture available in research and historical records, and through new stories that keep alive, or revise, the old ones. While the processes are similar, we can still evaluate their differences. Whereas frontier nostalgia often longs for the past in order to justify white European domination, Momaday's counter-nostalgia pinpoints the destructive continuities between past and present—primarily racism and colonial domination—and thereby demonstrates that more ethical social relations were, and are, possible.

Ultimately, *House Made of Dawn* reveals the fallacy of the linear trajectory of progress that identifies Abel as "crazy" and misrepresents both nature and Native American culture as disappearing, or as "empty and dead." Written within a context in which nostalgia for pastoral nature was prevalent and urban space was increasingly seen as overdeveloped and polluted—indeed, more and more cast as a fearsome, racialized "wilderness"—getting back to nature likely would have seemed forward-looking to many mainstream Americans. The novel thus exploits this dominant framework, and its identification of Indian culture with healthy, natural communities situates it as progressive and future-oriented.

Whether or not the term "renaissance" is an appropriate label, *House Made of Dawn*'s success did signal a new age for nature as well as for American Indian literature.[24] Momaday's focus on landscape marks the

text as very much of its time—a time when environmentalism priori-
tized natural landscapes over urban areas. However, Francisco's death,
Abel's struggles in the city, Ben's commentary on social change, and
Angela's tendency to see both land and people in economic terms signal broader changes in the ways humans were beginning to understand
their environments. More and more, man-made nature would seem
to replace, and even precede, unspoiled or "first" nature. Just as third-
wave American Indian literature would begin to transcend the opposition between traditional Native cultures and Anglo-European culture
to engage "urbanity and a more comprehensive, global perspective"
(Allen 14), so would many American writers begin to grapple with the
second and third natures that were reproducing with seemingly greater
and greater speed. The kind of relatively simple nostalgia Abel felt—for
a particular environment and a tribal community living in it—would be
complemented by other nostalgias, most notably, an acute sense of what
Momaday calls "psychic dislocation." While familiar nature narratives
continued to circulate in American literature and culture, the kinds of
nostalgia at work in the United States were becoming increasingly complex and varied.

In October of 1999, a now-defunct coalition of nonprofit organizations called the Turning Point Project[1] placed a controversial full-page advertisement in the *New York Times*. The ad features a hairless mouse with what looks like a human ear growing from its back, and the top third of the ad consists of a large-print headline: "Who plays God in the 21st century?" Two unsettling images—the mouse with the ear and a smaller photo of three identical-looking sheep—compete with the headline for viewers' attention. Well-placed in the dead center of the page and looking like some kind of bizarre optical illusion, the image of the mouse is jarring. Front feet perched on the edge of a glass dish as if trying to escape, the chimerical creature raises eyebrows and questions.

Despite the fact that the "ear mouse" contains no human cells and was not, technically, genetically engineered,[2] the picture insists this is no "natural" mouse. It must be an "alien species." The photo of the sheep is also startling, especially since just two years earlier Dolly the Sheep had made global headlines for being the first mammal cloned from an adult cell. All three sheep look in the same direction, heads and bodies aligned, slightly forward-pointing ears making them look a bit sinister. Asking readers whether we want our own species to follow suit, the caption reads: "*Coming soon: cloned humans?*" (original emphasis). The photos suggest frightening posthuman futures: One is monstrous in its deformity, the other robotic in its sameness.[3]

How did we get to this point? The ad tells a quick and dirty story of Earth's beginning that moves—within one paragraph—through the

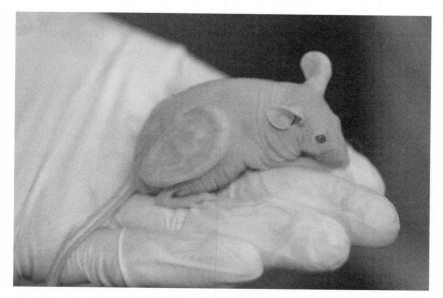

FIGURE 5. An experimental "ear mouse," similar to the one shown in the Turning Point Project's ad. (Courtesy of Dr. Joseph Vacanti and the Laboratory for Tissue Engineering and Organ Fabrication, Massachusetts General Hospital, Boston, MA)

emergence of sponges ("a billion years later"), dinosaurs ("only 215 million years ago"), and humans ("barely 50,000 years" ago). This large-scale perspective allows the writers to contrast natural history with human technology and foreground the fact that, even compared to the relatively new technologies of television and computers, developments in genetic engineering are very recent. The evolutionary story contrasts technological developments with natural ones—an opposition that is upheld throughout its text—and cautions readers that new genetic technologies could be catastrophic.

Viewers are asked to be nature's defenders in what the ad stages as a battle between corporations and the natural world. "Nature's creations" are being "invaded" and "altered" by big business and "the evolutionary process" "seized" by money-hungry corporations that want to "reshape life on Earth to suit [their] balance sheets." Reinforcing the battle rhetoric, the writers of the ad combat the argument that these "new creatures" can help save lives by emphasizing the "*truly* terrible scenarios" that might result from the new technology—like the potential to transfer viruses across species, or the risk of these animals disrupting a natural habitat in "unpredictable" ways (original emphasis). Just as the idea of combining components of different species is supposed to make us uncomfortable, the threat of these inventions "running amok" conjures sci-fi scenarios. The writers allude to H. G. Wells's *The Island of Dr. Moreau*, and Frankensteinian rhetoric haunts the text: "*These things are alive.* And they don't want to go back to their test tubes" (original emphasis). The conspiratorial, fear-inducing language invites intimacy and agreement. It is David versus Goliath, us versus the big corporations, and "we" are dared to side with the underdog to regain power: "When did we approve all this? Who appointed the biotech industry as Gods of the 21st century? . . . Have we lost our sanity?"

Certainly some readers must have wondered whether it was the ad's writers whose sanity was in question. Although the ad does not list any religious groups in its table of sponsors—and its evolutionary origin story indicates a secular perspective—it does acknowledge that the same objections can be raised "whether you give credit to God or to Nature." In both cases, the "integrity of the creation" is what's at stake (Brody 144). The ad's most powerful message is that we have reached a "turning point" by crossing the "*boundary between lifeforms*," a boundary they claim gives animals our "integrity" and our unique identities (original emphasis). Tapping into millennial anxieties with apocalyptic language, the ad warns of fundamental changes: "Nothing will ever be the same," it proclaims, "and we approach the gravest moral, social, and ecological crises in history."

Although it was published at the turn of the millennium, the ad responded directly to earlier developments in genetic research—most notably, the creation of the first transgenic mammal, a mouse, in the mid-1980s. In 1984 Philip Leder and Timothy Stewart, both at Harvard University at the time, developed a mouse that was genetically modified to allow it to carry an oncogene, which increases its susceptibility to cancer and makes it an ideal subject for cancer research. They were awarded a patent four years later for what became known as "OncoMouse," and they sold the rights to their invention to Du Pont.[4] The biggest legal precedent for this patent (and the one the Turning Point ad mentions) was the *Diamond v. Chakrabarty* decision by the U.S. Supreme Court in 1980, a 5–4 ruling that allowed Ananda Chakrabarty, a microbiologist working for General Electric at the time, to patent a bacterium that could break down crude oil. From this point forward, "an invention could not be treated as unpatentable in principle simply because it was comprised of living matter" (Bent 6). Despite the huge ramifications of this decision for the scientific community, the American public initially took little notice.

But by the end of the 1980s, a backlash to genetic research had begun. What attorney Stephen Bent describes as "an ad hoc coalition of animal protection, farm, and religious groups" brought a range of legal, ethical, and socioeconomic objections to the table (6). According to philosophy professor Baruch Brody, most ethical objections involve an "interconnected series of arguments about man's control over nature, man's responsibility toward nature, and the need to preserve species and protect their integrity" (144). Some opposition groups are certainly concerned about the suffering of animals, though many object to the commercialization of research (and the corporate possession of "life") and the potential unforeseen consequences that might emerge from such research. For this study, I am most interested in the objections about "excessive interference with the 'natural' world," as well as those that claim patenting animals "will devalue human life" (Bent 7). For many, the final frontier in scientific research is the human one, the line at which "we may alter our relationship not [just] with the rest of nature but with ourselves" (McKibben, *Enough* xii). When "human" requires quotation marks, people start to get nervous.

Some of the uneasiness involves patenting *"life itself"*—the point at which, as the ad submits, "natural evolution gave way to corporate evolution" (original emphasis). It is partly corporate involvement that is at issue here, the trend toward privatizing life. But it is also the research itself that some find disturbing. As the ad's creators emphasize, humans are "playing God," taking over processes that have previously been governed by a higher being—God, for some, and Nature, for others. Though some are against the practice of designing animals to suffer, more often the concern is less about the animals' pain and more about the process, which enables humans to "take over Nature's work." Closely related to this concern is an insistence that we are whole creatures, not, as the Turning Point ad cleverly puts it, "auto parts at a swap meet." For Jeremy Rifkin—one of the earliest and most vocal critics of the biotech industry—the loss of "recognizable boundaries" between species leads to a lack of respect for species integrity, a situation where "living beings are drained of their substance and life becomes a code to be deciphered."[5]

There is not just a kind of holism inherent in these arguments but a kind of nostalgia as well: a nostalgic assumption that capital-N "Nature" exists as a foundation for all life. "Nature," by this logic, constitutes a frontier that should not be breeched. This imagined line—which, by some accounts, has already been crossed—is the point at which nature is no longer natural. It is man-made. Along with this sense of abrupt qualitative change comes nostalgia for nature as it existed before we interfered. The Turning Point ad imagines a time prior to our earth-changing technological interventions, a time before we "broke the species barrier." Rifkin's writing and interviews often carry a trace of nostalgia—for species purity, for the "laws of nature" (which he fears will soon be completely rewritten), and for Darwinian evolution as a natural process. Beneath these objections lies the longing for a "pure" natural past: a time when mice were mice, sheep were sheep, and humans were humans, a time when humans were not yet tampering with the nonhuman—at least, not to the extent that we are currently.

Of course, even those who call for caution in genetic research can see the flaws in this logic. As Bill McKibben says about his own "end of nature" thesis, "Many critics claimed that we weren't really 'ending' nature because either we had been altering our surroundings for centuries, or we were a part of nature ourselves and hence couldn't destroy it" (*End* xix). In addition to calling opponents Luddites and their arguments "inchoate," defenders of genetic research often try to destabilize the idea of "pure Nature," arguing that the new research does not cross any line that hasn't been crossed long ago (Brody 142). As Bent explains, "There is a fairly long history to the patenting of multicellular life forms in the USA" (5). His legal origin is the 1930 Plant Patent Act, which "allowed the patentability of products of nature that were produced through the use of human intervention," including plant breeding (*Transgenic Animal Patent Reform Act*). (The horticulturist Luther Burbank, who appears in chapter 6 of this study, was one of the scientists who lobbied for this legislation.) Others point even further back, insisting that there was never a time when humans did not interfere with nature; there is, in a sense, no "Nature" at all.

Some high-profile academics echo the oppositional discourse insofar as they, too, identify nature as recently overtaken by capitalism. Fredric Jameson and Jean Baudrillard are two who seem to express dismay about the loss of "nature" and the "real." I will return to their points in the next chapter. But most scholars seem to side with the researchers, at least in theory. Among the many who are wary of nostalgia, Donna Haraway argues that "there is no room for nostalgia, purity, conspiracy theories of technoscience, appeals to culturally transcendent reason or dehistoricized nature, or any other reductionism" (*Modest_Witness* 101).

Haraway is relieved, then, to find that Nature, often "the key operator in foundational, grounding discourses," is tough to isolate in our current state, which she calls the "nature of no nature": a state in which the nature-culture divide has collapsed once and for all (102–3). She finds this condition "edifying" precisely because it eludes the *transcendental moves* of origin stories (121, 108, original emphasis).

In keeping with her anti-purity stance and dedication to complicating origin myths, her reading of OncoMouse sees the transgenic creature as breaching "the great divide between Man and Nature, and its gendered corollary and colonial racial melodrama" (120). Rather than subject nonhuman animals to our own mythologies, Haraway advocates seeing them as "companion species," with a shared history of "co-habitation, co-evolution, and embodied cross-species sociality" (*Companion Species* 4). In her work on Dolly the Sheep, Sarah Franklin shares these priorities and suggests that the "lineages" of Dolly are both "familiar," in the sense that humans have always manipulated their environments, and "newly hybridized, or mixed" (Franklin 13). Their hybridity is empowering, according to Franklin, since it enables us to pay more attention to "the shared genealogy of remaking that we and Dolly both belong to" and, so, to consider more carefully what kind of future we want (206).

These scholars are right to be worried about nostalgia for "pure" nature or, as Franklin puts it, for "life's imagined natural order" (206). It is true that myths of purity—the "all-too-full spaces of foundational, unmarked Nature and Culture"—have often been oppressive (Haraway, *Modest_Witness* 112–13). The time when mice were mice and sheep were sheep is, many fear, the same time when men were men and women were women—a worrisome line of reasoning for feminists in particular.[6] But even though more and more of us "can't keep good distinctions between natures and cultures straight," discourses of nature's purity persist (Haraway *Companion Species* 9). Plenty of people will gladly invoke original nature, whether sincerely or strategically, to combat what they see as change for the worse. Many are uncomfortable with the blurring of boundaries and the seeming limitlessness of human control. McKibben, for instance, finds it troubling that we can no longer know "what mixture of 'nature' and of 'us'" even basic things like weather contain (*End* xxiii).

Within a discourse that is too often polarized into "threats and promises," it is hard to feel confident that the "situated conversations" Haraway hopes for will necessarily come to pass, much less result in fruitful self-reflection (*Modest_Witness* 41, 121). I share Haraway's wish that "in these warped conditions, a more culturally and historically alert, reliable, scientific knowledge can emerge," but I am not especially sanguine that it will (*Modest_Witness* 121). What if conditions simply become, well, more warped? Who is to say that a broader awareness of our "contingent foundations" will lead to "hygienic" dialogue (*Companion Species* 9; *Modest_Witness* 121)? Indeed, one of the biggest concerns expressed by McKibben and Rifkin is that the American public, in particular, is not even paying attention to genetic research, much less participating in informed debate.

If our goal is more honest dialogue, then it is important to assess how nostalgia informs what discussion there is. While for some, a "residual naturalism" is the "main obstacle to full exploration and exploitation of life's potentials," others cling to a nostalgic naturalism (Rabinow 249). McKibben may be nostalgic in his formulation of a "human" species, or a nature prior to the "end of nature." However, it is not necessarily reactionary to be concerned for the future—to find the possibility of engineering one's own offspring somewhat unsettling, or to worry that identity might become a question of "design specs" (McKibben, *Enough* 53). This nostalgia can be accompanied by alarmist or reactionary rhetoric, as in the Turning Point ad, but it also marks the onset of uneasiness—a kind of emotional "check" or gut reaction. Those who, like McKibben, oppose genetic engineering for "intuitive and visceral reasons" often see a qualitative difference between past and present (McKibben, *Enough* 40). McKibben argues that the "change in quantity" humans have effected "is so large that it becomes a change in quality" (*End* xix). Rifkin suggests that the new research is qualitatively different because "in classical breeding, it is only possible to cross close relatives in the biological kingdom. Today, however, we are no longer constrained by these biological boundaries."[7]

Whether they are right about the qualitative difference or not, their uneasiness, that "visceral" reaction to change, could be the starting point for useful dialogue. As the idea of an essential nature, or an integral species identity, grows increasingly suspect, I wonder if more people will share McKibben's type of nostalgia. We should ask, What is nature, when even life can be man-made? When life is no longer what it once was, how do we value it? What does it mean, for instance, to be "pro-life"? If nostalgia results when humans take over previously natural processes, then how might nostalgia play a valuable role in our contemporary discourse—a role that is provocative but not misguided, visionary but not idealistic?

Chapter 5 examines a work of fiction that is particularly insightful in regard to the dissolution of human-nature boundaries: Don DeLillo's *White Noise*. Many readers agree that DeLillo's work helps think through the ideological and material changes associated with postmodernity, and that his approach to these changes is often ironic and ambivalent. My reading locates nostalgia in his approach as well. *White Noise*, DeLillo's most widely read and studied novel, is especially helpful for theorizing the new kinds of nostalgia resulting from our "posthuman" status, including the postnatural nostalgia manifested in the discourse about OncoMouse and other transgenic creatures. Although DeLillo himself does not seem to think we've "crossed a line" in our relations to the natural world, some of his characters share McKibben's intuitive uneasiness about social, technological, and environmental change. *White Noise* both elicits and ironizes our nostalgia for pure categories—for things like nature, death, and the human—and implies that even previously stable categories, like the human body, now face serious security threats. In the process, the text reflects broader American anxieties in the 1980s, a time when various natural frontiers were being crossed, a time when social constructions of nature seemed to have replaced the real thing—a time, indeed, "when the real [was] no longer what it used to be" (Baudrillard, "Precession").

5 /   Don DeLillo's Postmodern Homesickness: Nostalgia after the End of Nature

The cover of the 2006 edition of Bill McKibben's *The End of Nature* features a yellow bird, chest skyward, eyes half closed, feet curled in mortal repose. Combining fear and nostalgia in a way reminiscent of Rachel Carson's powerful fable, McKibben's introduction to this edition laments that the planet "means something different than it used to. Something less than it used to" (xxiii). To dramatize our environmental loss, he tells this short parable: "Imagine that you have hiked to the edge of a pond in the forest and stand there admiring the sunset. If you should happen to look down and see a Coke can that someone has tossed there in the rushes, it will affect you differently than if you see a pile of deer droppings. And the reason, or at least one reason, is our intuitive understanding that the person who dropped the Coke can didn't need to, any more than we need to go on raising the temperature of the planet. We *are* different from the rest of the natural order, for the single reason that we possess the possibility of self-restraint, of choosing some other way" (xx, original emphasis). The idea that "we are different" refers to what McKibben sees as the human capacity to decide when technological "progress" has gone too far, an idea he explores in his treatise on genetic engineering, *Enough: Staying Human in an Endangered Age.* The Coke can also represents another kind of difference, though—what McKibben sees as a qualitative difference between the human-made and the natural worlds.

McKibben began charting such difference in the late 1980s with *The End of Nature.* The first text to coin the term "postnatural," this book chronicles not just change but loss, as it mourns the demise of a "set of human ideas" in which we conceive of "nature as eternal and separate" (8). McKibben insists *"we have ended the thing that has, at least in modern times, defined nature for us—its separation from human society"* (64, original emphasis). Even if it is only our "ideas" that have changed, *The End of Nature* feeds into a prevalent version of nostalgia in which nature is a pure, originary, "separate" environment that humans have corrupted. The past serves as an idealized counterpoint to our steady decline.

Now that climate change is generally accepted as an urgent global issue, *The End of Nature* has warranted a second printing. But McKibben first published it in 1989—right about the time the Harvard researchers were patenting OncoMouse. In his new introduction he looks back on that decade as a time of relative innocence, marked by his own youthful prose and cautious optimism as well as genuine uncertainty about climate change in the scientific community. Even though scientists had not reached consensus, McKibben was not the only one worrying that fundamental changes in human-nature relations were under way. Scholars were noting similar shifts, sometimes with measurable nostalgia of their own. In his influential *Simulacra and Simulations*, published in 1988, Jean Baudrillard questioned the very nature of reality: "When the real is no longer what it used to be, nostalgia assumes its full meaning." Although Baudrillard himself asserted that "nostalgia for a primary Reality is . . . a primitivist fantasy that covers over our realization that there is no such thing as primary Reality," the phrase "what it used to be" reflects a broader cultural nostalgia for a time when "the real" presumably *was* real (qtd. in Hamming 32). A few years later, Fredric Jameson posited that under capitalism's most recent regime all that remains of nature is our nostalgia for "some organic precapitalist peasant landscape and village society, which is the final form of the image of Nature in our own time" (34). Jameson further argued that the "new decentered global network" of capitalism's latest stage had become powerful enough to infiltrate even the "precapitalist enclaves [of] Nature and the Unconscious" (38, 49). Capital had co-opted, penetrated, or colonized not only all of *culture* but all of *nature* as well.[1]

Just as Theodore Roosevelt, Owen Wister, Frederick Jackson Turner, and others in the early twentieth century were nostalgic for the American frontier, Jameson's metanarrative betrays a late-century version of this narrative-emotion, in which capital's final frontier, nature, is officially closed.[2] Some amount of nostalgia is understandable, perhaps even warranted. In a world where second lives, online pets, biotechnology, virtual landscape planning, plastic surgery, and hypoallergenic cats are

realities, it seems fair to say that nature has, in many ways, been denaturalized. New technologies, scientific theories, poststructuralist insights,
and other influences have redefined nature in material and ideological ways that "render it more ductile, less inflexible—subject to revision" (Ross, "Urban Ecology" 25). Indeed, today's nature is often twice
removed from its original state, becoming "third nature": a representational category that includes the "simulated natures of everyday TV
and magazines, games like SimEarth . . . [and other] powerful means of
manipulating nature as 'information'" (Braun and Castree 4). To make
things more complicated, the relationship between first nature and its
successive manifestations is not self-evident. As early as 1980, geogra-
phers Neil Smith and Phil O'Keefe were alerting us to this increasing
complexity, explaining how "the 'second nature' is no longer produced
out of the first nature, but rather the first is produced by and within the
confines of the second" (35, original emphasis). In other words, second
and third natures often precede first nature, to the point where they can
be said to actually produce it. With first nature's alarming disappearance—and its very autonomy in question—and with second and third
nature not just proliferating but taking precedence, nature's function in
the political economy is more complex than ever.

The late 1980s mark an ideological turning point, then—perhaps not
in terms of actually breaching a "natural" boundary but in regard to our
ideas about blurring that boundary. The trail in McKibben's story cannot be seen as some unmediated space for authentic experience; from
this ideological standpoint, comparing the presence of deer droppings
with a Coke can becomes a less straightforward task. As it becomes less
possible to distinguish a pure or unspoiled natural world that is separate
from humans, some people long for an imaginary Eden. Others, however, find cause for celebration. Donna Haraway, for one, relishes "crucial
boundary breakdowns"—human/animal, animal-human/machine, and
physical/nonphysical—in her well-known "A Manifesto for Cyborgs,"
which was first published in 1985 (176). Her influential essay sketches a
"cyborg politics" that might "suggest a way out of the maze of dualisms
in which we have explained our bodies and our tools to ourselves" (204).
Its publication shook up scholarly discourse, presciently raising many
of the issues that have since become central to cultural studies scholarship and to popular debates about biotechnology, posthumanism, nature
preservation, and animal ethics.

Anticipating a shift that environmental historian William Cronon
would help popularize a little over a decade later, Haraway's essay

decisively deconstructed the human-nature binary. Cronon's often-cited "The Trouble with Wilderness" does something similar through a brief history of the transformations in American understandings of wilderness, which he reads as socially constructed rather than strictly material. In this essay he takes aim at McKibben's "end of nature" thesis for reifying the human-nature binary through its misanthropic metanarrative of degeneration, which fosters a sense that we can escape history and ignore the "wilderness in our own backyards" (Cronon 86). Furthermore, Cronon notes, such a narrative often underlies cultural imperialism, either by privileging some environmental issues at the expense of others—national parks instead of urban environments, for instance—or by exporting an American environmentalist agenda abroad.

Most scholars today recognize that nature has always been social as well as material. But not everyone initially welcomed Cronon's essay, partly because of its risky rhetoric. In his foreword to *Uncommon Ground*, he addresses concerns that deconstructivist logic leads to "a world where anything goes, in which everything becomes relative to our own ideas and there is no stable ground on which we can hope to make a stand in defending the natural world" (21). Ursula Heise explains the uneasiness surrounding the extreme poststructuralist view of nature in similar terms: it "plays into the enemy's hand by obfuscating the material reality of environmental degradation" ("Ecocriticism" 512). Heise recommends "weak constructivism," a version of what Cronon suggests when he tells skeptics that we have to continue making value judgments and respecting the material constraints of nature if we are to elude moral relativism.

Arguably, an unclear distinction between humans and nonhuman nature can lead to a belief that anything we do is "natural," a kind of slippery slope that permits obfuscating corporate strategies like greenwashing—a common practice today, but one that was hardly necessary in 1980s America. Consumption had reached another peak, and environmentalism had lost momentum. The bipartisan consensus that had enabled progressive environmental legislation in the 1960s and '70s was fractured under the Reagan administration. Urban environmentalists split with mainstream groups, and more radical organizations—like the well-known Earth First!, which was inspired by Edward Abbey's anarchism—splintered the movement. Reagan's leadership and the relative prosperity of the 1980s encouraged "the deification of greed as the American Way" rather than the development of a public conscience based on environmental stewardship (Stegner, "Legacy" 244).

The Reagan era marked a decisive end to the "environmental decade." Reagan appointed far-right Republican James Watt as his first Secretary of Interior, and Watt used this powerful position to promote increasing development, deregulating natural resources, and shifting power to state and local governments. The Sagebrush Rebellion, a Nevada-based regional political movement that sought to "return" control of local lands to the states, was underway when Reagan and Watt took office, and it gained national attention under Watt's watch (Rothman 174–75). If Watt's environmental policies harkened back to mid-century conservation ideals (and anticipated the more recent "Wise Use" movement), then the Rebellion was also a kind of nostalgic movement, drawing on American myths about the West to fuel its populism. It also relied on ideas about local "culture and custom" that—in a way reminiscent of the Southern agrarians' pastoral nostalgia—were informed by a kind of revisionist history: that of a West whose lands had always been under the control of local inhabitants with little federal oversight (Rothman 175).[3]

Just as Watt looked backward, Reagan also drew on nostalgia, balanced by optimism about the country's future, to solicit the support of the American public. As Gary Wills explains, Reagan framed American identity as "poised between the Good Old Days and the Brave New World"; the past he imagined for the country was one of "perfection" and American exceptionalism, a view "largely shaped by the movies he saw or made" (xxiii-iv). Juggling complex imagery as perhaps only an actor could, Reagan has been called the "first hyperreal politician" (Hamming 40). His acting credentials—which included sharing the screen with Iron Eyes Cody in several Westerns—meant that he could embody the mythical cowboy past with ease. Following Vietnam and the challenges that war posed to "America's code of frontier-masculinity," Reagan crafted an image of himself as "a Western president" in order to make the country feel strong during the Cold War (Le Coney and Trodd 167–68).[4] While frontier nostalgia surely appealed to some Americans—indeed, even Earth Firsters "saw themselves as modern-day cowboys"—first nature suffered throughout the Reagan era (Rothman 182).

The goal-oriented approach of 1980s environmentalism and its lack of a "holistic" vision may have limited its potential, but mainstream environmentalism became stronger in reaction to the Reagan years, and the scaffolding was in place for a "global grass-roots movement" to be built (Rothman 192, 194). Membership in environmental organizations increased dramatically, partly in response to policies like those of Watt, and by the late '80s "loud protests, ecotage, and other forms of resistance" were occurring throughout the West (Rothman 191). Parks preserved many kinds of environments, not just the dramatic, obvious ones. The environmental justice movement emerged in the early '80s, primarily in response to toxic waste and other polluting hazards in marginalized communities, and began to redefine the environment in terms of everyday life, as "the place you work, the place you live, the place you play" (di Chiro 301).[5] By the 1990s, the movement had taken on national dimensions and begun to complicate the traditionally white, middle-class, mainstream environmental movement, which had been less than attentive to the concerns of urban environments and their often non-white inhabitants. One of the biggest divergences of environmental justice from mainstream environmentalism was the insistence that the "invention of a universal division between humans and nature is deceptive, theoretically incoherent, and strategically ineffective" (301). This insight helped prompt the mainstream movement to expand its understanding of what "nature" meant. Environmental justice has enriched ecocritical work as well, pushing academics to pay attention to works of literature that engage "nature" in broader, social, terms and expand the kinds of texts that might be called "nature writing."

* * *

One recent addition to the ecocritical canon is Don DeLillo's widely read and frequently taught novel *White Noise*. DeLillo has long been known as an insightful theorist of postmodern culture. I am among those who situate him as a theorist of postmodern nature as well. As I have argued elsewhere in regard to *Underworld*, DeLillo's work is characterized by an alternately worshipful and irreverent treatment of nonhuman nature.[6] Like *Underworld*, *White Noise* is a simultaneously nostalgic and ironic text in its representations of both nature and culture. As such, it both maps and engenders a radicalized postmodern nostalgia. For this study, the earlier text is especially insightful since it offers a glimpse of 1980s America and its anxieties about entering a postnatural era. In particular, this novel poses questions about life and death in a posthuman world. What new definitions of nature emerge, and what new kinds of nostalgia result, in a world where first, second, and third nature overlap in more complex ways? What happens when even our own deaths seem unnatural, man-made? Contrary to the many critics who have expressed nostalgia's limitations, *White Noise* shows how nostalgia responds to these and other questions, as well as how it can be harnessed and utilized to spark social and environmental critique.

One should start by recognizing that DeLillo's nostalgia is not always for "nature." The nostalgia in *White Noise* points to various cultural objects: authenticity, community, childhood, originality, unmediated experience, a unified self, the cohesion of signifier and signified. DeLillo's writing shuns closure and instead foregrounds the failure of all narrative: its inability to "offer pattern and insight by virtue of its capacity for transcendence" (Stewart 22–23). Even our language, our ability to tell stories, seems irreparably severed from the real world, and this narrative inadequacy generates its own unique form of nostalgia, a troubling result of poststructuralist insight. If Susan Stewart is right that postmodern nostalgia longs for "a genesis where lived and mediated experience are one, where authenticity and transcendence are both present and everywhere," then DeLillo signals nostalgia's omnipresence in the postmodern moment (23).[7]

White Noise's characters all seem to feel this kind of diffuse nostalgia. They utter self-reflective, post-existential comments like "I am the false character that follows the name around" (17). They seem to be mourning the absence of an essential identity that is not constructed by arbitrary signs, or by television and other media. In addition to the vague wish for signifiers to match signifieds, there is a pervasive longing for cohesiveness, identified obliquely with life before television, intimate nuclear families, small-town communities, and pleasant pastoral environments. Along with this mood of longing, the fear of death haunts Jack and Babette Gladney's neo-nuclear family and their quiet life in Blacksmith—a town that is located only vaguely, somewhere in Middle America. Despite their seemingly quaint American dream (Jack is a professor at the "College-on-the-Hill"; Babette cares for the children and volunteers her time to work with the elderly), theirs is a world in which the characters are strangely out of touch with their surroundings.

The novel's nostalgia has a spatial, material component along with the more diffuse postmodern kind. *White Noise* reveals a postnatural nostalgia that overwhelms characters in a range of everyday environments—supermarkets, college campuses, overpasses, shopping malls, and their own homes. This nostalgia draws on familiar American nature narratives—in particular the wilderness, the sublime, and the pastoral—but compounds them, juxtaposing them alongside new circumstances and new ways of making meaning. Both the nostalgia for nonhuman nature as a category or idea, and nostalgia for nature as a real, material entity, are at play in the novel, and they do not always play nicely. Together, these conflicting longings elicit and ironize nostalgia for the human-nature binary, for the notion of nature as somehow distinct from the human. Nostalgia has found new possible origins, beyond pristine land-scapes, agrarian villages, or wilderness enclaves—although these classic forms of nostalgic narratives operate alongside the new kinds, confusing all sorts of boundaries. With the interplay of these various nostalgias, daily life takes on a nostalgic aura of its own—a situation Murray Jay Siskind, the novel's witty cultural theorist, describes as being "homesick for a place even when you are there" (257).

Murray's linkage of nostalgia with geography is crucial to understand-ing this novel. Following Frank Lentricchia's declaration that *White Noise* is "an ecological novel at the dawn of ecological consciousness" (7) and John Duvall's observation of DeLillo's fascination with "the eco-threat of consumer culture" (561), a handful of critics have addressed DeLillo from an ecological perspective. Scholarship by Cynthia Deitering, Dana Phillips, Ursula Heise, and Jeanne Hamming, in particular, indicates *White Noise*'s prominent position in the ecocritical canon. Although critics have recognized the significance of the everyday in DeLillo's writ-ing,[8] the environmental dimensions of his characters' day-to-day nostal-gia remain undertheorized. Part of DeLillo's socioeconomic critique, for instance, proceeds not just through an indictment of global capitalism but also through a relocation of nature within this political economy and an identification of capitalism's effects on specific environments. *White Noise*'s nature—which includes, most notably, human bodies and pas-toral landscapes—is both material and ideological. Sometimes its social production precedes its material manifestations. In DeLillo's literary world, first nature is inextricable from the nostalgic narratives we tell about it, the products we make from it, and the effects those products then have on the natural world and on our own bodies.

I argue that DeLillo's postmodern nostalgia reveals and defines itself primarily through a sense of lost nature. Thus, *White Noise*, like Jame-son's theory of postmodernity, posits nature, especially the human body, as a frontier that capitalism has conquered. However, this formulation—which reifies nature as distinct from culture—is only partly accurate. While postmodern nature retains the broad, often binary, meanings so important to American cultural myths, it also blurs those binaries through its emphasis on man-made nature, a nature that is present in parks, shopping malls, urban streets, supermarkets, toxic chemicals, and our own bodies. In this context, familiar nature narratives, recycled and redefined through new kinds of postnatural events and settings, generate a new kind of nostalgia, manifested in the sense of perpetual homesickness DeLillo's characters feel.

Rather than falling prey to nostalgia, as Jameson and McKibben seem to, DeLillo uses it as his ally even while holding it at a critical distance. Nostalgia becomes both a mode through which to read and describe the past and the present, and an ideological affect to be approached warily, with a healthy dose of skepticism. Functioning disjunctively, manipulating readers, and inciting critique, DeLillo's deployments of nostalgia for nature alternate between sincerity and irony. We might say DeLillo's nature is "doubled," in the sense that it is simultaneously (and self-consciously) real and imaginary, material and socially constructed, sincere and ironic, serious and funny, eulogized and ever-present. Linda Hutcheon also uses the term "doubled" to describe both irony and nostalgia in postmodern culture: nostalgia doubles two different times (past and present), while irony doubles two meanings (the said and the unsaid). Hutcheon suggests that irony and nostalgia share the "twin evocation of both affect and agency—or, emotion and politics" ("Irony" 199). Moreover, if modernity engendered nostalgia, then postmodernity is a time in which "nostalgia itself gets both called up, exploited, *and* ironized" (205, original emphasis). In *White Noise*, irony contends with a nostalgic longing that is frequently tied to nature—a nature that is itself "called up, exploited, and ironized." A few critics have hinted at the coexistence of irony and nostalgia in *Underworld*; however, none have analyzed this ironic nostalgia in any sustained way nor attended to its treatment of nature.[9]

DeLillo's fictional worlds are ironic, in large part, because second and third nature have begun to coexist alongside first nature. In *White Noise*, nature still "is," but its meanings proliferate in new ways; nature "is both what it is and an image or metaphor of what it is" (Phillips 243). In an America where many landscapes have become "unplaced" (Phillips 237), material nature seems to have been colonized by technology; people are their phone numbers, television generates reality, and present-day constructions of nature are heavily shaped by late capitalism. Dana Phillips explains that, in DeLillo's work, what is striking "is not so much the replacement as it is the displacement of older forms by newer ones, and the potential overlapping or even the merger of all those forms in an increasingly crowded cultural and natural landscape" (239). Even while the definition of nature shifts, familiar narratives and genres—the pastoral, the sublime, the wilderness—continue to circulate. Classic nostalgic nature narratives may be "displaced" by newer forms, but the classic forms continue to occupy space in the "single, seamless landscape" of postmodern America (Phillips 239). As DeLillo's Americans gather around toxic chemical clouds to experience a beautiful sunset or worry about their man-made deaths, simulated nature becomes a powerful accompaniment to the first-nature narratives that have circulated throughout the century.

Man-made events and environments can even improve upon nature itself. Should we be disturbed by the spectacular postnatural sunsets the characters in *White Noise* enjoy, or by the pile of waste at an urban landfill in *Underworld* that takes on the first-nature aura of an iconic desert feature? Against suggestions by Lyotard, Baudrillard, and Jameson that "the disappearance of nature is a turning point in global culture," Phillips reads DeLillo as demonstrating that nature and culture have never been distinct (245)—an observation Terry Gifford attributes to post-pastoral literature.[10] It may be true that nature has never existed apart from human conceptions of it, but it is also true that we have only recently become aware of this fact. Our conceptions have changed, and that kind of change can certainly feel like a turning point. DeLillo responds—playfully, irreverently, provocatively, and nostalgically—to these changing conceptions as well as to other differences between postmodernity and its historical antecedents, including the increasing coexistence of first, second, and third nature, and in some cases, the priority of the revised forms over the "original."

With Heise's astute observations about *White Noise* and risk theory in mind—in particular, her suggestion that its "destabilization of distinctions between the real and the nonreal can itself serve specific realist objectives"—I would like to suggest that destabilizing *nature* serves a similar function ("Toxins" 756). That is, destabilizing distinctions between the natural and the nonnatural draws attention to the "real" environments these characters must negotiate, the risky environments of their everyday lives.[11] Combining a sincerely nostalgic mood with an ironic approach to consumption, to nature, and even to nostalgia itself, *White Noise* encourages active participation by its readers and advocates an engaged, thoughtful approach to daily life. DeLillo plays with postmodern American nostalgia in order to incite a critique of late capitalism and make a provocative argument for environmental and social justice.

* * *

Attentive readers will notice traces of American nature narratives from the book's opening lines. *White Noise* begins with a scene reminiscent of the American Western: "The station wagons arrived at noon, a long shining line that coursed through the west campus" (3). Several critics have noted the resonance of this sentence with the Western: the image of a slow-moving wagon train; the "noon" that evokes heated shootouts and the film *High Noon*; and the location of the action on the west part of the campus. DeLillo even takes the scene to the national level when he calls the arriving students "a collection of the like-minded and the spiritually akin, a people, a nation"—a description that invokes Turner's pioneers (4). Laura Barrett calls the reference to the Western "both nostalgic and parodic"—a coexistence I will discuss in more detail below (100).

After the evocative opening, DeLillo moves into a description of Blacksmith that reads like an elegy to pristine nature. Jack locates their home "at the end of a quiet street in what was once a wooded area with deep ravines. There is an expressway beyond the backyard now, well below us, and at night as we settle into our brass bed the sparse traffic washes past, a remote and steady murmur around our sleep, as of dead souls babbling at the edge of a dream" (4). Later, Jack and Babette lie in bed "listen[ing] to the gently plummeting stream of nighttime traffic"; the expressway "washes past" in a "steady murmur" that sounds like a "babbling" brook (29). The language here might be describing campers slumbering in a tent near a creek except that these streamlike sounds are produced by cars, not water. The natural imagery is an early indication of the ways in which these characters experience man-made environments *as* first nature. The loss of a nature that "once" existed is thus felt from the novel's opening pages. It seems we have become postnatural both in terms of our real landscapes—ravines have been replaced by expressways—and our national stories: the neo-Western and the neo-pastoral take place against a fully commodified landscape, where all nature is second nature. From the first scene, we are invited to make value judgments about these shifts.

Much as he does with the Western, DeLillo recycles and updates other familiar American nature narratives. For example, one of Babette's sons from a previous marriage—Eugene, who is living in the Australian outback with his father—is represented in terms of a new postmodern definition of savagery. Eugene is "growing up without television," which makes him "a sort of wild child, a savage plucked from the bush, intelligent and literate but deprived of the deeper codes and messages that mark his species as unique" (50). These "deeper codes" are technological ones; to be civilized—indeed, to be human—is to be media-savvy. Anyone not versed in the rhetoric of television is, in a sense, "a savage." In another passage, the shopping mall becomes a new wilderness: a place of fear and disorientation, far removed from everyday life. When an elderly brother and sister disappear from Blacksmith, they are found "alive but shaken" in a "vast shopping center out on the interstate." They had been "wandering through the mall for two days, lost, confused and frightened" before holing up, the sister "venturing out to scavenge food scraps" in this "landscape of remote and menacing figures" (59). Situating the mall in opposition to civilized, safe Blacksmith, DeLillo plays with traditional American conceptions of wilderness as a frightening place by identifying the shopping mall as "remote and menacing" in its own right.

While the shopping mall might be understood as a pastoral setting, of sorts, in other instances,[12] the example I cite here clearly relies on wilderness rhetoric. The fact that the same place can host a range of American nature myths underscores the ways in which signifiers of nature can be applied in new contexts. It might also suggest a heightened placelessness that is unique to the mall—a distinctly homogenous, vacuous space, in which any and all signifiers might float, as long as they ultimately land on a commodity. More specifically, conceiving of the mall as wilderness has a defamiliarizing effect: through being rendered "nature," the mall as a space of consumption is denaturalized. In passages like these, DeLillo's nostalgia rewrites familiar nature myths for a postnatural America by transposing old myths onto new environments.

In more general terms, nature rhetoric often lends the novel's incidents an "epic quality" (122). Representations of humans in natural landscapes abound in the text. For instance, Wilder's seven-hour stint of crying is described as a sort of vision quest, likened to "wandering in some remote and holy place, in sand barrens or snowy ranges" (79). When a toxic cloud of chemicals hits Blacksmith and the town's families are forced to evacuate, their journey recalls westward migrations—"a whole history of people trekking across wasted landscapes" (122). DeLillo picks up the wagon train image again when he compares the returning evacuees in their merging vehicles to "wagon trains converging on the Santa Fe Trail" (159). The toxic cloud itself, known as the "airborne toxic event," generates a sense of sublime "awe that border[s] on the religious" due to its "terrible" and "spectacular" qualities. Its viewers respond to it "in a simple and primitive way, as some seasonal perversity of the earth like a flood or tornado, something not subject to control" (127).

Descriptions like these demonstrate that in postmodern America nature has become Martin Heidegger's "standing-reserve," "a representation which man both produces and consumes" (Valdez Moses 65).

White Noise comments extensively on this treatment. If nature is "on tap, on cable" and otherwise rendered as just another object for technological consumption, then DeLillo's language retains the faintest traces of a nostalgia for more familiar, reassuring narratives about the natural world (Valdez Moses 64). There is a sense from the novel's start that second nature, and even third nature, generate similar kinds of sights, sounds, and effects as first nature, even though the materials have changed. This is a world where a busy overpass doubles as a "scenic lookout" and the supermarket possesses "dense environmental texture" (DeLillo 171, 168). The characters—and, presumably, readers—have mixed feelings about these transformations.

On one level, DeLillo's characters seem unfazed. Indeed, what Thomas J. Ferraro astutely calls "a sparkling quotidian naturalism" enlivens many passages with a seemingly sincere appreciation for the auras of postmodern environments (31). The visit to "the most photographed barn in America" is a case in point. By the time Murray and Gladney arrive at this tourist destination, they have already seen five road signs introducing the barn. They are greeted by tour buses, cars, cameras, and hordes of tourists snapping photos. Murray pronounces, "Once you've seen the signs about the barn, it becomes impossible to see the barn." Yet this lack of authentic perception does not distress him. They are, he acknowledges, "not here to capture an image" but "to maintain one" (DeLillo 13)—an image mediated by the "gaze of cultural nostalgia" (Hamming 33). Nonetheless, Murray describes the event as a "collective" and even "religious" experience. Although he claims they can no longer know what the barn looked like prior to being photographed, never mind what made it unique in the first place, Murray does not mourn the inability to "get outside the aura" of this tourist attraction. Rather, he notes, he and Jack are "part of the aura. We're here, we're now." In case the reader doubts this is a positive experience, DeLillo adds: "He seemed immensely pleased by this" (12–13).

The presence of simulacra is highlighted here and throughout the novel, but the function of these simulacra is debatable. Frank Lentricchia suggests that "DeLillo's point, unlike [Walter] Benjamin's, is not the nostalgic one that aura is in decline, but that its source has been replaced" (92). Lentricchia reads the barn scene as an anti-nostalgic one, in which the precession of simulacra, evidenced by the road signs and barn photos, is treated "not with nostalgia for a lost world of the real but with joy" (196). In scenes like this one, DeLillo plays with familiar nature narratives, applying first-nature rhetoric to a second-nature environment in order to generate readerly nostalgia and then ironize or even mock that very nostalgia. One gets the impression that the experience of sublime or religious awe at the barn is no different from—or at least, not inferior to—that same experience of awe on a mountaintop. On one hand, then, the novel suggests that man-made nature is no better or worse than first nature. As John Frow puts it, "The realm of signs becomes not simply a 'second nature' but a primary 'reality'" (182). Looked at this way, nostalgia seems inappropriate, even silly, and readers who might have felt a sense of longing are quickly checked.

On the other hand, and in combination with this ironic nostalgia, DeLillo's novel also engenders a deeper sense of loss—a nostalgia that is not just for nature, but for authentic experiences that are less mediated, not legitimated solely through representation. I would argue that while there does seem to be joy, there is also a sincere, even dire, nostalgia in Murray's proclamations and, perhaps, in readers' affective reactions. While Murray might enjoy the absence of originality and solitude, his reaction runs counter to what tourists traditionally hope to find in nature. Even if today's tourists no longer prioritize first nature and are content not to see the barn, it is not entirely true that the aura's "source has been replaced." Second and third nature spark nostalgia, in part, because they evoke the spectral traces of first nature. Nature still serves as a powerful primary source, even if that power comes from it being an "absent presence."

Although some critics deny any "sentimental regret for a lost world of depths," I would argue that there is a sense of lost authenticity, and that nonhuman nature serves as its primary marker (Frow 189). This nostalgia implies a "real" nature to return to and contributes to the novel's postnatural feel. Deitering, one of the first scholars to read *White Noise* as a postnatural novel, also notes that it "evokes nostalgia" because "the planet itself no longer feels like home" (201). Phillips, too, acknowledges nostalgia's role in the text when he concedes that the one emotion Gladney's otherwise flat character betrays is "a certain lingering nostalgia about and interest in 'nature in general'" (243). When Jack tells his doctor that he "gets high just walking in the woods," Jack's clichéd posturing is both funny and sad, tinged with a sense that this type of experience isn't accessible in the ways it used to be (DeLillo 279). In conjunction with the more ironic passages that seem to celebrate second and third nature, nostalgia for first nature works as an affective counterpoint to question late capitalism's consumerism, materialism, and so-called technological advances.

One of the strategies for this questioning is the novel's foregrounding of the negative effects of a late capitalist economy on both nonhuman nature and human cultures. For one thing, there is the ironic fact that, despite greater access to information, we are losing knowledge of everyday environments, including our own bodies. There is a strong sense of lost innocence as information increases and we become "the sum total of our data . . . the sum total of our chemical impulses" (202). As the debates about genetic research in the late '80s illustrate, a certain nostalgia results when "we reduce [the body] to cells and molecules" and our behavior to "a tangle of neurons" (200). Heinrich, Jack's son from a previous marriage, foregrounds this loss several times in the novel. The precocious teen poses questions that challenge readers to ask whether we have lost touch with fundamental environmental realities in a world where everything is connected to everything else. For instance, he wonders, "How can people live their whole lives without knowing the names of their own parts of the body?" (158). Murray alludes to "brain fade" resulting from the "wrong kind of attentiveness"; in one of his classic ironic-nostalgic observations, he claims people have "forgotten how to listen and look as children" (67). Babette's father, who appears in Blacksmith for a surprise visit, echoes Murray's comments when he wonders, "Were people this dumb before television?" (249). These characters and their anxieties hint that "progress" has had a paradoxically dumbing-down effect on humanity.

Taken together, these assertions suggest a nostalgia for authentic and useful knowledge: for a time when people read books and told stories that were passed down over generations, for a time when having conversations—rather than going shopping or watching television together—was considered a way to spend quality family time. More than that, Heinrich's interrogation combines a critique of environmental toxics with an attention to global politics. His argument with his father about whether or not it is raining outside (Heinrich insists they can't be sure) is an example of how this process works: "How do you know it's not sulfuric acid from factories across the river? How do you know it's not fallout from a war in China? . . . What *is* rain anyway?" Heinrich asks (24, original emphasis). Heinrich's objections to everyday ignorance and the toxic risks they all face suggest a younger generation who is ready to compensate for the older generation's complicity. His parents' obsessions with death seem especially selfish in the face of his real-world concerns. Setting the stage for Heinrich's comments, Jack wonders directly before this conversation if he has "raised [Heinrich], unwittingly, in the vicinity of a chemical dump site, in the path of air currents that carry industrial wastes capable of producing scalp degeneration, [and] glorious sunsets? (People say the sunsets around here were not nearly so stunning thirty or forty years ago.)" (22). Even Jack, albeit at a detached, almost cynical level, shares Heinrich's concerns.

One reason the majority of characters in *White Noise* exhibit such environmental ignorance is that "the environment of the image *is* the landscape—it is what (for us) 'landscape' has become" (Lentricchia 195, original emphasis). DeLillo suggests a similar point in an interview when he says television—particularly "bad news, sensationalistic news, over-whelming news"—is "all that we've got left of nature" (qtd. in Remnick 48). Television, radio, words, and images bombard the Gladneys and DeLillo's readers, creating an environment of constant representational stimulation in which it is easy to confuse images with what Deitering calls "the Real" (202). Unexplained quotations are interspersed with characters' voices to create a constant flow of information that mimics reality; lines from television and radio advertising, the "white noise" of everyday life, become indistinguishable from live dialogue. During the airborne toxic event, media, especially the radio, dictate reality. In a humorous caricature of the increasingly blurry line between nature and technology, the Gladney girls experience the physical symptoms the radio warns them about *before* they hear them announced on the air. When the family gets together for a night of television watching, they witness "floods, earthquakes, mud slides, erupting volcanoes" (64). Jack's colleagues suggest the following explanation for the widespread fascination with televised natural disasters: "For most people there are only two places in the world. Where they live and their TV set" (66). Television is itself as much of a "place" as one's hometown. In a strange way, then, watching natural disasters on television is its own form of traveling—a kind of postmodern tourism.

Just as televised nature feels unreal, Blacksmith is a town that feels unplaced. Murray says he "can't help being happy in a town called Blacksmith"—a town that, for him, is a kind of "pastoral home site." The reasons for his happiness are twofold: his location in a "small-town setting," and his ability to be a part of "higher learning in some impossibly distant and tree-shaded place" (10–11). Academia and the natural world combine to form a sort of neo-pastoral setting in which intellectual labor replaces agrarian, a shift in which the ivory tower stereotype reinforces the sense of detachment from place that the novel theorizes. Although Jack chairs the department of "American environments," he is out of touch with even his own intellectual territory since, despite his role as founder of the field of Hitler Studies, he has been able to get away with not knowing German. The "environments" Jack and his colleagues study are more cerebral than visceral, more technological than natural, more placeless than placed. The College-on-the-Hill is sheltered, inconspicuous and disconnected from the rest of the world: it "occupies an ever serene edge of the townscape, semidetached, more or less scenic, suspended in political calm" (85). Moreover, the town of Blacksmith is neither urban nor rural; it is not proximate to any city, and so it seems isolated to its inhabitants, who have "no large city to blame for [their] sense of victimization. No city to hate and fear" (176).

Murray seems to glory in his "impossibly distant" and privileged intellectual life, but Jack, rather comically, struggles with feeling disconnected from his labor and his neo-pastoral town. As Jeanne Hamming points out, Gladney, like the town, has been "domesticated by the conversion of a once wild nature," and he experiences a reciprocal "longing to return to nature" (27). Especially after Babette confesses her affair, Jack "retreats into essentialist conceptions of masculinity" in which maleness was most at home in a natural setting (think Roosevelt); he seeks a "previously impervious masculine corporeality" that seems to have disappeared (27). Hamming makes a good point about Jack's masculinist urges, but such nostalgia for a stable embodiment—though certainly gender-specific in its manifestations—is not restricted to male readers any more than it is restricted to male characters. Indeed, Babette fears death as much as, or perhaps more than, Jack does. The appeal of "impervious corporeality" would have resonated with a broad 1980s audience, poised as they were at the "end of nature" and amid new kinds of boundary- and body-blurring technologies. If Jack's body is under siege, then so are the rest of our bodies.

Even though Blacksmith's residents prefer to think of themselves as "semidetached," the presence of everyday toxics and televised natural disasters should remind them of the "technocultural encroachments" upon their lives (Hamming 27). They are already "environmental exiles" (Deitering 200) when the "airborne toxic event"—a "high-definition event" signifying a "whole new generation of toxic waste"—hits Blacksmith (DeLillo 138). Caught off guard, Jack tries to reassure his family with the following wisdom: "These things happen to poor people in exposed areas. Society is set up in such a way that it's the poor and the uneducated who suffer the main impact of natural and man-made disasters. People in low-lying areas get the floods, people in shanties get the hurricanes and tornadoes. I'm a college professor. Did you ever see a college professor rowing a boat down his own street in one of those TV floods? We live in a neat and pleasant town near a college with a quaint name. These things don't happen in places like Blacksmith" (114). A short while later, Jack makes his point again, claiming, "I'm not just a college professor. I'm the head of a department. I don't see myself fleeing an airborne toxic event. That's for people who live in mobile homes out in the scrubby parts of the county" (117).

Given Jack's tongue-in-cheek humor and DeLillo's frequent mocking of his character, it is hard to pinpoint the tone of these statements. Nevertheless, several things stand out. First, the phrase "society is set up in such a way" suggests that the unfortunate overlap between disaster and poverty is the product of a range of social forces. Although he does not clarify what these forces might be, Jack makes the implicit claim that disasters affect "the poor and the uneducated" disproportionately for real, social reasons. Coming on the tails of the confident assertion that "these things happen to poor people in exposed areas," the passive construction ("society is set up") stands out for its ambiguity, demanding attention from readers. We should wonder who, or what, is the subject of this sentence.

Second, the coupling of "natural and man-made disasters" is provocative; throughout the novel, the line between these two classifications becomes increasingly blurry. The airborne toxic event itself is, in a sense, both. Although it is often described in language that evokes sublime nature, the chemical involved in the event, Nyodene D., is man-made, "a whole bunch of things thrown together that are byproducts of the manufacture of insecticide" (131). Third, these passages are notable for the conspicuous absence of an important factor in environmental injustice: race. In the very white town of Blacksmith race is an absent presence. At some points—for instance, when Willie Mink says to Jack: "You are very white, you know that?" (310)—race comes to the fore. By cleverly dramatizing white flight, the airborne toxic event underscores the central characters' whiteness by foregrounding their social class and the protections they expect from it. An observant reader will note that the Gladneys' race, as much as their class, contributes to their privilege, the limits of which are highlighted here.

Finally, Jack's statements are ironic: the airborne toxic event *is* happening in Blacksmith, and he and his family *are* fleeing it, even if he doesn't "see himself" in this story. Jack is no longer safe in his ivory tower or secure in his middle-class identity. Environmental toxics have reached his "pleasant town." Had Jack been paying more attention to daily life in Blacksmith rather than obsessing about his mortality, he might not have been so surprised; the airborne toxic event is not the first incident in the novel. Readers may recall several references to toxic environments earlier in the text, including one incident at the local grade school where "kids were getting headaches and eye irritations, tasting metal in their mouths. A teacher rolled on the floor and spoke foreign languages. No one knew what was wrong. Investigators said it could be the ventilating system, the paint or varnish, the foam insulation, the electrical insulation, the cafeteria food, the rays emitted by microcomputers, the asbestos fireproofing, the adhesive on shipping containers, the fumes from the chlorinated pool, or perhaps something deeper, finer-grained, more closely woven into the basic state of things" (35). When the "men in Mylex suits" go to investigate, the situation is complicated further: since Mylex is "itself a suspect material," the investigation yields suspect results. The sheer number of possible causes for these mysterious physical ailments is overwhelming, and the fact that the cause could be "something deeper" adds to the impression that toxics are everywhere—in our environments, and as a result, in our bodies. Toxics have become "woven into the basic state of things," with the (natural) human body being the final boundary that capitalism—and its toxic byproducts—crosses. As the nostalgia inherent in the objections to OncoMouse suggests, the human frontier is for many people the most sacred one.

When we are told a few pages later of a "rumor" that one of the investigators died suddenly during the inspection, the uncertainty surrounding the death is what's alarming (40). In a postnatural world, death becomes the last natural limit. Winnie Richards, another colleague of Jack's, posits that death is necessary to appreciate life: "Isn't death the boundary we need? Doesn't it give a precious texture to life, a sense of definition?" (228). Barrett puts it another way when she writes that, in this novel, "the only virgin land is death" (98). Like "virgin land," death is a heavily fraught symbol, a natural line that *White Noise* suggests is being crossed. In a sense, capitalism has penetrated even death. When Jack is exposed to the airborne toxic event after stopping to buy gasoline, his body is infiltrated by toxic chemicals. Like the second nature around him, Jack's death is man-made—a (by)product of human causes. Murray describes "the nature of modern death" in terms of objectivity, predictability, and knowledge. Denaturalized and represented as information, death has become merely a "network of symbols" subject to interpretation—an "entire awesome technology wrested from the gods" (150, 142). This rhetoric mirrors the opponents of OncoMouse and other genetic technologies in its discussion of human beings as "playing God." Murray, characteristically, is more thrilled than afraid.

However, readers may be less certain about their feelings. Lawrence Buell's concerns are especially helpful when making sense of the novel's heavily thematized fear of death. For Buell, *White Noise* exemplifies how "toxic discourse may repress, fail to fulfill, or swerve away from itself according to the drag of other discourses with which it cross-pollinates" (*Writing* 51). To him, these "other discourses" include DeLillo's "framing" of the airborne toxic event as "a postmodern symbol of inauthenticity" and the novel's subsequent focus on the "death obsessions" of both Jack and Babette (51).[13] I would argue, though, that DeLillo's treatment of the "(non)event" (Buell 51) as a marker of postmodern inauthenticity is itself a kind of environmentalist statement. The feeling that the airborne toxic event is inauthentic resonates with the nature-as-limit trope I have been discussing—the idea of nature as a final frontier that late-capitalism has crossed. If even ecocatastrophes are nonevents that empty out materiality and elicit a remote nostalgia for an actual catastrophe, then we are pointed back to the everyday detachment we feel from our environments and the unforeseen consequences that stem from our treatment of those environments.

In the same vein, the novel's fear of death reflects a broader anxiety about humankind's increasing ability to control, via science and technology, all of nature. When Jack tells Babette that scientists have invented microorganisms to consume the harmful chemicals in the airborne toxic event, this is little consolation to her. Babette expresses a range of emotional responses to this new knowledge:

"The very idea, the very existence, the wondrous ingenuity. On the one hand I definitely admire it. Just to think there are people out there who can conjure such things. A cloud-eating microbe or whatever. There is just no end of surprise. . . . What scares me is have they thought it through completely?"

"You feel a vague foreboding," I said.

"I feel they're working on the superstitious part of my nature. Every advance is worse than the one before because it makes me more scared."

"Scared of what?"

"The sky, the earth, I don't know."

"The greater the scientific advance, the more primitive the fear."
"Why is that?" she said. (160–161)

Interestingly, Babette slips from fearing the "advance" to fearing nature itself. This slippage is telling: technology ultimately alters nature so that it becomes impossible to distinguish a nature that is unaltered. Even the sky and the earth are subject to revision—in some cases, already revised. The fact that Babette can't precisely describe her fear but rather feels "a vague foreboding" indicates her inability to differentiate between human and non-human nature with the same kind of "intuitive, visceral" reaction McKibben trusts to tell him when enough's enough (*Enough* 40). She also displays a corresponding need to assuage this fear by transposing it onto the material world. Her suspicion that "they're working on the superstitious part of [her] nature" conjures the age-old definition of nature as a pure, interior, essential part of human beings. Her fear of technology is grafted onto external nature—the sky, the earth—but it ultimately points back to human nature, and human responsibility for nature. More than that, her reaction suggests, like McKibben does, that our intuition will tell us when we have crossed a line.

Of course, it is much more than intuition that is required to make sense of the complexities of genetic engineering and postnatural nature. Underneath a purportedly collective faith in human ingenuity lies serious doubt, even fear, about living in an entirely man-made world, where the "very existence of custom-made organisms" no longer warrants surprise or nostalgia (DeLillo 160). While Babette uses her intuition to tell her when things aren't right, Jack goes to his doctor, who breaks the news to him about his new, postnatural status. Bringing environmental hazards as close to home as possible—to the presumably "safe" place of middle-class suburban America, even to the body itself—makes the novel's environmental justice critique difficult to ignore. By inserting toxic chemicals into the protagonist's body, *White Noise* embeds fear and doubt in readers as well.

Taken together, the "vague foreboding" Babette identifies combined with Jack's ironic disavowal of the toxic event's threat to his middle-class family foreground the fact that it is a (white) privilege to ignore environmental hazards. This point is perhaps even more powerful today, as the unequal effects of environmental hazards on the poor and people of color are becoming ever more visible. The devastating impacts of Hurricane Katrina revealed to the world the degree to which those Americans living in poverty are disproportionately people of color and exposed the fact that it is these people who are most victimized by natural disasters. Moreover, "natural" disasters often have man-made causes—such as global warming, which some scientists think contributed to the severity of Hurricane Katrina—and as such are (like the airborne toxic event) byproducts of consumer capitalism. Revisiting the passage where DeLillo's schoolteacher responds to toxics at the school by "[speaking] in foreign languages," we might interpret this remark as a direct challenge to American exceptionalism (35). Such exceptionalism—represented by the Gladney family's (shattered) faith in its own immunity to environmental disasters—dovetails with the national tendency to ignore the environmental effects of excessive consumption and the ways in which these effects are unevenly distributed across geographies.

White Noise poses one question that is especially haunting in regard to toxic chemical incidents and their frequent representations "on the news": "How serious can it be if it happens all the time?" (174). As Heise explains, the everydayness of toxic threat extends its relevance beyond "an ordinary family's encounter with one exceptionally dangerous technological accident"; rather, the novel is about the inescapable "risk society" in which most of us find ourselves ("Toxins" 752). Heinrich shares her assessment, informing his family over dinner that "the real issue is the kind of radiation that surrounds us every day" (DeLillo 174). As the representation of environmental hazards in the form of "terrifying data" becomes "an industry in itself," and disasters are, in effect, naturalized through being televised, readers are challenged to consider their own risk levels and their own complicity in the processes that produce the risks (174). Nostalgia for uncontaminated nature, and for an everyday life free from the "everyday drift" of toxics, underscores the novel's environmental justice critique. More broadly, nostalgia for "real" nature—for pure environments, unchanged by technology and unmediated by television—helps foreground what has been lost as second and third nature begin to dominate everyday life.

* * *

Nine days after the airborne toxic event, life in Blacksmith returns, more or less, to normal; the kids go back to school, the shoppers once again browse the supermarket shelves, Jack recommits himself to finally learning German, and Babette resumes teaching basic life skills to the elderly. There is, however, at least one important difference: the sunsets are out of this world. Deeply colored and longer-lasting, they have become "almost unbearably beautiful" (170). Although the causal connection cannot be proven, the word on the street is that Nyodene D. "(added to the everyday drift of effluents, pollutants, contaminants and deliriants)" has contributed to an "aesthetic leap from already brilliant sunsets to broad towering ruddled visionary skyscapes, tinged with dread" (170). The sublime awe inspired by the sunsets not only draws crowds but also compels readers to reassess postmodern nature. As Joseph Tabbi argues, even if DeLillo's postnatural world is one in which "created objects" and "reproductive images" are in some sense primary, "we need not accept such conditions passively" (174). Precisely because nature and culture have become more complexly intertwined, we are forced to confront the "dread" that results.

DeLillo's toxic sunsets provide an ironic counterpoint to McKibben's sunset parable. Clearly, the qualitative difference McKibben sees between the Coke can and the pile of deer droppings does not apply in DeLillo's world. Where McKibben locates nature's end, DeLillo finds only the inability to determine a precise turning point. DeLillo disrupts the very origins on which nostalgia usually relies, replacing purity with uncertainty and competing "schools of thought" that can only try to sort and organize flows of information into some kind of recognizable "narrative sweep" (227). Perhaps this is all human beings have ever been able to do. Yet when Jack witnesses "another postmodern sunset, rich in romantic imagery," that sense of romance compels contemplation (227). Whether we see irony or nostalgia in the sunsets—or, as I do, both—we are asked to make value judgments about them and to reflect on our emotional responses. Do we agree with McKibben, who would presumably say that a frightening, probably toxic, sunset observed from a highway overpass is fundamentally different, "lesser," than a nontoxic sunset enjoyed from a more "natural" location—a remote mountaintop in a national park, for instance? Or do we agree with DeLillo, who seems to suggest that first nature and sublime experiences have always been preceded and colored by our own "romantic imagery"?

The likelihood that a particular environment's source is man-made, and the increasing difficulty of identifying nontoxic environments, are in some ways beside the point. The fact that the characters still gather to watch the sunsets—indeed, still feel inspired, even awestruck, by their overwhelming beauty—implies a lingering admiration, a need, for non-human nature, or at least, for the experiences such nature has traditionally fostered. As *White Noise* illustrates, in an era of "cable nature," there remains some nostalgia for "walking in the woods," even if those woods are unlikely to be wilderness (DeLillo 231, 279). There remains a desire for transcendent experience, even if that transcendence is achieved by watching one's daughter mutter "Toyota Celica" in her sleep (155). There remains an urge to describe a pastoral aesthetic in one's environment, even if the sounds are generated by traffic. The second- and third-nature qualities of these characters' experiences either accentuate a reader's sincere nostalgia for first nature or cause us to reflect on the instability of this category—or both.

It is not exactly right to conclude, then, that "DeLillo mimics nostalgia for an audience who no longer believes in it" (Parrish 703). People do believe in nostalgia, perhaps more than ever. DeLillo's nostalgia is both a mode through which to read and critique the past and the present, as well as an ideological affect to be approached warily, with a critical irony. By compelling a self-consciousness about nostalgia, *White Noise* disrupts organic narratives of the past. Still, there is a sense that something has been lost, a loss manifested in a postmodern "sadness without an object, a sadness which creates a longing" (Stewart 23). Nostalgia in *White Noise* is an everyday condition, partly because its characters are always "at a loss" to communicate, or experience, what they consider to be authenticity. But this loss is a productive one insofar as "nostalgia . . . may depend precisely on the irrecoverable nature of the past for its emotional impact and appeal" (Hutcheon, "Irony" 195, original emphasis). Hutcheon is right that the past is always irrecoverable, but I would emphasize a different word in her statement: nature. Despite first nature's increasingly irrecoverable quality, *White Noise* suggests we might still use nostalgia as a way of channeling and reflecting on our collective longings.

As they recreate experiences typically associated with nonhuman nature, DeLillo's characters also create new ideals of community, which are partly inspired by the shared longing for familiar nature narratives. The crowds of onlookers gathered on the highway overpass (now an unofficial "scenic lookout") reflect at least a dim impulse toward neighborliness, even if their "nervous" chatting suggests they are out of practice for such communal events (171). The crowd at the billboard in *Underworld*'s epilogue is even more indicative of the potential for such gatherings to inspire "the hope that grows when things surpass their limits" (818). The final word in this more recent novel—"a word that spreads a longing"— is, significantly, "peace" (*Underworld* 827). While DeLillo remarks somewhat wistfully that "most of our longings go unfulfilled," his writing challenges us not to simply accept this perpetual lack of contentment but instead to ask questions about what it means that we experience longings at all (*Underworld* 803). If nostalgia is understood as a longing for an ideal of sorts, then what are those ideals? Who establishes them? Who benefits from our belief in them, from our continually unfulfilled longings? And could those ideals ever, in some present-day form, be achieved? DeLillo's work suggests that some of nostalgia's power comes from exposing the gap between the "real" and the "ideal," which can compel an analysis of, for instance, the negative byproducts of a capitalist economy.

Put another way, if our present is a site of near-perpetual longing, then that chronic lack of fulfillment helps raise questions about the causes of our longing. 1980s America was a time in which previously stable boundaries—between species, and between human-created and natural environments, in particular—were becoming noticeably more permeable. Jack Gladney has his finger on the pulse of the decade when he wonders: "What is a thing and how do we know it's not another thing?" (126). Ours is a world in which, Paul Rabinow reminds us, "older cultural classifications will be joined by a vast array of new ones, which will cross-cut, partially supersede and eventually redefine the older categories in ways that are well worth monitoring" (245). McKibben is right that we should not sit by and passively accept these redefinitions if they run counter to our intuition, though we should be self-conscious about where things like intuition come from.

McKibben may also be right that, given current environmental conditions, "what's nostalgic and sentimental is to insist that we keep doing what we're doing now simply because it's familiar"—in other words, to refuse to change (qtd. in Morrow). Whether we agree with him or not, nostalgia can and does play a role in helping us monitor broad cultural shifts. As an emotional response—a reader's or a character's—nostalgia can help us negotiate a cultural montage that is ever more elaborate. Nostalgia marks our discourse and deserves serious scrutiny, not just for its reactionary impulse but for its call to self-reflection. This is where irony becomes a crucial helpmate to nostalgia. DeLillo's book is deliberately ironic, both in the sense of being a sarcastic caricature and in Haraway's cyborg-political sense of using irony as "a rhetorical strategy and a political method" in which "contradictions . . . do not resolve into larger wholes" ("Cyborg" 173). *White Noise* goes beyond the usual categories of nostalgia and demonstrates that ironic "distance [is] necessary for reflective thought about the present as well as the past" (Hutcheon, "Irony" 207).

Finally, DeLillo reminds us that the alternatives to change are not either nostalgia or celebration; this is a false choice. We can be nostalgic and celebratory, cautious and forward-looking, sincere and humorous, at the same time. In fact, embracing multiple perspectives, multiple affects, at once might be wise as we face our increasingly posthuman and post-natural future. Even if it seems like "things have no limits now . . . no level of values" (DeLillo, *Underworld* 76), we don't have to consider our future in terms of a "wholesale loss of meaning" in which the value of being human, or any other species, is lost (McKibben, *Enough* 205). What we should do, DeLillo implies, is sift through and evaluate the prolifera-tion of meanings, natures, and emotions that constitute our postnatural world—a task that has not gotten any simpler in the new millennium.

Most Americans need no introduction to *Survivor*. Since its premier in the United States in 2000, the "reality" show has been among television's most watched programs.[1] For those who may be marooned on desert islands of their own, culturally speaking, here's an overview. In each series, contestants ("Survivors") are taken to an exotic destination, such as a remote island, separated into "tribes," compelled to exist without most of the luxuries of modern life, and recorded for television audiences while they struggle to "negotiate the tensions between cooperation and competition" (Kellman).[2] Each episode features physical challenges that pit one tribe against the other, and each concludes with a meeting of the "tribal council," where members of the losing tribe vote to cast one of their teammates out of the game. As the process continues, the tribes merge and a sole Survivor remains at the season's end. This winner takes home one million dollars.

Although this may sound like fun and games, *Survivor* actually reveals much more about American ideologies and their exportation across the globe than it does about good-natured competition between individuals. To Mark Burnett, the show's executive producer, the show illustrates nothing less than the "core essence of humanity," an essence apparently best demonstrated by success in a society ruled by corporate capitalism (qtd. in Murray 43).[3] While the show purports to strip individuals down to their "underlying humanity" by re-creating a primitive environment, it simultaneously markets and reinforces a "discourse of social Darwinism" defined by the "naturalized terms of corporate

capitalism: individualism, competition, scarcity, domination, and elimi-
nation" (Murray 45, 44). Within these terms, the contestants' abilities
to remain popular among their fellow contestants take precedence over
any real need to adapt to the physical environment, though nonhuman
nature remains a powerful symbolic force in the show.

Wilderness, usually conceived of as antithetical to the workplace,
becomes the proving ground for an equally savage corporate nature—
the place where "humanity" and corporate capitalism merge. Viewers
learn next to nothing about the real geography of the show's locations
or the lives of these regions' inhabitants. As Philip D. Beidler writes
of James A. Michener's *Tales of the South Pacific*, the "real terrain" is
obscured by "a mythic geography firmly in possession of its real owners, the American audience" (Beidler 211).[4] Both setting and character,
Survivor's nature plays some familiar roles for this audience. In place of a
particular local environment, viewers "discover" one of America's favorite, and most enduring, nature myths: the frontier. Not surprisingly, the
product of this reinvented frontier environment—and perhaps what
contributes to the appeal of the show for Americans—is a "cannibalistic
system" that "encourages factions and rewards opportunists" (Kellman).
Nostalgic nature narratives reinforce the show's problematic ideological
consequences. Nature is upheld as a moral authority, a nonhuman space
apart from our everyday lives. Race is reified as a skin-color distinction
and, thus, rooted in the body. At the same time, a superficial multiculturalist impulse to blur cultural boundaries paves the way for American
imperialism in the forms of touristic exploitation, a consumer-oriented
capitalist economy, and the commodification of non-white cultures.

The nostalgic mystique of frontier ideology is especially dominant
in *Survivor*'s ninth season, "Vanuatu: Islands of Fire." Host Jeff Probst
prefaces this season's first episode by explaining that eighteen American
"strangers from different walks of life" will be "forced to work together
to create a new society, while battling the elements and each other." The
Survivors "must learn to adapt" to this new environment and to the people
they interact with if they want to stay in the game. In language that resonates with Turner's famous thesis, Probst's description highlights several
tenets of a pioneer society—notably, the individual's struggle with savage
elements and the democratic society that struggle supposedly produces.
And yet, as in Turner's version of westward expansion, the narrative the
show ultimately tells is an imperialistic not a democratic one.

The first episode in the Vanuatu series enlists Native people as part
of its cast and equates these modern-day noble savages with the natural

world. The CBS website provides this written description of the "tribal welcome": "The Survivors were awestruck to see hundreds of indigenous Vanuatu tribe members quickly rush the boat while shouting out a fierce battle cry. Host Jeff Probst explains that before the castaways were going to be welcome on these islands, they would first have to pass local initiation rites."[5] In the video clip chosen by CBS to represent this episode, the contestants do indeed seem "awestruck"; various stages of fear and amusement are revealed on their expectant faces while high-pitched shrieks resound as the Natives surround their visitors on the water.[6] The clip begins with footage of the active volcano, Mount Yasur, which Probst warns "displays its anger" regularly. In sweeping terms that equate nature's mysterious wrath with the primitive "warriors" who live there, Probst alludes to the island's "fascinating history of cannibalism" in addition to warning that sorcery and black magic are practiced here. A skull in front of a fiery volcano serves as this season's icon.

The opening montage that kicks off each episode includes a range of rapid-fire images: Survivors with painted faces sporting leafy crowns on their heads; what appears to be a Native Vanuatuan bungee jumping; smoke, fire, and ash erupting from Mount Yasur; and various shots of mostly white Survivors juxtaposed against dark-skinned Natives in the background. Interspersed very briefly are a skull and a Native lunging forward with a primitive-looking knife. Finally, a spear-throwing Native caps off the pastiche—a complex visual text consistent with Fredric Jameson's theories about our growing "appetite for a world transformed into sheer images of itself and for pseudo-events and 'spectacles'" (18). The spectacular features of this montage work in two ways. On one hand, our white male host reinforces cultural difference when he assures us that the Chief is a "real chief" and the ritual is "an authentic Vanuatu tribal tradition," undertaken by people who "take their spirituality very seriously." On the other hand, despite Probst's reminder that the Americans "are in a foreign country" and "must be granted access to the land," the sequence of images facilitates a blurring of cultural lines between American Survivor and Native. Subjecting Vanuatuan culture to the gaze of American television audiences, the montage exemplifies the worst kind of multiculturalism: one that renders cultures interchangeable, evacuates historical and material differences, and provides a clean slate for the inscription of American ideology.

The primary ideology at stake here, as I've indicated, is the frontier myth; accordingly, wilderness is the main form nature takes in the show. More broadly, wild nature performs two seemingly paradoxical functions, both helping to smooth over cultural difference and, conversely, reinforcing racial distinctions. A floating signifier that is easily manipulated by global technology, nature can be a symbolic stand-in for a culture, a race, or the frontier myth, as well as, more broadly, a gateway to spirituality. At the same time, wild (or first) nature is still a strong presence: a biophilia Burnett describes as "man's intrinsic longing to be one with nature" is presumed to be shared by participants and spectators alike (qtd. in Murray 45). Still, what "being one with nature" means today is conflated with spectacle. Getting back to nature has become something to do not by oneself but with everyone else, as publicly and socially as possible. The show reifies our American nostalgia for an "organic precapitalist peasant landscape and village society" at the same time that it effaces the possibility of such a society's existence—except on "reality" television, where nature is catapulted into the "now" of multinational capitalism (Jameson 34). Even as the show conjures Turner's nineteenth-century pioneers, it indicates just how far Americans have come; not only have we tamed the wilderness but we have moved beyond the pastoral stage to a new phase of human-nature relations, which is both postnatural and hyperreal.

"Real" nature is superseded by televised myth as modern-day Americans replay a frontier adventure story that is at once familiar and new, nostalgic and contrived. *Survivor* exemplifies the observation by DeLillo's "American environments" department chair that television is a kind of ironic "place" in its own right (66). Jennifer Price echoes this insight when she suggests that television, being simultaneously real and unreal, poses new challenges, including the imperative "to tell the difference between TV Nature, as an absolute ur-Reality at the edge of modern life, and real nature, as something we can use and change" (256). "Reality" television can uphold nature's mythic qualities. But what we see on television often matches the ways we define and encounter "real" nature. For instance, by reifying nature as first and foremost a backdrop for recreation and adventure, *Survivor* encourages the separation between nature and everyday life that often leads to environmental destruction.

Of course, not everyone is so pessimistic about the show. In *Reality TV: The Work of Being Watched*, Mark Andrejevic admits there is "nothing natural about the second nature—the capitalist jungle—in which [*Survivor* suggests] we struggle" (209). However, he gives more credit to contemporary viewers, who he claims are better able to negotiate this postnatural reality; indeed, he suggests that part of viewers' enjoyment of the show stems from their pleasure in "debunking the ruse of naturalization" (196). He argues that reality TV exposes the artifice of capitalism, rather than simply naturalizing it in viewers' minds: what we see, then, is "the reality of contrivance" (209). Still, Andrejevic has to admit that, even as viewers realize the artificial nature of the show, there remains a simultaneous "foreclosing [of] the possibility of anything beyond contrivance" and, so, an "acceptance of its version of human *nature* as competitive, Darwinian, and so forth" (209, 206–7, original emphasis).

While his reading differs from mine, we agree that the show naturalizes U.S.-based global capitalism. *Survivor* exemplifies what can happen when a postnatural understanding of nonhuman nature collapses the nature-capital distinction. The wilderness becomes a corporate world of sorts—a place where all must guard themselves against "the snake lurking in the next cubicle"—while, on the flip side, nonhuman nature is offered as ripe for consumption (Burnett, qtd. in Murray 50). Survivors who successfully complete challenges are rewarded with American products—for instance, in episode 5, all the Pringles they can eat and all the beer they can drink. The fact that the winning tribe enjoys these indulgences against a natural backdrop of dramatic waterfalls contributes to the confusion of boundaries between nature and consumer culture. On this show's set, nature is the environment of daily life and consumption represents a vacation, in a reversal of the more typical positioning of nature as an authentic antidote to consumer culture. This reversal situates nature as both part of and external to human culture: nature is proximate insofar as it is subject to capitalism, but nature is still distinct from our everyday lives, which enables its domination.[7] When corporate competition is framed as a jungle, where tribal politics must be negotiated to achieve success, nonhuman nature serves as a vehicle for gaining and legitimating capital. In the process, capitalism is marketed as natural law.

Ultimately, the show celebrates the American ideology that frontier adventure—now interchangeable with and kept alive by competitive capitalism—can still build character over a century after the frontier's closing. As such, *Survivor* illustrates one of America's contemporary renditions of cultural imperialism via an explicitly racialized tourism—a tourism manifested in previous decades by white patrons visiting Native American schools, white tourists slumming in Harlem's cabarets, and the counterculture's romantic appropriations of American Indians. The show establishes racist binaries as transnational: it conjoins non-whites of all nations with nature and erases any historical, economic, or political distinctions between the non-whites in question. In a telling statement, the only African American Survivor in the Vanuatu series, Rory, notices that the Natives are "jabbing spears" at everyone—everyone, that is, except for him. He concludes that "a black man coming onto the island is not particularly unwelcome." As "a black man," Rory is likened to the Vanuatu Natives; he is also immediately pegged as "different," even "a bad seed," by his male tribe and marginalized accordingly.[8] In effect, global technology and multicultural ideology have enabled the United States to export its racism—in which race is a bodily trait, manifested by skin color, and dark skin color makes one "different"—across the world.

Operating through racial distinctions, capitalism's evolution is reinforced as a teleological narrative, in which the ideal Survivor rises from simulated savagery to millionaire status in the ultimate "bootstraps" legend for the twenty-first century. Meanwhile, knowledge of indigenous people is eulogized, commodified, and even auctioned off to support the upwardly mobile Americans.[9] *Survivor*'s nostalgic representations of nature, especially of the particularly American wilderness associated with the frontier, suggest that ours is a meritocratic world, a zero-sum game where the playing field is equal and individuals' "natures" are accountable for their successes and failures. As Keat Murray suggests, the show works to "naturalize the increasingly polarized social structure produced by cutthroat competition" within an economy of scarcity (Murray 44). The show also affirms observations by New Western historians about the durability and flexibility of the Turnerian frontier myth. The fact that these familiar frontier narratives can now play out in so many spaces and via so many mediums means that the process of evaluating their ideological stakes is both more difficult, and more important, than ever.

The next, and final, chapter features a twenty-first-century literary text that fictionalizes many of the issues in *Survivor*: the new, flexible frontiers of global capitalism, the shifting conceptions of nonhuman nature currently circulating, and the ease with which nature and race—while increasingly unstable as definitive categories—still inform one another. Ruth Ozeki's *All Over Creation* envisions a neo-agrarian community that values the sanctity of natural "life" and its autonomous processes; the novel's "bad seeds" are not people of color who have been equated with nonhuman nature but rather global capitalists who refuse to honor that sanctity. If *Survivor* reinforces Jameson's point about nostalgia's "incompatibility . . . with genuine historicity" (19), then Ozeki's novel strongly suggests otherwise. Indeed, if we attend to the nostalgic longing in her text we can see how this backward-looking emotion can indicate *attention* to history rather than mark its absence. Drawing on both familiar and new kinds of nature narratives and challenging the lingering belief in racial and species purity, Ozeki generates nostalgia for hybridity in order to incite a critique of the American brand of global capitalism *Survivor* celebrates. Nature's very survival, according to her novel, depends on how thoughtfully we navigate the increasingly complicated routes and roots of nostalgic narratives.

6 / Nostalgia and Nature at the Millennium: Ruth Ozeki's Green Culture of Life

By the start of the 1990s, nature, nation, and identity had become radically unstable categories. End-of-nature rhetoric and other "discourses of terminal lament," along with a shift away from "ecosystem equilibrium," or "balance," as an ecological paradigm, shook the foundations of the American environmental imagination (Frederick Buell 547, 573). Identity, too, had lost its roots, thanks in large part to the dominance of critical theory in the 1980s. Despite the gains of civil rights movements, intellectuals from both ends of the political spectrum—albeit for different reasons—now opposed identity essentialism.[1] Many scholars had come to embrace "the postmodernist view that identities are purely arbitrary, and hence politically unreliable . . . ideological fictions, imposed from above"—meaningless at best, divisive and oppressive at worst (Alcoff and Mohanty 3–4).

Even nations had begun to seem obsolete, at least in theory, since multinational corporations appeared to wield more power in the world than national governments. This seemingly "postnational" political arena, combined with a vital American economy in the 1990s, provided opportunities for the U.S. to reassert global dominance. Some, like Frederick Buell (who, except where otherwise indicated, is the "Buell" I'm referencing in this chapter), resisted the idea of the postnational precisely because they saw globalization as little more than a "new frontier for American business and society" (553). According to Buell, this "new frontier" operated within several major realms, including multiculturalism—which was "reconstructed during the Clinton presidency as a new form of national consensus"—and environmental problems, which he thought would "provide the site for regaining global economic and political leadership" (562, 576, 559). Buell's concerns resonate with other scholars of neoliberalism who describe an oppressive state of consensus politics that generates consumers rather than citizens, shopping malls rather than communities, and, ultimately, "an atomized society of disengaged individuals who feel demoralized and socially powerless" (McChesney). Wendy Brown explains how neoliberalism resurrects a classic liberal economic model that values "a maximization of free trade and competition" and "minimum interference from political institutions" (6). This market-knows-best approach reduces humans to "*homo oeconomicus,*" since every aspect of our lives can be "cast in terms of market rationality" (8, original emphasis).[2]

Part of what enables such marketability is, ironically, the very fluidity of meaning many scholars embrace. A complete absence of foundational narratives can lead to a world where images and narratives are more easily manipulated, commodified, and exported—a world where texts like *Survivor* carry as much cultural currency as, say, *An Inconvenient Truth.* By some measures, a "postmodern ecology" (Garrard, *Ecocriticism* 15) driven by a dynamic, even chaotic, model of ecological change, rather than a "balanced" one, is more easily yoked to late capitalist values.[3] Likewise, it is partly the widespread destabilizing of cultural identities within an ahistorical "multiculturalist" discourse that enables a reassertion of American cultural imperialism, as Buell and others worry. However appealing unstable meanings may be to cultural theorists who fear race essentialism and other oppressive purities, anti-foundationalism can also be dangerous. As Ursula Heise explains, "Like feminists and race theorists who emphasized the cultural rather than biological grounding of their objects of study," ecocritics who adopt a poststructuralist extreme risk erasing any notion of "the real" that could be used as a basis for creating (or defending) an environment or an identity ("Hitchhiker's Guide" 512).

With these concerns in mind, many scholars, writers, and other intellectuals have begun to develop more nuanced ways of theorizing our posthuman, postnatural status. Theoretical frameworks like "postpositivist realism" in ethnic studies resonate with ecocritical approaches like "weak constructivism" and "postpositivist ecocentricity"[4] to reflect a growing sense that, in the new millennium, we must be both real and hyperreal, natural and postnatural, human and posthuman—at the same time. If "identities are theoretical constructions that enable us to read the world in specific ways," as Satya P. Mohanty argues in his formulation of postpositivist realism, then a "theory-mediated" approach to the world can produce a qualified, but still helpful, sort of objectivity (*Literary Theory* 216, 211).

This approach requires a "real world" to be read, of course, and the categories of nation and nature are still useful in describing this world. Informed by the insight that national boundaries are not discrete, scholars must also recognize that "nation-states are alive as mechanisms of control and domination," despite the rising influence of transnational corporations (Lionnet and Shih 8–9). The U.S. invasion of Iraq is but one example that illustrates how the nation-state continues to be influential. Likewise, reports of nature's demise have been, to paraphrase Mark Twain, greatly exaggerated. One need only look at the latest natural disaster in the headlines, or compare contemporary photographs of the earth from outer space with those taken in the 1960s—which, as McKibben and others show, reveal a shockingly different planet—to mark some of the real environmental consequences of human activity. Buell is right that "it would be senseless to abandon the old wilderness preservationist (pre-death of nature) activisms" and their corresponding imagery just as, on the flip side, it would be "folly to deny that we are entering an era of postnature" in which various new eco-linkages are spawned (581). Since "pre-death of nature" narratives still circulate in obvious and sometimes troubling ways, as *Survivor* illustrates, it is imperative to monitor, engage, and rewrite nature stories rather than overlook them in a fascination with the "post-."

American literature is very much engaged in this rewriting. As my previous chapters have shown, sometimes literature imagines alternatives to the American cultural nationalism Buell and others lament.[5] In this chapter, I read Ruth Ozeki's second novel, *All Over Creation*, as an articulation of such an alternative. Although her novels may not do the cultural work of a show like *Survivor*, Ozeki is becoming, if not a household name, at least a quasi-canonical one. *My Year of Meats* (1998) won the Pacific Rim Book Prize, *All Over Creation* (2003) was a best seller, and more college classrooms are starting to feature her work. If *Survivor* markets American competition abroad—reaffirming capitalist values as it reenacts the frontier on foreign soil—then Ozeki's novels use nostalgia to work against this sort of national marketing. I hope to show not only that Ozeki eludes the brand of neoliberal multiculturalism that Buell, Brown, Lisa Duggan, and others decry, but also that she exposes some of the ways in which "free" trade is debt-ridden.

Moreover, Ozeki's work shows that nostalgia does not always escort American hegemony across new frontiers. In the same way that Paula Moya recuperates identity and experience as not necessarily "either dangerously reactionary or hopelessly naïve," Ozeki makes it clear that appeals to nostalgia can also diverge from these functions ("Postmodernisim" 25). Her re-placed nostalgia anchors the diffuse, abstract sentiment in the particularities of bodies, species, plants, and landscapes to rewrite the national story that is "rooted in the racist fiction of primordial white American universality" into a new narrative of social and environmental justice (Kim xii). In Ozeki's hands, nostalgia becomes a tool for recreating "pre-death of nature activisms" for a postnatural world.

Specifically, *All Over Creation* reinvents the pastoral American nature myth by redeploying it counter-nostalgically and updating it for a global readership—in the words of Michael Pollan, "bring[ing] the American pastoral forward into the age of agribusiness and genetic engineering" (qtd. on book jacket). Indeed, Ozeki's novel might be read as one of the rare but "remarkable" texts that contain all six of the attributes Terry Gifford associates with the post-pastoral (*Pastoral* 150).[6] Though I will gesture toward these attributes in my analysis, I am not interested in reading the novel via a sort of "checklist" approach but rather in examining Ozeki's updating of the pastoral as it occurs in its particular context. That means paying attention to the novel's critique of global capitalism, its wariness of genetic engineering, its reflection of the recent "realist" theories I outlined above, and its strategic participation in millennial nostalgia. Its nostalgia illustrates what Gifford calls the pastoral's "impulse towards retreat, renewal and return," which, for Ozeki, involves combining a sincere nostalgia for idealized notions of "roots, neighbourhood and community" with an attention to how these notions are negotiated in a cyclical way, through a "renewal and return" that is self-aware and ongoing (Gifford, *Pastoral* 174). By characterizing both human cultures and nonhuman nature as hybrids and redefining what a nostalgic ideal of community might look like in the contemporary world, *All Over Creation* follows the complex roots and routes of identity, nation, and nature as they appear in a small corner of the world: rural Idaho.

I have been arguing that the difference between troubling nostalgic narratives and more progressive nostalgia often lies in the sort of "home," or origin, to which characters, authors, or readers long to return. Ozeki's fiction envisions "home" as a space where "a political culture based on community-governed and network-oriented social organization" can emerge and thrive (di Chiro 310). *All Over Creation* deploys nostalgia in a way that parallels earlier environmentalist texts, like those of Aldo Leopold, Rachel Carson, and Edward Abbey;[7] yet the novel updates these tactical eulogies for our contemporary political economy. Ozeki's counter-nostalgic treatment of nature instigates a condemnation of exploitative human relationships and contributes to a vision for a more just society.

Because her literature enters so directly into conversations about political economy, cultural identities, and the fate of human and non-human nature in a globalizing world, it makes sense to call Ozeki an environmental justice writer.[8] Ozeki's novels model what Lawrence Buell calls an "environmentalist double vision," which includes attention to both social justice and traditional environmentalist concerns (*Writing* 12). In her fictional worlds, human relationships forged in close connection to natural environments provide a space for critique and a site of possibility within which healthy, sustainable, ethical relationships between humans and other species might flourish. Ozeki is able to foreground nature's social dimensions without overlooking its materiality; she reveals nature's endangered position within our political economy but does not foreclose its agency. She thus capitalizes on deep ecology's abilities to generate affect and instigate ethical interrogation in order to develop a political critique in terms of social ecology.[9]

While I wish to read Ozeki as a "nature writer" of sorts, her work also engages issues of home and identity that are at the heart of Asian American studies and ethnic studies more generally. Echoing Lisa Lowe's claim that Asian American literary texts often deal more in "heterogeneity" than in "cultural unity or integration" (53), Elaine Kim describes Asian American literature as "a literature of protest and exile, a literature about place and displacement, a literature concerned with psychic and physical 'home[s]'" that are "fluid and migratory" (ix). Kandice Chuh expresses a related desire "to disarticulate 'nation' from 'home'" in order to "further the work of creating home as a space relieved of states of domination" (124).[10] Within the broader realm of ethnic studies, the recent anthologies *Reclaiming Identity* and *Identity Politics Reconsidered* make similar moves to "disarticulate" and destabilize identities while retaining the rights to rearticulate identities on their own terms. These theoretical attempts to have it both ways—to "reclaim" identity as a knowable, useful category, not just a socially constructed one—are invigorating contemporary scholarship. Ozeki's two novels can be seen as participating in this ideological framework of "both/and," since they approach nation, identity, and nature from this sort of "realist" perspective.

With the notable exceptions of Heise, whose work I engage below, and Rachel Stein, who tracks *All Over Creation*'s exposure of the "dangerous intersections" of genetically engineered crops and women's reproductive justice (178), most critics have attended to Ozeki's first novel, *My Year of Meats*. David Palumbo-Liu's reading of that text is especially pertinent to my analysis of *All Over Creation*. Palumbo-Liu sees *My Year of Meats* as a literary expression of what "affective community" looks like in a world too often guided exclusively by rationality and a market-driven set of rules for behavior ("Rational and Irrational" 54, 59). Echoing Scott Slovic's suggestion that we take nostalgia more seriously, Palumbo-Liu insists the affective "might be the most powerful tool in persuasive storytelling, and progressives should reclaim that as a tool" (66). Because it is more nostalgic than *My Year of Meats*, Ozeki's second novel has more to teach us about how this particular affect is a "powerful tool"—one environmentalists and other activists might be wise to "reclaim."

Through nostalgic nature narratives, *All Over Creation* brings together unlikely allies—including "young radical environmentalists" and "old fundamentalist farmers"—in a multivocal exposure of globalization's negative impacts on various forms of "life" (*Creation* 267). Ozeki successfully sketches the "dynamic possibilities of the work of border-crossing friendships, collaboration" and political relationships, though she does not have to move "beyond the nostalgic" to do so (Lionnet and Shih 21). The novel cultivates a green "culture of life,"[11] a political alliance that, unlike conservative and religious appropriations of the idea of "life," imagines a world where respect for natural and cultural diversity inspires a dedication to rectifying geopolitical inequality. By constructing a diverse affective community, *All Over Creation* illustrates how nostalgia can help imagine new ways for pre-death-of-nature stories to circulate more productively within a transnational, postnatural world, to the benefit of both nonhuman nature and human cultures.

* * *

Set amid the millennial anxieties of 1999, *All Over Creation* is driven by characters coming to terms with a common past and an uncertain future. Lloyd Fuller and Momoko, his Japanese war bride, are unable to run their Idaho farm; Lloyd is nearing death after a series of heart attacks, and Momoko has begun to feel the effects of Alzheimer's disease. Cassie ("Cass") Quinn, whose family's farm has neighbored the Fullers' for years, and her husband, Will, have been caring for the aging couple. Through a series of legal exchanges, the Quinns are poised to take over the Fullers' land. Cass and Yumi Fuller, Lloyd and Momoko's daughter, were childhood friends until an affair with their high school history teacher, Elliot Rhodes, led to Yumi's pregnancy and subsequent abortion. Her father's outrage prompted Yumi to run away from Liberty Falls, and she has not been back since—until Cass beckons her home to help sort out the finalities of the land transfer, make arrangements for Momoko, and bid farewell to her dying father.

Yumi's return home—the enactment of nostalgia's literal meaning—is the catalyst for the novel's plot and the node around which all the other events pivot. Almost immediately, Yumi begins a new affair with Elliot Rhodes, who happens to be in town on behalf of his public relations firm, Duncan & Wiley. History repeats itself, yes, but with some crucial differences. Elliot, once a hippie who became a teacher to avoid serving in Vietnam, has shed his countercultural beliefs and entered a world of public relations "spin." He has returned to Liberty Falls to monitor a group called the "Seeds of Resistance," a gang of activists who drive from town to town in a biodiesel-fueled van (the "Spudnik") spreading information about genetically modified (GM) foods to local communities.[12] The Seeds land in Liberty Falls to investigate Fullers' Seeds, Lloyd and Momoko's business that sells exotic seeds to buyers around the world.

During the quarter century Yumi has been away, the rules of the farming game have been rewritten by the emergence of global agribusiness and the ubiquity of GM foods. Ozeki's fictional Cynaco—the corporation represented by Elliot's employer, Duncan & Wiley—is a thinly disguised Monsanto, the agricultural biotechnology corporation frequently targeted by activists for promoting harmful products and putting small farmers out of business. The novel's "NuLife" potatoes are the fictional double of Monsanto's NewLeafs: potatoes that are genetically modified to produce *Bacillus thuringiensis* toxins (Bt), which kill insects that threaten crops. The New Leafs were the first bioengineered Bt crop on the market in the 1990s, as well as the only one to be removed from the market after farmers, consumers, and some corporations responded negatively (McHugh 27). The "GroundUp-ready" NuLifes are, like Monsanto's RoundUp-ready seeds, genetically engineered to withstand potent (and patented) herbicides. In Susan McHugh's convincing reading of *All Over Creation*, these potatoes are metaphors for a heterogeneous, rhizomatic identity that opposes the homogeneity of genetically modified organisms (GMOs) as well as the polarizing, reductive discourse that surrounds their production, marketing, and opposition. As Ozeki explains in an interview about the book posted on her website, potatoes are "a staple crop that has co-evolved with human beings" ("Conversation") and as such, what Donna Haraway would call a "companion species."[13] Key characters in the novel, potatoes are shown to be co-evolving with humans and other species in ways that demand historical attention and nuanced discussion. Like all good fiction writers, Ozeki "shifts the burden onto readers" to sift through the complicated issues at hand (McHugh 37).

All Over Creation's chaotic plotlines are woven together via "a dizzying array of perspectives," as narrative voices fluctuate, diverse characters collide, and past and present converge (McHugh 28). Characters' memories often overcome them and transport them back in time "in a flash" (Ozeki 196). The expression "after all these years" becomes a wistful refrain suggesting that both everything and nothing has changed. When Cass complains she "couldn't get the phrase out of her head," the reader likely feels the same way (59). Between Yumi's abortion, Cass's father's beatings, and Lloyd's heart attacks, there is little to be nostalgic for in this group's past. Even as Ozeki's characters indulge in backward-looking narratives, then, the beginnings they imagine are, like Kim's idea of home, contentious and fraught. From the start, Ozeki's novel stresses that nostalgia is an invented and malleable narrative—like nature, always "vulnerable to correction" (212).

The phrase "in the beginning" (another of the novel's wistful refrains) opens the text; however, what "the beginning" holds is constantly shifting. Resonating with Edward Said's description of beginnings as insistently "historical" rather than mystifying (xiii), her characters embrace complex origins—"events" rather than sites of truth or coherence (Foucault, "Nietzsche" 154). The religious and environmental overtones of this phrase are among the book's first indications of nostalgia for an Eden in which humans live in harmony with each other and with their environment. The novel's "first" section (titled "in the beginning") instructs readers to "imagine you are a seed" (3). With this mandate we are asked to situate ourselves at a "beginning" of our own, to participate in coauthoring the story, and to engage with the text's environmental and social politics on an affective level. "Creation," in this sense, is about negotiating the proliferation of stories in the novel's "decentered network," knowing there is no "easy answer" (McHugh 33).

Just what kind of seed to "imagine" remains ambiguous. Yumi is thought by some of the other characters to be a "bad seed," and some readers might be put off by her self-centeredness and poor decision making (79). Even the "good" activists, the Seeds of Resistance, are in some ways hard to take seriously. Their political tactics—pie-ing the face of Cynaco's CEO or dressing up as Mr. Potato Head and visiting grocery stores—might seem juvenile to some readers. With no one character entirely sympathetic, readers must listen to all of their stories and evaluate their perspectives. As Geek, one of the Seeds, explains, "Every seed has a story . . . encrypted in a narrative line that stretches back for thousands of years" (171). Readers are asked to trace the "narrative line" of the degeneration of the farming industry, which is the novel's political focus. Seeds are metaphors for beginnings insofar as their lives are cyclical; as Momoko reminds us, "Grown-up plant is seed too" (332). Time is often measured in seasons, as when the Seeds ask to stay at the Fullers' "through a growing season" (161). The seed metaphor offers an alternative model to a linear view of history—one in which nature's cycles trouble any fictitious human narratives of progress. Unlike the discourse surrounding transgenics, which tends to categorize people as "good/bad seeds," readers are asked to consider the ways in which beginnings are always "beginning-again" (McHugh 26, Said xiii).

One thing that consistently marks the beginning of any narrative line is nature: "It starts with the earth. How can it not?" (3). In the elegiac tradition of Leopold, Carson, Abbey, and others, Ozeki eulogizes nonhuman nature even as her characters encourage readers to do whatever it takes to protect what remains. Nostalgia for nature saturates the novel from the first page—indeed, from the first words: "It used to be the best topsoil around. Used to be feet of it, thick, loamy. There's less of it now" (3). In a passage that resonates with Carson's provocative warning at the beginning of *Silent Spring*, Geek asks Yumi to "picture the whole planet as a garden, teeming with millions upon millions of flowers and trees and fruits and vegetables and insects and birds and animals and weevils and us" and then to "picture it gone" (409). Geek invokes nostalgia for a fertile pastoral nature to enlist his audience—not just the skeptical Yumi but also Ozeki's readers—in "picturing" a world that is not yet destroyed by unchecked global capitalism.

Similar declensionist stories abound, but as often as nostalgia is invoked it rarely finds a pure origin. Even the original Burbank potato is both cultural and natural, the result of "centuries of cross-pollination, human migration, plant mutation, and a little bit of backyard luck" (4). In 1872 the renowned plant breeder Luther Burbank discovered a "seed ball" on his farm, planted all of its seeds, selected the two best plants, and proceeded to develop the Russet Burbank, which became the

Plant Patent Act
1930

"prima donna of potatoes" after "the industry calibrated itself around [it]" (McHugh 34, Ozeki 246). Burbank helped inspire the passing of the Plant Patent Act in 1930, the landmark piece of legislation that allowed the patenting of new hybrid plant varieties—and provided a legal precedent for the patenting of other life forms, including OncoMouse, later in the century.

As the book's "original" capitalist, Burbank marks the blurry line between natural and human creations as well as the seemingly inevitable influence of the market on both. The original Burbank potato is unnatural, in the sense of being, at least partly, a human creation; but it is also natural, since its origin (the seed ball) was a product of naturally occurring reproductive processes. Ozeki's potatoes are also postnatural, since they are GM versions of Burbank's original. Through uncovering this potato's natural-postnatural status, Ozeki is able to trace its material impacts in the present: Burbank's ability to produce "a whopping ten-ounce tuber with excellent fry color" rendered other potato species obsolete, much as an exotic species might wipe out the natives. The irony, as the book shows, is that the potato's "wildly heterozygous" properties have been used to create monocultures that might extinguish the "wild" cross-pollinations, migrations, and mutations that have governed farming until relatively recently (Ozeki 56).

It is unclear whether we are supposed to "worship" Burbank or fear him. In Ozeki's re-telling of the history, the "radical nature" of Burbank's potato involved harnessing the potatoes' natural tendencies, establishing "total control" over their "haphazard" characteristics, and effectively cloning a new species (56–57). Rather than reifying capitalism as natural, though, the novel deploys nostalgia for naturally occurring hybrid species—before they become favorites of industry. To a degree, "natural" is equivalent to "pre-market," and the book seems to idealize an imaginary origin that is as yet untouched by socioeconomic forces, even as it recognizes the increasing impossibility of such a state of affairs. The novel deploys this nostalgia to characterize global agribusiness as a destructive force that works, in a sense, against nature. Rather than reify a pure, static, natural world, the book's nostalgia targets processes: the characters long to return to a dynamic model in which nature functions according to its own "wildly heterozygous" rules without excessive human intervention. The challenge, of course, is to define what counts as excessive.

Lloyd Fuller, whom McHugh dubs a "latter-day Burbank," has opinions about this, and his character helps illustrate the primary ways nostalgia works in the novel (McHugh 36). On one hand, Lloyd exhibits a sincere nostalgia for earlier, presumably better, times for farmers. He reflects Ozeki's own father's stories, which she says were "steeped in nostalgia, of how things used to be, back in the old days, when tomatoes tasted like tomatoes, and eggshells were sturdy and didn't crumple in your hand, and bread was baked fresh every day" ("Conversation"). To the Seeds, Lloyd is a "guru"—a romantic "icon": "Totally salt of the earth. The American farmer making a lonely stand, defending his seed against the hubris and rapacious greed of the new multinational life-sciences cartel" (104, 106–7). When they arrive in Idaho, Lloyd tells the Seeds, "Soil's dead now. Water's dead, too. You should have seen the birds when I was a boy! Oh, my goodness, the sky would be black with 'em!" The Seeds reply: "Oh man! . . . You are so *cool!*" (146, original emphasis). While they deify him because of his age, wisdom, and knowledge of farming practices, his nostalgia is also, in part, what makes Lloyd "cool" to the activists. Lloyd longs for the days when farming communities worked closely with a healthy natural environment, produced healthy food for humans to consume, and controlled their own labor.

On the other hand, Lloyd also expresses the novel's anti-nostalgic recognition that humans have always capitalized on nature through agriculture: "This is what planting is all about—the ancient human impulse to harness that miracle and to make it perform for our benefit" (171). Despite the fact that Lloyd sounds like an agricultural purist at times, he is also one of the novel's proponents of hybridity. Even if he is too ill to articulate it very well, he is aware of "the age-old story of agriculture as an ongoing intervention into plant genetic material" to insure crop viability (McHugh 41). He has lived this story. In effect, then, Lloyd's view of farming's past is counter-nostalgic in that it combines sincere nostalgic sentiment with anti-nostalgic critical distance. He disagrees with the direction of contemporary farming and laments what has been lost as a result of these changes, but he is realistic about farming as an anthropocentric "intervention." Lloyd's "environmentalist double vision" contributes to the dialogue regarding present-day farming technologies.

Retelling Burbank's legacy through Lloyd's hero worship also allows Ozeki to theorize human-nature relationships more generally. What matters, Lloyd and Burbank suggest, is how we use nature—what kind(s) of nature we produce, and more important, whether we treat nature like a partner or a competitor. As Yumi explains, "Fuller Farms seemed living proof to us all that with the cooperation of God and science, and the diligent application of seasonable cultural practices, man could work in harmony with nature to create a relationship of perfect symbiotic mutualism" (6). Such "mutualism" is reflected in Burbank's philosophy as well. For example, the "third" epigraph cites Burbank's determination "to find the vulnerable spot in Nature and make her [his] co-worker" (109). "Co-worker," rather than, say, "employee," implies equal status, even if the desire to find "her" vulnerability reveals his antiquated andropocentric view. Despite what are clearly ideological limitations to his philosophy, Burbank's conception of nature implies a nostalgic respect for natural processes that the novel generally upholds.

Both Burbank's philosophy and Lloyd's adaptation of it are predicated on a belief in nature's agency. For all its emphasis on social ecology, *All Over Creation* insists on some aspects of nature that are independent of human knowledge, that operate according to intrinsic rules, that are "self-propagating"—that are what some deep ecologists call "wild" (Snyder, *Practice* 8–12). Nature's wildness does not mean we should mystify it, however. Rather, autonomous nature is treated as a co-creator of the world. This insight is an essential component of the Seeds' view of farming. Geek explains to Frank, "The pea trains the farmer, and the farmer trains the pea. The pea has learned to taste sweet, so that the farmer will plant more of it" (124). Since the Seeds understand nature and humanity's co-evolutionary interdependence, the group's environmental ethic is neither totally anthropocentric nor totally ecocentric, but a combination of the two. Nature's agency in *All Over Creation* retains part of the deep ecological ideal of an independent natural world (there are some things we can never "know" about nature) in order to temper social ecology's utilitarianism (there are some elements of nature we shouldn't "use" for our own good). The result is a view that replaces mainstream environmentalism's emphasis on individual responsibility with an understanding of nature as an able partner in social affairs, not a child in need of parental guidance.   *actor network*

Still, in its frequent reminders that autonomous nature "knows" things humans don't, the text replicates the overly ecocentric, even misanthropic, stance often associated with deep ecology and echoes the "end of nature" rhetoric that was commonplace in the 1990s. For instance, the Seeds remind readers that "we depend on plants. They depend on us. It's called mutualism. The balance between nature and culture. At least, it used to be. But now the balances are shifting" (124). This sounds a lot like the now-discredited "balance and harmony" model of ecology, and the idea of shifting balances informs the Seeds' historical narrative (Garrard 78). With statements like the following, they argue we've reached a breaking point in our relations with nature: farmers "for thousands of years . . . saved seeds from their harvest, planted them, harvested them, and so it went . . . Until now" (268).

Sentiments like these are reminiscent of McKibben's rhetoric—both in *The End of Nature* and, more recently, in *Enough*—as well as that of the 1999 Turning Point Project's "Who Plays God" advertisement, with its startling "ear mouse" and cloned sheep. Like McKibben's argument that humans are changing the earth's atmosphere and now, our own species identity, in qualitative and irrevocable ways, Ozeki's characters suggest humans are threatening to cross a similar line in food production. As Lloyd's speech near the novel's end cautions, "Whatever base corruptions man has inflicted upon nature, there were certain of our Maker's laws, sacred and inviolable, that even man could not breach. In this assumption we have been sadly mistaken" (301). In these desperate moments, the narrative juxtaposes nostalgia and fear to create an aura of crisis. Echoing Jeremy Rifkin's concerns about genetic engineering, Lloyd laments that scientists "are now able to create novel life forms that have never before existed on God's earth" (105). In her online "conversation" about the book, Ozeki reproduces this rhetoric when she mentions "the ways in which, particularly in this modern age, we try to play God and control nature's every move, and the myriad ways nature outfoxes us" ("Conversation"). Taken together with the concerns of Lloyd, the Seeds, and even Luther Burbank more than a century earlier, there is a distinct trend of worrying about crossing a line or reaching a turning point in human-nature relations.

More than human control, the characters fear the changes this control might cause. Though DeLillo's Babette may have felt a "vague foreboding" about human technologies, Ozeki's characters can pinpoint their anxieties precisely. For instance, they worry that "nature's own varieties [of seeds] are slowly dying out. Soon all we'll have are genetically modified mutants" (173). Genetic engineering encroaches on nature's agency, and it might eventually limit human agency as well, since "we're trying to usurp the plant's choice" when we "barely know the root language" (124). The results of this usurpation are unpredictable at best, and potentially disastrous. While such concerns can come across as naïve, reactionary, or alarmist (as the Turning Point Project advertisement shows), the concerns in Ozeki's novel are made more palatable by a constant awareness that farming has always been "an exercise of human will" ("Conversation"). Even Lloyd realizes that there was never a time when humans did not use nature. This realization complements the Seeds' deep ecological tendencies with a social ecological perspective and suggests that what is at stake, finally, are natural processes.

The novel's nostalgia implies—much like McKibben's does—a time when natural processes were less mediated, less tampered with, less effected, a time when humans exercised their will after nature had already set certain processes in motion, not before. This was also a time when farmers had more agency to control their own labor, when they "saved seeds from their harvest, planted them, harvested them," and so on, in a cyclical fashion that was not dictated by corporations with financial investment in the results. With genetic technologies like the terminator seed, Ozeki suggests not only that humans alter this process but also that we create something new—something not previously found in nature. Indeed, legal patents like the one granted in the *Diamond v. Chakrabarty* case make similar claims.

For readers who are uncomfortable with this kind of nostalgia, which implies clear boundary distinctions and species purity, Ozeki complicates the narrative by having her characters retain a broader ideological conception of interspecies relations as co-evolutionary, never a one-way street. What matters most is our attentiveness to these co-evolutions and how they generate "multi-species communities" with implications for individual as well as large-scale, even global, politics (McHugh 46–47). Acknowledging hybridity at the origin, as she does with her genealogy of the Burbank potato, enables historical trajectories to be traced more readily than origin stories based on myths of purity, which tend to reify the present as having evolved "naturally" from a fundamental moment of truth. Ozeki's characterization of natural origins reflects the wisdom of a "new" (or "postmodern") ecology that highlights "disruptive disasters, perturbations caused by the 'individualistic' activities of species, and nonequilibrium states, randomness, and instability as more fundamental than order in understanding nature" (Buell 570). But she does not leave us with only randomness and instability. Her novel traces the real trajectories that "random" beginnings take—paths that are routed through interspecies communities, human political systems, public relations spin, and industry's constant recalibrations.

* * *

Nature may sometimes "outfox" humans, but there are limits to its agency. For one thing, as Kate Soper notes, "[Nature] may recommend certain types of action, and it will always have its say in determining the effects of what we do, but it does not enforce a politics" ("Nature/nature" 33). Ozeki's characters, however, do enforce a politics, and they employ nature as their number one ally.[14] Even as the characters remain acutely aware that material nature—landscapes, plants, human bodies, indeed, "life itself"—is at stake in their debates, nature's postnatural status renders it a versatile political category. *All Over Creation* pits public relations spokespersons against environmental activists and local community members as each attempts to narrate a version of nature that will aid their political agendas. Nostalgia, with its capacity for "both affect and agency," becomes a key discursive strategy for each of them (Hutcheon, "Irony, Nostalgia" 199).

Elliot Rhodes (the closest thing to a "bad seed" in the novel) embodies one side of the feuding forces.[15] Once a history teacher, Elliot has taken a more cynical view of the past: he now sees history as "just someone's spin of a set of events. It's only a matter of who's more skillful at getting his version on the public record" (226). His skepticism toward historical truth aligns him with some postmodern insights.[16] Yet his character shows how, when these insights are taken to extremes, they can lead to a kind of moral relativism, a total loss of foundations, a world where "anything goes" (Cronon, Foreword 21). Elliot and his boss, Duncan, use familiar arguments in support of Cynaco's seeds, claiming, for instance, that their products will directly benefit starving people in India (277). This neoliberal narrative masks less generous goals of global capitalism, by which corporate involvement in seed control generates "technologies of dependency" rather than humane aid (Shiva 721).

The Seeds articulate quite another perspective. A "heckler" at a Cynaco public relations event translates Duncan's version of company policy in the following loaded question: "Is it Cynaco's long-term policy to mine Third World genetic resources, engage in globalized biopiracy, and rob developing countries of their ability to produce food independently and sustainably?" (258). Geek extends these observations by suggesting the real reason people are starving, despite a global surplus of food, is that "food isn't being distributed fairly, to those in need"; the scarcity myth is "just corporate marketing" (272). Through Geek and the other protester-characters, Ozeki demonstrates what Andrew Ross has shown: that scarcity is, to some degree, a function of capitalism, an ideology that can be manipulated to propagate "unequal social organization, maldistribution, and political injustice" (*Chicago Gangster* 16).

Juxtaposing these contradictory political stories, the novel exposes how the ways we talk about GMOs in popular discourse are "severely limited" (McHugh 41). Both perspectives—the Seeds' and Cynaco's—are, in their own ways, reductive. Likewise, their characters are not as fleshed out as Yumi, who remains aloof from their political concerns for most of the novel. For readers who might be put off by the Seeds' angry criticism or Cynaco's calculated self-interest, Ozeki offers a third perspective: that of the Idaho farmers. While far from idealized, Ozeki's farmers are depicted as well-meaning men and women who experience the conflicts and compromises of global agribusiness in their everyday lives and who are all the more sympathetic for being "economically endangered" (McHugh 35). Illustrating not just the corporate party line and the radical left critique, but also the more complicated rock-and-a-hard-place predicament of some farmers, Ozeki gives us several views and asks us to assess them.

To some degree, the farmers have internalized corporate "spin." Echoing Cynaco's claim that its technology is helping to feed the world's poor, Will Quinn claims, "Monoculture is efficient. We got six billion humans on earth, and a lot of them are starving" (272). Cass recites the logic of scarcity when she offhandedly remarks "some things had to die so that others could live" (270). During more reflective moments, Will likens himself and the other farmers to drug addicts, where "corporations are the pushers, the farmers are the users, and the fields are our bodies"; although he and Cass are "trying to cut back," going "cold turkey would kill [them]" (272). There are pragmatic reasons why the Quinns are stuck using pesticides they don't believe in: not only are the new technologies supposed to make their lives easier—by cutting down on labor time and pesticide application—but, also, "banks don't lend money to farmers who don't use inputs. Not sound farming practice" (77). Farmers lament their predicament but remain caught in the economic traps set by free trade policies; what constitutes "sound farming practice" is mandated by external forces. Elliot overhears the following discussion between several farmers—who, as if to advertise their conflictedness, are "wearing caps with company logos and coveralls stiff with dirt"—concerning the limits to their agency:

> "Can't do anything about the weather," Spudee said doggedly. "But we can change our farm policy. With this kind of economy, it all comes down to whether we ought to be market driven or depending on government."
>
> The third man, in an Acme Metal Fab cap, spoke up. "I say the government *should* pay. They're the ones that go and make

dumb-ass decisions like NAFTA, letting in all them Canuck spuds to drive the price down. I still got last year's crop in the cellars that I can't sell. Cheaper to dump it."

Fertilizer paid for his gas. "And now with the Europeans boycotting the GMO crops . . . What did you decide about the NuLifes, Will? You planting them?" (219)

As this tense dialogue shows, nature, the economy, the market, the government, and the farmers are all players in this free trade drama, and each—even "the weather"—has a degree of agency to influence how farming is conducted. The reference to "Canuck spuds" reminds readers that genetically engineered foods are not just an American issue but a transnational one. Their concern about the European boycott helps decenter the American nation by reminding readers that other countries are more wary of corporate-backed techno-foods. In effect, this dialogue—taking place as it does around the similarly fraught gasoline pump, another reminder of natural capital flowing unevenly across national boundaries—hints that the American push to unload genetically engineered crops on unwilling nations is a form of imperialism.

Pitting individual choice—"You planting them?"—against global economic forces highlights a serious power discrepancy between agribusiness and the "entrepreneurial actors" who try to make a living in this economy (Brown 15). Their situation also accentuates the "increased sense of futility" embedded in such formulations of local-global relationships as those encapsulated in the environmentalist slogan "think globally, act locally" (Buell 582). Interestingly, Will dodges the question of whether he will plant the NuLife potatoes and shifts the terms of the conversation to interrogate the nation-state. Mentioning his service in Vietnam, he tells his fellow farmers "there was a time [he] laid down his life for [his] government and was glad to do so" (219). But his own bodily ailments, which may be caused by either Agent Orange or the "exposure factor on the farm," are causing him to doubt this allegiance. The link is more than coincidental: Cynaco (like its real-world double, Monsanto) is responsible for manufacturing both Agent Orange and the chemical product GroundUp that keeps the NuLife potatoes growing. By making the connection between the nation-state and agribusiness explicit, Will reminds us of our simultaneously national and postnational status and models how to follow power flows across global, national, and local scales.

Overall, the farmers offer hopeful evidence that concerns about the neoliberal free trade agenda do exist at the local level, where detrimental effects are often most noticeable. In particular, the farmers' observation that they can either be "market driven" or "depending on government" means that they have not completely bought into the neoliberal message that the free market is the only choice. Although Will is only somewhat sympathetic to the Seeds' concerns, and although he remains ambivalent about his use of chemicals at the book's end, he does show an inkling of an environmental justice consciousness. He voices suspicions about the fact that his wife, his mother-in-law, and his neighbor, Lloyd Fuller, have all struggled with cancer; Will himself has also developed worrisome symptoms. However, he doubts his own experience, conceding that he is "just a farmer," not a scientist, and so he "can't say" whether these diseases are effects of environmental toxics (219–20). His predicament illustrates how "expert" knowledge too often trumps local, experiential, even bodily knowledge; combating this sense of individual powerlessness is one of the biggest challenges for the environmental justice movement. In the final analysis, a single perspective is insufficient for understanding complex problems of environmental justice. We can better understand the Quinns' helplessness when we hear them spouting corporate rhetoric, and when the Seeds reshape the Quinns' views, a more complete picture emerges—one that avoids reductive, polarizing discourse.

In an effort to resist global forces, foster local knowledge, and nurture the "seeds of resistance" that are growing in Liberty Falls, the Seeds organize the Idaho Potato Party, which serves as the climax of the novel. Inspired by the Boston Tea Party and hosted at Fuller Farms on the Fourth of July, the Potato Party is "an educational event, like a teach-in, to wake people up to the magnitude of this hazardous corporate agenda" (265). The teach-in offers informational workshops on things like "worm composting and gene splicing, the secret to effective protest letters and the ethics of patenting life, the latest in biotech research and European boycotts of American GMOs" (291). Some protesters take direct action and plot to uproot the GM crops, in a modern-day enactment of the monkey-wrenching tactics popularized by Edward Abbey. The Potato Party is infused with a mood of '60s nostalgia, perpetuated by the countercultural crowd of long-haired, braless, VW van–driving hacky-sackers it attracts. Cass observes that the event feels "like a rock concert or something" (288). Indeed, readers might easily imagine a soundtrack of rambling Grateful Dead tunes or Joni Mitchell's soulful lament that we've "paved paradise, put up a parking lot."[17] Just as Yumi feels nostalgic when she first sees the Seeds, readers who "were there" in the '60s (even if they only claim to be so in retrospect) might experience longings of their own as the Potato Party gathers its diverse celebrants—out-of-towners as well as local residents.

Of course, some of the Fullers' neighbors think the couple has taken up with the wrong crowd, especially once word gets out about the "Garden of Earthly Delights," the Seeds' semi-pornographic website on which Lilith, one of the group, performs erotic acts with vegetables (152). The main purpose of the site is fundraising for their travels, though Lilith has a more profound agenda. In her words: "I become a symbol of Earth, begetting life, the primeval Mother" (121).[18] When Charmey, another of the Seeds, acknowledges that "somebody must work and make the money," she illustrates Ozeki's investment in refusing to separate political economy from cultural identities (152). Specifically, these debates—which are carried out by Ozeki's characters—highlight the troubling ways in which feminist concerns are caught up in global capitalism. Although the Fullers do receive one complaint letter calling Lilith a "harlot" and "whoremonger" and invoking religious rhetoric, the majority of Liberty Falls's residents are unconvinced that the questionable morality of Lillith's virtual nudity outweighs more pressing issues, like keeping their farms under local control (230).

At the teach-in, natural life proves to be an ideal capable of uniting disparate political factions and rallying them in a more or less coherent protest against the harmful effects of global agribusiness. Lilith begins her speech to the Potato Party–goers with the phrase "It starts with the earth," returning us to the novel's beginning and inviting the audience to join her in tracing the "narrative line" of the local crops (289). As it does elsewhere in the novel, a nostalgic ideal of a tolerant, pastoral community counters narratives about privatization, scarcity, and overpopulation by romanticizing a time when nature was more than just a commodity, and when natural processes dictated agricultural practices. The nostalgia promoted by the Seeds, although reductive, can come across as sincere and refreshing when compared to the market-driven rationalization of Cynaco. Refusing to be dismissed as modern-day hippies who just want to "drop out," the Seeds supplement their nostalgia with well-researched critiques of particular corporate practices—including self-serving technologies like the "terminator" seed, which benefits the company by forcing farmers to purchase new seeds every year—as well as broadly formulated worries about the acquisition of "intellectual property rights over the planet" (266). Moreover, they understand the need to unite disparate groups into a political faction that can address a variety of problems. It is the range of issues that attracts the range of attendees at the Idaho Potato Party and rallies them against the harmful effects of global agribusiness. The event suggests that nostalgia—for a pastoral community, for "family" (loosely defined), and for wild natural processes—might be a useful affect in imagining a socially equitable future for a diverse world.

Of course, from the perspective of Duncan & Wiley, the best reaction to this multifaceted manifestation of "liberty" is to reduce it to terms that are easy to dismiss: "anticorporate, antigovernment, antiglobalization. And most offensive of all, anti-American. These so-called radical environmentalists represent the latest fad in the protest movement that traces its roots to the sixties" (165). Casting the protestors as posturing rebels with no focused agenda is a familiar move; marking them as "anti-American," or, worse, as "terrorists," is another rhetorical approach that is often used today to dismiss environmentalists with more radical agendas (168, 263). Elliot wants to tell "a story of domestic terrorism—honest American farmer, salt of the earth, his crops targeted by the antiprogress forces of the Luddite left sort of thing. A vicious attack on the American way of life" (278). Elliot's "spin" on the Idaho Potato Party writes these ideologies into a tight narrative that also attempts to deploy a nostalgia, of sorts, as he, too, invokes the "honest American farmer" of the pastoral tradition. Ultimately, his nostalgia fails to mask the political realities experienced by the farmers themselves, and it fails to measure up to the affective urgency with which the Seeds bring their concerns to the table.

By enabling her characters to maintain the spirit of radical politics (and by running the villain, Elliot, out of town), Ozeki's novel contests the linkage of radical environmentalism to terrorism. Reagan-era dismissals of environmentalism—which cast it as threatening to "American traditions of freedom, liberty, and private property" and charged it with "help[ing] cause the U.S. slide from global dominance" by tying up natural resources—continue to be effective in anti-environmentalist rhetoric at the millennium (Buell 572). In Ozeki's novel, private property is linked with Americanism and used as ammunition to combat the Seeds' protests. As Rodney, Elliot's local spy, says, the Seeds are guilty of "trespassing for starters. Destroying crops is criminal mischief and malicious damage to private property, not to mention un-American" (296). Though the story is set earlier, the novel was published in a post-9/11 climate of fear, a time when the label "un-American" was slapped on protesters of all stripes and the word "terrorism" carried enormous weight. Elliot's rhetoric becomes more than just "spin" when the Liberty Falls police force follows explicit orders to treat the protesters' crop destruction "as an act of terrorism" (306).

Up against powerful rhetorical and economic forces like these, radical activism in the new millennium requires more than conjuring '60s nostalgia. In fact, antiglobalization movements have had to work against representations of their protests as "a shallow and anachronistic echo of the 60s" (Yuen 7). Although mainstream environmental activism has its "roots in the grassroots activism of the 1960s," its limited attention to race and other social categories has disconnected it from the civil rights agendas of that era (Cole and Foster 30). Duggan worries that today's political left, more generally, has overlooked how neoliberalism "organizes material and political life *in terms of* race, gender, and sexuality as well as economic class and nationality, or ethnicity and religion" (3, original emphasis).

Ozeki's savvy Seeds update environmental activism for today's political economy. For one thing, Ozeki's inclusion of Momoko as, essentially, an activist—as indicated by her valuation of nonhuman nature (she is "a born gardener" [5]) and her role in Fullers' Seeds—prevents the novel from perpetuating the image of whites as default environmentalists and reflects the more multicultural demographics of twenty-first-century activism. More broadly, the novel's nostalgia for the '60s seeks to harness components of the civil rights movement that are still useful today—most significantly, the abilities to see isolated problems as symptomatic of larger systemic forces and to understand economic inequalities as negotiated through race, gender, and class. Thus, although Ozeki's emphasis is primarily on foregrounding the damaging effects of global capitalism on humans and nature, *All Over Creation* locates the overlapping cultural categories Duggan mentions—as well as, I would add, age and disability—within the multi-scalar economic forces that both structure and operate through them. Since I cannot tackle all of these issues here, I will focus on the one that is most pertinent to my discussions of nature: race.

Ozeki repeatedly points out that natural hybrids are mirrored in human inter-races: like the "mutant" squashes spawned by some of Momoko's seeds, Yumi's children are "all mixed up" (118). Thus, the nostalgia for natural "hybrids" that fuels the book's critique of agribusiness and its monocultures parallels the hybridity of human beings, and of human cultures. Indeed, nostalgia for hybrid nature underscores a celebration of multicultural human identity. Like our companion species, the potato, humans have always been "wildly heterozygous" in our own reproductive practices; the idea of a "pure" race is a fiction. Some readers may be tempted to read *All Over Creation*'s depiction of cultural hybridity as a substantiation of the "superficial 'multiculturalism' compatible with the global aspirations of U.S. business interests"—a charge Monica Chiu levels at *My Year of Meats* (Chiu 44). However, such a reading becomes untenable given *All Over Creation*'s explicit critiques of these very business interests, the critiques of racism included in the novel, and the ways in which these critiques are connected to Ozeki's more overt challenge to global capitalism.[19]

Ursula Heise argues that the novel participates in a larger trend in "some strains of environmentalism, ecocriticism, and ecologically oriented fiction," in which "cultural diversity is presented as a substitute, complement, or metaphor for biological diversity as a way of endorsing the cultural encounters that globalization processes enable, even as many of its economic and political dimensions are rejected" ("Transnational Turn" 20). Put another way, Ozeki's approach to diversity allows her to celebrate cultural globalization and its "cross-breedings" while rejecting the problematic effects of economic globalization (19). Heise is, of course, right to point out the worrisome consequences of such an approach, which include an unquestioned embrace of immigration (which would not appeal to Native Americans, for whom immigration meant colonization), an inaccurate suggestion that "non-native species are harmless," and a reliance on the often problematic strategy of looking to nature for a model of how humans should live (23, 19).

I agree that Ozeki wants to suggest a "'natural' affinity" between environmentalists and multicultural proponents, and I do think the text uses environmental "cross-breedings" to support the value of human diversity, but I do not see the same problems Heise does in the novel (19). To the extent that we can deduce the book's environmentalist argument, I would say that Ozeki's cross-breedings work, primarily, to critique the homogeneity of genetically engineered plants, which she situates as "against nature" in the sense that they alter natural processes. Her characters do fear the kind of "invasion of wild ecosystems" by transgenic plants that Heise mentions in reference to Lloyd's embrace of exotics (19). GMOs are the new, postnatural "exotics," and Ozeki's characters are very wary of them. She posits first nature as an idealized space that these exotics could destroy, even as she recognizes the hybridity of that original space. Heise's attention to transnational routes neglects the more rooted ad hoc communities that are developed in the novel and how these communities bring the more abstract concerns about routes "home" to a particular location. This "homecoming" allows readers to judge for themselves whether such "invasions" are appropriate or acceptable.

Nostalgic origins that are hybrid in nature prevent any simplistic romanticization of human cultures and point us toward a more careful historicization of our co-evolving pasts. The novel's treatment of Native Americans is a case in point. Ozeki is clear that their oppression is predicated on both ideological and economic grounds, with the latter operating through the former, and that nostalgia can help highlight the relationship between a material past and a romanticized one. Early in the novel, Yumi is chosen for the coveted role of "solemn Indian princess" in her school's Thanksgiving performance, while Cass (who is white) plays a potato. Ozeki hints that the students' social hierarchy mirrors a national hierarchy in which "romanticized reconstructions of early American history" delineate the roles of racialized groups (Heise, "Transnational Turn" 17). In Ozeki's fictional Idaho, as on *Survivor*'s Pacific Rim frontier, non-whites are lumped together as "exotics." An Asian American child is perceived as an appropriate substitute for a Native American, and both groups' histories are effectively erased by such substitutability. When the young Elliot Rhodes pegs Thanksgiving as "revisionist bullshit" and "genocide," readers may be inclined toward sympathy (Ozeki 22).

Twenty-five years later, Elliot's belief that history is little more than "spin" enables him to see Native Americans as just another "pest" for his PR firm to contend with—or to exploit. As *Survivor* illustrates, natural-cultural images are easier to uproot from their histories with new media and the globalization of multicultural ideology, even while familiar nostalgic narratives threaten to romanticize real concerns out of existence. When Elliot sees that the farmers are "being sued by a local Indian tribe demanding compensation for groundwater contamination from agricultural runoff," he wants to form an "InterTribal Agricultural Council" to mask the material realities and political tensions with an illusory multiculturalism. With any luck, he thinks, they will "get a Shoshone spokesperson to endorse the NuLife—fewer pesticides mean clean water for our people, that sort of thing. Wisdom. Heritage. Indians always made for positive imaging" (188).

As Iron Eyes Cody's famous PSA showed in the 1970s, the image of the American Indian as uber-environmentalist carries tremendous cultural currency. Ozeki's novel draws attention to the ways in which Indian-ness becomes a floating signifier that "erase[s] the complex histories of

Indians and others" (Deloria 174). Instead of contributing to this erasure, Ozeki makes it clear that a neoliberal economic system—represented, here, by Cynaco and its "free trade" agenda—is predicated on ideas about culture that are often detached from reality. Ozeki exposes the complex interplay of image, stereotype, and material reality by inventing a tribal lawsuit and juxtaposing it against Elliot's desire to use Indians for "positive imaging." The lawsuit conjures a colonial history as well as a present-day situation some would describe as ongoing colonialism, helping Ozeki demonstrate the negative impacts some non-Native humans continue to have on indigenous "species."

Suggesting that racism in America has not vanished but, in fact, may be more entrenched with the spread of multicultural ideology across the globe, Ozeki refuses to situate the United States as a world leader in promoting diversity and tolerance. In rural Idaho, not only are Momoko's plants "truly exotic," but her fellow townspeople clearly think their "yeller" neighbor is exotic as well (5). Elliot sees Yumi as similarly exotic. It is partly because "he admire[s] Asian Culture" that he seduces (or, the law would say, rapes) his fourteen-year-old student (21). This orientalism has not gone away by the time Yumi brings her own children to Liberty Falls. Her oldest son, Phoenix, winds up in jail for defending himself against the sheriff's son, who holds him at gunpoint and threatens him. Phoenix describes the other boy's philosophy as an attempt to eliminate difference: "Get rid of everybody. Niggers, Japs, queers, wetbacks, hippie scum, whatever" (237). He clarifies that Ocean, his younger sister, is safe because "she's blond" (238). For the inhabitants of Liberty Falls, race is still rooted in the body.

Ozeki refuses to see the town as an isolated pocket of ignorance, even though Idaho's history as a haven for white supremacists might make this a tempting choice. Instead, she identifies forms of violence that range from private, personal, and localized to public, economic, and globalized, and shows how all are enabled by a common racism. The type of exploitation Cynaco participates in, the novel suggests, purveys racist ideology across the globe and, so, is hardly less harmful than Elliot's sexual conquest of the young Yumi or Phoenix's classmates' threatening behavior toward him. As the American Indian example illustrates, Cynaco's marketing strategies are comparable to the ideologies perpetuated by *Survivor*: domestic racism is exported abroad, and Asia continues to be imagined as a frontier for American exploitation. Ozeki's celebration of hybridity works against the essentializing nostalgia that enables such racism to function.

She's arguing for a more complex nostalgia
that doesn't essentialize or romanticize but encompasses
the complexity of the past —
Counter nostalgia —

* * *

In the end, when it is clear that Lloyd and Momoko are unable to manage Fullers' Seeds any longer, the technologically savvy Seeds help move the company online. The new Internet-based company allows users to "adopt" seeds that interest them, grow them into plants, and distribute them to other online registrants. Yumi operates the website from Hawaii, and Cass manages the distribution from Idaho. This techno-communal stewardship of nature, whereby pockets of interested parties propagate all kinds of plants, including exotics, offers an alternative to private property-based patriotism. The promotion and sustaining of "life," rather than the accumulation of wealth, is the mission.

At first, not all the characters are drawn to "pro-life" rhetoric. In a moment of frustration, Yumi accuses her father and the Seeds—both, in her view, "fanatics"—of propagating "the kind of pro-life bullshit that drove [her] out of [Idaho] in the first place" (267). And yet, the environmentalist pro-life agenda the novel develops is quite different from the "culture of life" that was popularized during the Bush administration, which took strong political stances against abortion and euthanasia and was predominantly Christian. Ozeki's pro-lifers share a conception of life that prioritizes personal choice, compassion for others, and respect for diversity, along with a dedication to social and environmental justice. What brings them together, ideologically, is a belief that some aspects of life are not commodifiable—or shouldn't be. The novel's suspicion of genetically modified foods reminds us that food is life, and so are the bodies that eat that food. Women's bodies become especially important, since these are the producers of new life for humanity and often the most affected by environmental toxins. The morality of global agribusiness—and by extension, any other producer of environmental toxins—becomes subject to scrutiny.

Of course, merely "having a common enemy" will not necessarily lead to long-term political alliances (Alcoff and Mohanty 3). In using the rhetoric of "life," Ozeki seems aware that "environmentalists have a great deal to learn from conservatives"—especially in terms of articulating new values (Shellenberger and Nordhaus 31). The "life" the characters believe in conjoins moral conservatives (like Lloyd) with deep ecology-minded activists (the Seeds) in ways that are attentive to social ecological concerns. Although Lloyd believes the Seeds' action "is not about politics" but "about life," "life" is exactly where their politics overlap. A common nostalgic ideal of nature, encapsulated by the word "life," unites such disparate groups in resistance to neoliberalism's reduction of human subjectivity to "*homo oeconomicus.*" Ozeki's novel becomes part of the global movement Vandana Shiva says is "calling for a ban on patents on life and recovering of the generic basis of life as 'commons' which cannot be owned and privatized" (721). "Life as commons" is an integral facet of the social dynamic Ozeki's characters outline.

Drawing the line at privatizing nature, *All Over Creation* articulates objections to the neoliberal trend of supporting markets as "sacred" (McChesney 7).[20] Lloyd's religious fundamentalism seems out of step with the Seeds' liberal choices, but Ozeki brings these two worshippers of life together in provocative ways.[21] While Lloyd situates God as the Maker of all living things, the Seeds substitute Nature for God. But in some ways, it doesn't matter (to cite the Turning Point ad) "whether you give credit to God or to Nature." In fact, reading Lloyd's political speeches, one is struck by how easy it would be to substitute "nature" for "God" without losing any of his meaning. At other times, the relationship is reversed and the earth—a metonym for natural creation more generally—seems to stand in for God. For instance, the "second" section begins with an epigraph from Genesis: "And the earth brought forth grass, and herb yielding seed after his kind" (45). Lloyd's religious fervor does not alienate him from the environmental activists, because his respect for "creation" transcends partisan politics or disagreements about more personal "moral" choices. Most of the town's religious residents overlook what they see as Lilith's inappropriate acts, and Yumi and her father put aside their opposing views on abortion so that they may see eye-to-eye on more wide-ranging social issues.[22] Indeed, Lloyd's interaction with the Seeds seems to help him become more tolerant of those with different beliefs, and his forgiveness of Yumi by the novel's end hints that his own beliefs are shifting. Lloyd even takes the lead in critiquing his neighbors when he articulates policies about how "anti-exoticism is Anti-Life" and "explicitly racist" (66–67).

In their attempt to convince consumers to demand labels on genetically engineered products, the Seeds personalize their politics and position nature at the bodily scale with slogans like "Food is life. You are what you eat" (184). As in DeLillo's *White Noise*, bodies are the most noticeable scale at which environmental toxics manifest themselves. When Yumi's youngest child, "Poo," ingests dirt from the Fuller Farm, Cass's doctor explain that while "geophagy" is nothing new, the prevalence of lawn chemicals in today's soil means that "the earth . . . isn't what it used to be. Dirt isn't clean these days" (389). If nature "isn't what it used to be," then longing for a less toxic earth fuels an investigation of the forces that have corrupted it. Through nostalgia for a "purer," healthier nature, one that is less affected by human impacts, Ozeki sets up a contrast between this imagined space and the neoliberal political agenda that often contributes to its destruction. Whether such a space ever existed is beside the point. What matters is the kind of society we want for ourselves now, and the past is as valid a place as any to find an ideal toward which to strive. In keeping with its skepticism about "easy answers," the novel never condemns GM foods outright, nor does it give us a clear indication of whether Ozeki believes (with Haraway) that "transgenics are not the enemy" or whether she merely wants her readers to make their own decisions (Haraway, *Companion Species* 11). It is first and foremost information that we need, Ozeki implies, if we are to make good decisions about what to put in our bodies.

The moral of the story, which is spoon-fed to us through a reflective Yumi at the book's end, is that "we are all responsible. Intimately connected, we're liable for it all," even if we are also "powerless to forecast or control any of our outcomes" (410). Nostalgia for nature compels Yumi's revelation. Her heart "crack[s] open at the hopeless beauty and fragility and loss of all that is precious on earth" while she is sitting in the greenhouse that reminds her of her Hawaiian home. Part of relinquishing control is coming to terms with the inevitability of "fragility and loss," which engenders nostalgia. The reader might feel a sense of loss when Fuller Farms is left to the dubious agricultural practices of the not quite reformed Quinns, and Momoko's garden is opened up to the elements.

There is some hope, however, in the fact that "life is evanescent, but left to itself rarely fails to offer some consolation" (411). Nature will take its course, as "volunteers" and perennials and transplants from migrating humans take root in the earth. Ready to accompany Yumi to Hawaii, Momoko leaves behind her gardening tools, since, in Hawaii, "everywhere is garden. It is enough" (414). This ending celebrates both nativism, in terms of local communities that are "enough" for their inhabitants, and exoticism, as human "transplants" take root in new environments and "voluntarily" become responsible for their stewardship. While Heise might cringe at the comparison of seeds to colonists when the novel mentions how "you and your offspring will put down roots to colonize that foreign shore," I would argue that this is an instance of the text demanding reflection about such processes (171). Far from naturalizing them, Ozeki asks us to trace the "roots" of colonial histories to their contemporary trajectories, their "routes," in the present—a process she models through her history of the Burbank potato and its market-driven evolution into dominance.

In its reminder that "we are all responsible," Ozeki seems to substitute personal responsibility for broader social change, echoing the liberal ideology of voluntarism that prevails in contemporary American politics. However, Yumi quickly adds that we are also "intimately connected": our decisions have far-reaching effects, and no individual—indeed, no *species*—is autonomous. Rather than promoting personal responsibility in lieu of public accountability, then, Yumi advocates both; personal responsibility is not "an abdication of public, collective caretaking" but something to be undertaken within such a public context, with environmental and social "caretaking" as primary goals (Duggan 87). The fact that Yumi takes charge of Momoko after Lloyd's death indicates that she has come to understand such "caretaking" as an important part of nurturing the collective "life" this novel promotes.

By refusing to cohere neatly into a happy ending, Ozeki's novel foregrounds the complexity of contemporary families, migrations, and transnational allegiances. Yumi's personal journey, in which she forgives her parents and takes responsibility for them, mirrors another of the novel's messages. Developing an affective community can become a corrective to the displacement, disconnection, and moral relativism that foster lonely lives like those of Elliot and, prior to his engagement with the Seeds, Frank Perdue. As in *My Year of Meats*, the kinds of communities Ozeki imagines are not constricted by kinship in any conventional sense. Cass and Will are able to fulfill their own desire for a child when they adopt the daughter of Frank and Charmey after Charmey is killed in a tragic accident. Their action demonstrates the complexities of global commerce and suggests that the process of "becoming sympathetic community members" is as valuable as being "responsible scientists or informed consumers" if we are to develop more ethical relationships to other species, and to each other (McHugh 44). Ozeki's unconventional families illustrate that promoting "life" can take many forms—from Fullers' Seeds, to adoption, to political activism, to neighborhood or community-wide caretaking.

The final images in the novel, two photos Frank sends to his daughter, illustrate the dynamic between nostalgic nature imagery and political action. The first is a photo of Frank dressed in a gas mask and all-black anarchist garb at the WTO protests in Seattle, his smiling eyes conveying a message of hope to his daughter in Idaho. The second photo is a snapshot of "a glacial lake, azure and sparkling, set high up in the mountains." Nonhuman nature was what inspired Charmey, and Charmey, in turn, inspires Frank as he tells his daughter, "I gotta make sure there's still some nature around for you when you grow up, in case you decide you dig it, too" (416). The spectacular vista motivates the transnational protest not just for Frank but perhaps also for readers, since by the end of the novel we have learned to see nature as part of our everyday lives. Nature is crucial to our existence, not just in our national imaginary or in wilderness areas (or in the photographs we take of them) but essentially—in food, and in the chemicals that go into making food, which end up in our bodies. Locating nature at the bodily scale helps Ozeki inspire readers to uncover its role at other scales as well—the local, the regional, the national, and the global.[23] As Frank's comments remind his daughter—and by extension, the next generation of activists—nostalgic rhetoric, by itself, is not sufficient to effectively generate critique; it must be linked to political economic connections at these various scales.

If "seeds tell the story of migrations and drifts," then Ozeki asks us to do more than just skim those "books" (171). It becomes increasingly important to understand "nature" as simultaneously everything that is other-than-human and as that which encompasses us. Even as it is nostalgic for a nature that is not yet "dead," her work recognizes nature's complex imbrication in capitalism's imperial projects, especially as these projects are now, to a degree, both postnational and governed by global technologies. In the end, this "realist" approach to nature allows her to formulate her own programs for social and environmental justice: localized communities of makeshift "families" that share common goals, the evolution of Fullers' Seeds as a publicly owned and traded techno-commune, and the mobilization of activist forces to contest neoliberalism.

Nostalgia proves a powerful affective force contributing to each of these environmentally and socially just endeavors. In *All Over Creation*, nostalgic "longing can make us more empathetic toward fellow humans, yet the moment we try to repair longing with belonging, the apprehension of loss with a rediscovery of identity, we often part ways and put an end to mutual understanding" (Boym xv). What unites Ozeki's characters is not a shared identity—not a religious affiliation, or a racial category, or a national allegiance—but a shared longing. This longing is for socially just communities that are not realized in the present, and a respectful, sustainable understanding of nature provides the common ground on which these communities are founded. The nostalgic origin, then, is a nonviolent, nonhierarchical community that values human and environmental "life," yet recognizes the contingency of such life as lived within a global political economy. Although this origin is an ideal, its creation remains a real possibility.

Conclusion

In 2010, eighty-seven of Yellowstone National Park's bison took up residence in a new summer home: Ted Turner's Flying D Ranch, a 12,000-acre span of western Montana terrain. In a controversial agreement with Montana Fish, Wildlife, and Parks, Turner arranged to keep a portion of the historic bison herd's newborn calves (approximately 188 animals, according to a *New York Times* article) in exchange for letting the herd stay on his property (Johnson). Most of the animals will return to the park after their five-year ranch "vacation," but the fate of the calves is uncertain. They could be sold to another ranch, or they could end up on a patron's dinner plate in one of Turner's restaurants.[1] I suspect even Edward Abbey, who was alarmed by the direction the parks were headed in 1968, might be shocked by this flagrant example of the government "contracting out its essential sovereign functions and bartering the yield"—in this case, the bison (Johnson). Although the National Park Service was not the primary agency involved in brokering this deal, the "bartering" of its resident bison reflects one of the new challenges park managers face: pressure to outsource to private partners, with questionable impacts on what managers routinely call "the resource."[2]

It is not just the act of the government giving federally managed (and publicly owned) animals to Turner—a move many see as privatizing nature—that raises eyebrows. The circumstances are compounded by the fact that these calves are considered a genetically pure species, since, unlike ranch-raised bison, they have not interbred with cattle. The Turner ranch compromise thus raises the classic American question:

"What does it mean to be wild?" (Johnson). The bison situation reflects a postnatural destabilization of the idea of "pure" nature and a corresponding awareness of natural-cultural hybridity that makes it easier to see humans—and our impacts—in every corner of the more-than-human world. Today's bison are not out roaming on the open range; they are corralled in public parks and private ranches, featured on websites, honored in activist literature, stuffed into souvenirs for tourists' children, and, as the Turner situation illustrates, traded as assets in the messy political game of natural resource management. The writer of the *New York Times* article is not alone in wondering whether we've reached a "turning point" for this particular species (Johnson).

Along with more complex conceptions of nature come new forms of nostalgia. The story of the bison elicits nostalgia for familiar objects, like wildness and the "Frederic Remington" West (Johnson), as well as for new ones, like pure species boundaries, which are accentuated in a postnatural world. New forms of nostalgia include longings for authenticity, for certainties, for connectivity—to "nature" and to other people—and for intact natural processes. As categories seem less and less stable, there is a reciprocal, intensified longing for clear lines that help us keep nature in its place and "the human" safely bounded. Many people want bison herds to roam on their side of the park boundary, where we can still consider them "wild," not on Turner's ranch, where they confuse our distinction between wild and domesticated animals.

In a contemporary context characterized by an increasingly "tangled web" (Johnson) of human-animal, public-private, pure-hybrid, natural-technological dynamics, it has become both more difficult and more important to identify what we mean when we talk about "nature" and to assess who benefits, and who doesn't, from our understandings of it. Each of the texts in this study encourages readers' judgments by invoking nostalgia in ways that draw our attention to fraught histories, contemporary injustices, and large-scale changes. N. Scott Momaday's "psychic dislocation," Don DeLillo's "homesick[ness] for a place even when you are there," and Bill McKibben's "visceral" reaction to genetic engineering describe affective responses to broad social, economic and technological developments. They also point to specific nostalgias: for natural processes, for less mediated connections to people and landscapes, and for "impervious corporeality" (Hamming 27). Whether we see things like cloning as turning points or as mere blips in an always-dynamic evolutionary history, the nostalgic sentiments such new technologies inspire in some people challenge all of us to gauge our affective responses to

FIGURE 6. State workers and livestock agents herd bison back into Yellowstone, a process called hazing. (Nicole Bengiveno / *New York Times* / Redux)

change—or as Aldo Leopold and Rachel Carson urge, to consider what the absence of such responses might mean.

Other authors in this study foreground specific displacements from environments, cultures, and homes, and the nostalgia that often results. For authors such as Zitkala-Ša, Claude McKay, and Momaday, who describe characters that are uprooted from a homeland, looking backward reveals an "interweaving of natural beauty and trauma" (Outka 173). These authors deploy a reflective, skeptical, and probing counter-nostalgia to spotlight such tense "interweaving," contrast the beauty with the trauma, and, in the process, implicate the human forces at fault. Nostalgia performs a valuable critical function when it illuminates a traumatic event—for Zitkala-Ša, the uprooting of indigenous children in the name of education; for McKay, the forced migrations of slavery; or for Momaday, mismanaged government relocation projects. This sort of nostalgia does not simplify or elide history; rather, it reveals a complex past with legacies like poverty, ongoing racism, oppressive working conditions, and the paradoxical mandates of assimilation.

In all of the literary texts surveyed here, a re-placed nostalgia connects an otherwise "free-floating" emotion to the material world and to its complicated politics in the present. Even an idealized origin—whether a species, community, or environment—located in a mythical past can serve as a model for the future, especially insofar as it helps us trace material shifts and, if necessary, prompts us to change course. Since nostalgic narratives can serve many functions and—as McKay's and Ruth Ozeki's novels show most clearly—circulate at local, regional, and transnational scales, it becomes imperative to track both the routes and roots of such stories.

For ecocritics and other scholars invested in the pursuit of a more just world, such tracking is imperative. Some scholars have already begun to link nostalgia with environments and to recognize its role in progressive politics. For example, eco-cinecritics Robin L. Murray and Joseph K. Heumann argue that the 2006 cinematic phenomenon *An Inconvenient Truth* shows how environmentalist messages can "gain rhetorical force when an environmental nostalgia with emotional appeal is evoked" (196). These scholars are cautiously optimistic that "eco-memory," especially personal memories that are conjoined with historical, collective memory, might help us "learn from the past" and "recuperate real community" (201). Lawrence Buell, too, has made the productive potential of environmental memory the subject of his next book, and he has lectured widely on the topic.

Ecocritics are on the right track with our renewed attention to the pastoral, too, though the relationship between nostalgia and the pastoral deserves more attention. For all of the authors in this study (though perhaps least for DeLillo, whose complex pastoral is more ironic), a nostalgic pastoral ideal helps challenge social injustices and provide a vision to strive toward. Indeed, it seems that the pastoral is the nature narrative most frequently called upon to imagine more ethical human-nature and human-human relationships. This seems to work best when the pastoral is wrenched free from its historical status as the evolutionary byproduct of the frontier, and when it breaks ties with the Rooseveltian adaptation of Turner's frontier thesis that has dominated American culture.

As ecocriticism works to circumvent the American-British hegemony that has characterized the field, nostalgia—with its transnational routes—could be one catalyst for initiating more cross-cultural, interdisciplinary dialogue. Perhaps nostalgia might be fruitfully classed as what Buell terms an "ecoglobalist affect," since it has the potential to bridge a "specific site and a context of planetary reach" ("Ecoglobalist Affects" 232). Postcolonial ecocriticism, with its interest in displacement, in "unhomed" subjects (Bhabha 13), and in transnational, often diasporic, migrations, is especially well positioned to benefit from a renewed attention to nostalgia. In addition to questions of home and exile, biopiracy and environmental racism as forms of "ecological imperialism" (Tiffin and Huggan 4) should be considered in relation to nostalgia, since this longing is closely linked to bodies as well as to species and racial categories.

A greater engagement with ethnic studies—a crucial next move for ecocritics—will likely require more attention to nostalgia as well. Books by Kimberly Ruffin, Paul Outka, and others, as well as collections like *The Colors of Nature*, signal new dialogue between ecocritics and ethnic studies scholars, but so far nostalgia has not been a key element of this dialogue. We would do well to pay attention to nostalgia's role in not just perpetuating but also challenging pure racial and ethnic categories, as Ozeki and Momaday are adept at doing with their nostalgia for hybridity. For individuals, nostalgia is a valid kind of memory that can motivate personal identity explorations—in the way that, for example, a feeling of loss or "regret over lacking knowledge" of one's ancestry can prompt the quest to recover a "racial memory" (Su "Ghosts" 378). More broadly, as Momaday's novel suggests, nostalgia might be a useful way of remembering the past that points us toward issues of social and environmental justice and promotes understanding across racial and ethnic lines.

Environmental activists, too, might reconsider nostalgia as an effective tool for navigating a global political arena in which environmental concerns are increasing urgent. Especially since the "death of environmentalism" has been called for by some of its biggest proponents,[3] the question of how to articulate environmental problems and solutions most persuasively demands reconsideration and—as Scott Slovic's call to engage nostalgia suggests—an "all hands on deck" approach. For some tastes, environmentalist rhetoric is still too self-flagellating, or too misanthropic, to be compelling.[4] Elegies risk playing into the guilt and shame that have plagued environmentalism, but they can also offer more positive visions of the future. As the work of Leopold and Carson suggests, a nostalgic attempt to recover an ethical relationship to our environments could have an "emotional appeal" and perhaps prompt action in ways that guilt and shame might not. That said, the "wild" nature Leopold valued seems outdated when notions of purity are obsolete and when—as Yellowstone's bison herd exemplifies—nature is so materially and representationally mobile. Can nostalgia for "wildness" still function today, or have people already passed the point where such nostalgia is possible? Would generating nostalgia for undisturbed natural processes, as Ozeki does, be a better strategy?

New theories of nostalgia that recognize its flexibility and range could be valuable in addressing broad strategic questions like these as well as the specific instances of dislocation that people, bison, and other species face in the new millennium. The editors of *Postcolonial Green: Environmental Politics and World Narratives* begin their collection by discussing the number of people killed and left "homeless" by the devastating Indian Ocean tsunami in December of 2004 (Roos and Hunt 1). While this incident shows how "our world is locked in a dance of cultural, economic, and ecological interdependence" (Roos and Hunt 3), it also invites assessment of the nostalgia that accompanies such uprootings. Several months after the tsunami, a front-page *New York Times* article described the displaced residents from the Sri Lankan town of Navalady in terms of a nostalgic recovery process: "Placeless people can find themselves nostalgic even for homes linked with horror. More than the longing for a specific piece of ground, it is the ache for normalcy, familiarity, routine, the ability to locate themselves in a web of known people" (Waldman). For these refugees, nostalgia was a natural response to a traumatic event, and a way of connecting with one another in the face of tragedy. Like all nostalgia, theirs conjured both a material environment—a "specific piece of ground"—and less tangible components of home: "normalcy, familiarity, routine," and one's place within a community.

Even when a place is "linked with horror"—as the wilderness is for some African Americans, even today[5]—nostalgia sometimes still surprises us with its presence, and its potency. Of course, many people have not experienced the tragedy of losing a home to a natural disaster or the "horror" of being uprooted or displaced by human forces, and Edward Said is right to caution against romanticizing exile or making it "serve notions of humanism" ("Reflections" 174). Still, homelessness is expected to become more common in the new millennium. Who can say how many more "placeless people" there will be when global warming causes the oceans to flood low-lying countries? As the editors of *The Colors of Nature* write, climate change experts forecast large-scale displacement, and we will need to hone our "ability to listen and empathize across differences" and distances if we are to address these trends as a globe (Deming and Savoy 11). Nostalgia can highlight the material and political dimensions of dislocations. Who knows but that it might also inspire empathy and, potentially, alert more people to a future we should take steps to avoid?

The longing to be located, to feel at home in a place, remains strong in many people, and we should not rule out nostalgia's ability to inspire cross-cultural and transnational empathy in ways other emotions might not. Like all narratives about the past, nostalgia is imperfect, incomplete, and sometimes simplistic. But then again, sometimes it is a legitimate, provocative reaction that prompts evaluation or enhances existing perspectives. Too long considered antithetical to politically progressive movements, nostalgia could be enlisted to visualize new kinds of natures and cultures. As a powerful, often collectively shared, affect, nostalgia is certainly a tool for mapping social and environmental injustices in both past and present. Perhaps getting "back to nature" can also help steer us toward a different, better future.

Notes

Preface

1. Although the NPS is a relatively well-liked government agency, not everyone supports it. American Indians, for example, might justifiably harbor antagonism toward parks and park managers. Some local residents of towns bordering national parks feel deprived of access to "their" backyards and angered by park fees. Perhaps most crucially, the parks are not as democratic as they could be; the touring public remains predominantly white and middle-class. For studies of diversity (or rather, the lack of it) in national parks, see Floyd and Stanfield et al.

2. Some credit George Catlin's vision of a "nation's Park" in 1833 as the first expression of the national park ideal (Spence 10).

3. Grand Teton National Park's "video rivers" are streaming videos shown beneath four-by-fifteen-foot glass screens embedded in the floor. Accompanied by a "nature soundtrack," the footage provides a bird's-eye view of park scenery that visitors can view while strolling through the center ("Video Rivers"). One of the park's partners, the Grand Teton Association, offers a "preview" of the videos on its website, so you can watch the footage even before visiting the park (*Grand Teton Association*).

Introduction

1. Many environmentalists and writers, including Edward Abbey in *Desert Solitaire*, have grappled with this rhetoric. The tension between present "enjoyment" and leaving the resources "unimpaired" for the future continues to be an underlying paradox in park management, although recent legislation has emphasized that preservation should be the priority.

2. To their credit, the NPS employees I've had the privilege of working with do genuinely want to protect park resources; however, the agency's ability to do so fluctuates with administrations and budgets.

3. In addition to Ritivoi's helpful overview, Linda Hutcheon provides a brief history of nostalgia in "Irony, Nostalgia, and the Postmodern" (2000). For a recently published history of nostalgia from 1780 to 1917, see Austin.

4. Roberta Rubenstein mentions "re-placing" nostalgia, but her meaning—"to override or neutralize loss through reparative transformations of emotional pain associated with past experience"—differs substantially from mine (164).

5. Hutcheon defines this word as pointing to "the process . . . by which writers of history, fiction, or even theory render their materials coherent, continuous, unified— but always with an eye to the control and mastery of those materials, even at the risk of doing violence to them" (*Politics* 62).

6. Barry Lopez voices a common critique, for instance, when he blames nostalgia for helping to create "spurious geographies," which are marketed by industries that exploit Americans' nostalgia for the "virgin landscapes of their fathers" ("American Geographies").

7. Ecocriticism's leading scholars have remarked on its overlap with cultural studies. See Heise ("Hitchhiker's Guide" 506) and Buell (*Future* viii).

8. Hochman reminds us that "cultural studies began in green"; "nature" has been central to the field since Frankfurt School philosophers began theorizing its domination in the 1940s (5).

9. The "Radical Pastoral" panel was one of the conference's most popular sessions. Its content can be found online at http://radicalpastoral.blogspot.com as well as in the *Journal of Ecocriticism*'s July 2011 issue at http://ojs.unbc.ca/index.php/joe/issue /view/24/showToc.

10. Rosaldo focuses on the ways in which "nostalgia makes racial domination appear innocent and pure," only briefly mentioning the environmental implications of his oft-cited phrase (107).

11. See Gifford's chapter, "Post-pastoral," for a discussion of these traits.

12. Though not directly applicable to my study, Oona Frawley's work deserves mention here. She argues that in some Irish pastoral texts, "nostalgia, far from being an indulgent, sentimentalizing exercise, provided a political impetus that allowed, in many ways, for the movement from 'homesickness' to 'home rule'" (157).

13. I am informed by Foucault's use of "genealogy" here, as treatment of the past that "rejects the metahistorical deployment of ideal significations and indefinite teleologies. It opposes itself to the search for 'origins'" (*Discipline* 140). I also model the concept (and phrasing) of "counter-nostalgia" on his formulation of counter-memory.

14. See Rothman for a historical discussion of this fluctuation.

Having a Field Day

1. Cothran reads the Baby Show as a manifestation of "Progressive Era campaigns of racialized health reform" (201).

2. Whether the right tribes receive credit for the art is a matter of dispute. There is controversy over the tribal affiliations of some of the best-known Yosemite-area basketmakers. According to a recent article in *Indian Country Today*, most of the baskets were made by Paiutes, not Miwok Indians. The Yosemite Museum says otherwise. http://www.indiancountrytoday.com/yourict/49511947.html.

3. I refer here to Philip J. Deloria's book *Playing Indian*, in which he examines the long-standing practice of non-Natives performing Indian identity—a practice he

argues has "afforded a powerful foundation for subsequent pursuits of national identity" while subjugating the interests of real Indians (7).

4. See Spence for an overview of the shifting criteria for inhabiting park lands—including ancestry, popularity of crafts, and employment by the NPS—and the eventual destruction of the village as part of a fire-fighting practice session (120–30).

5. Spence's project reveals the extent to which various tribes—including the Crow, Shoshone, Bannock, Blackfeet, and Yosemite—used or inhabited park lands at the time of park designation. Of these tribes, "none ever fully relinquished their claims to these areas in a treaty with the United States" (6). For a more comprehensive overview of interactions between Indians and national parks, see Robert H. Keller and Michael F. Turek.

6. In her discussion of the Blackfeet Indians in Glacier National Park, Marguerite S. Shaffer shows how, while tourism was being promoted as a patriotic act of American consumption, the Blackfeet were rendered a historic group of people whose lives and culture were part of the nation's past, not its present.

7. See Limerick (*Legacy of Conquest*) for an analysis of the ideology of innocence.

1 / Longing for Wonderland

I use the term "post-frontier" to indicate the time following the official "closing" of the frontier by the U.S. Census Bureau in 1890. This is not to suggest that the trope of the frontier does not continue to circulate—in updated manifestations and often in troubling ways—throughout the century.

1. Cronon's essay was controversial when first published. See rebuttals by Dave Foreman and Gary Snyder in *Wild Earth* (Winter 1996/7). *Reinventing Nature?* also details arguments against Cronon's anthology, *Uncommon Ground*. Over ten years later, Cronon's insights are widely known and commonly accepted.

2. I explore the pioneering aspects of tourism in my article on Marianne Moore's "An Octopus" (2005). Terry Gifford, in his introduction to *John Muir: The Eight Wilderness-Discovery Books* (1992), also asserts that the closed frontier was rediscovered as "an essentially inner experience in National Parks" (13).

3. See Richard White's essay in *The Frontier in American Culture* for a more thorough discussion of the emergence of the cowboy figure.

4. Gail Bederman's insightful chapter in *Manliness and Civilization*, "Theodore Roosevelt: Manhood, Nation, and 'Civilization,'" provides a more extensive discussion of Roosevelt's life and politics. See also Slotkin's *Gunfighter Nation*, especially chapter 1.

5. Robert Gottlieb, for one, critiques the NPS as, at its inception, "an institution run for and by the elite" (31).

6. The extent to which Zitkala-Ša abandons oral tradition is debatable. In her reading of *American Indian Stories*, Vanessa Holford Diana argues that, in fact, "Zitkala-Ša affirms the oral tradition in which she was raised" through the way she tells her stories, which recollects the "traditional cycle story" (171).

7. See Bernardin for a discussion of how Zitkala-Ša exploits sentimental ideology. By contrast, Laura Wexler argues that her autobiographical writings are so sentimental that they "had no Indian in them that was left untouched by western codes" (33).

8. As Andrew Ross (1994) has shown, positing nature as a moral authority can be a problematic approach to environmental politics and social justice, especially when this ideology is wielded by potential cultural imperialists.

9. Cronon and other scholars note the tendency of sublime wilderness to "reinscrib[e] the notion of nature's otherness" (Hitt 603). See Christopher Hitt for a helpful overview of these problems and a more hopeful reading of the sublime's potential.

10. Myers insists that her work "brings together environmental awareness with social justice" and imagines the "possibility for coexistence of white people and people of color with each other and the land" (138). While this possibility is less apparent in her autobiographical stories, passages like the one in "The Great Spirit" do lend themselves to his reading.

11. For an alternate but complementary reading, see D. K. Meisenheimer Jr., who argues that the reference to herself as a tree stripped bare might invoke the Sun Dance pole and "a tribal, collective consciousness" (118).

12. Foucault defines discipline as "a type of power, a modality for its exercise, comprising a whole set of instruments, techniques, procedures, levels of application, targets; it is a 'physics' or an 'anatomy' of power, a technology" (*Discipline* 215).

"Plucked Up by the Roots"

1. The anthology also reached out to other predominantly white regions—notably the West—in order to advocate a "national agrarian movement" that valued "the defense of individualism, the small community, [and] the state," as opposed to the federal government (xi).

2. See James R. Grossman and Joe William Trotter Jr. for examples.

3. This appeal might also be linked to Ransom's foundational role as a New Critic. In a sort of New Critical analysis, Ransom reads the "text" of Southern experience as a unified one and embraces a universal humanism that skews and simplifies reality.

4. Another Rooseveltian reference occurs in the final essay, when Young champions the "primitive man" over the "nervous, busy, softened" type created by industrialization (354).

2 / "Home Thoughts"

1. See Jennifer Haytock for an explanation of Cather's phrase and why she chooses the year 1922 to signify this "break."

2. For a discussion of "New Deal regionalism," see Lauren Coats and Nihad M. Farooq. They suggest that while the interest in folk culture was perhaps meant to be inclusive, it often upheld the "pre-existing architecture of a national narrative" that erased cultural difference (90).

3. For one piece of scholarship that shares my assessment of *The Professor's House*, see Michael Hobbs.

4. John Steinbeck's *The Grapes of Wrath*, for instance, might be read as a counternostalgic text insofar as it complicates the Edenic myth of California.

5. Campbell's chapter "Toward an Expanded Critical Regionalism" in *The Rhizomatic West* provides a useful overview of recent trends.

6. I invoke the phrases of choice, respectively, of Mary Louise Pratt, Neil Campbell, and Arjun Appadurai.

7. See Evelyn White and Eddy Harris for two interesting engagements with the issue of black experience in wilderness.

8. As Dorman explains, most regionalists were "nationalistic" in that they wanted to reconstruct American culture out of domestically available materials (23).

9. Both Robyn Wiegman and Donna Haraway have observed how twentieth-century technologies of race relocated it from external (via strategies like craniometry) to internal (via technologies like gene mapping) and "lodged" both race and white supremacist logic "more fully in the body" (Wiegman 31). See Wiegman's chapter "Visual Modernity" in *American Anatomies* and Haraway's "Race" chapter in *Modest Witness*.

10. Michael Omi and Howard Winant provide perhaps the most influential overview of "racial formations" in the United States, although their discussion of this period is brief.

11. See William Maxwell, qtd. in http://www.english.illinois.edu/maps/poets/m_r/mckay/mustdie.htm.

12. McKay completed a novel called *Color Scheme* several years earlier, but he burned it after American publishers deemed it "much too explicit in its sexual frankness and language" (Cooper xvi).

13. James Weldon Johnson was an earlier, outspoken critic of U.S. intervention in Haiti. He also celebrated the country's revolutionary history, claiming Haiti was "the one best chance that the Negro has in the world to prove that he is capable of the highest self-government" (*The Crisis*).

14. See studies by George Hutchinson (1995) and Ann Douglass, in particular.

15. See Baker Jr. for a discussion of the critical phenomenon of constructing the Harlem Renaissance as a "failure." See Lowney for a mention of the limitations of critical discourse caused by the focus on Jake's primitivism.

16. For one compelling reading of how McKay negotiates racial identity, see Sylvia Xavier.

17. The reference to Jake's sister resonates with Du Bois's "Of the Coming of John," in which the protagonist's sister longs to have his educational opportunities. Both authors delineated their struggles for equality in predominantly masculinist terms, addressing female identity to a limited degree.

18. See Leon D. Pamphile's *Haitians and African Americans: A Heritage of Tragedy and Hope* (2001) for an account of the political and cultural connections between the two countries.

Born Free and Equal

1. See Michael Cooper and Wakatsuki Houston for accounts of life in the camps.

2. See Melody Graulich for a discussion of the rules of photography in the camps—observed by "outsiders" like Adams—and a provocative juxtaposition of Adams's work with the "insider" photographs taken by Toyo Miyatake.

3. I would be remiss not to give a nod to John Okada's classic *No-No Boy*, which explores these issues in much greater depth.

4. David Palumbo-Liu addresses some of the problems with this figuration in *Asian/American* (174).

3 / Nostalgia's Caring Capacity

1. I use Benedict Anderson's phrase here to suggest that the spread of television in the 1950s generated an "imagined community," not unlike the process by which

print-capitalism helped define national consciousness through the "imagined link-ages" created by novels and newspapers (33–35).

2. I follow Fredric Jameson's distinction between the 1950s and the "fifties," in which the former indicates the historical period and the latter refers to the decade as reconstructed by media representations (281).

3. McKibben's *Deep Economy: The Wealth of Communities and the Durable Future* is a contemporary example of a text that asks us to rethink our understanding of environmentalism as, necessarily, economic sacrifice.

4. Remarkably, Carson is still criticized today for being alarmist, narrow-minded, and scientifically inaccurate. For an overview of recent debates, see Aaron Swartz.

5. Interestingly, Buell points out that "only in retrospect does *Sand County Alma-nac* loom up as Leopold's magnum opus. He himself would have thought it to be *Game Management* (1933), the leading textbook in the field" (*Writing* 185).

6. As Buell and others have begun to explain, these environmental perspectives shared some common ground and have converged at various historical moments, making them more "complementary" than antithetical (*Writing* 13). See Ted Steinberg's chapter "Conservation Reconsidered" for a detailed account of the dynamic between conservation and preservation.

7. See Harold Fromm for a discussion of Leopold as anthropocentric. Rogers and Callicott (in "The Land Aesthetic") offer divergent views. Many of the essays in Callicott's *Companion*, including the essay by Roderick Nash, provide more nuanced readings.

8. Nash reminds us of Leopold's many predecessors, including Thoreau, George Perkins Marsh, Muir, Darwin, Edward Payson Evans, J. Howard Moore, Albert Schweitzer, and others (64).

9. See Peter Fritzell for discussion of the book's trajectory and Tim B. Rogers for analysis of the role of "embodied dialogue."

10. Of course, animal studies scholars have called such a facile opposition into question, especially as we learn more about nonhuman animals' capacity for emotion. See, for example, Jacques Derrida.

11. Marx identifies Jefferson with pastoralism, not agrarianism, since, unlike late-eighteenth-century agrarian doctrines, Jefferson "explicitly rejected productivity, or the material standard of living, as the chief criterion in framing social policies" ("Pastoralism" 50).

12. Fromm sees such aestheticization as precisely the kind of anthropocentric thinking that leads to environmental injustices in the first place.

13. Cronon is working on a history of Portage, Wisconsin, that I hope will explore these historical overlaps in detail. See Slotkin, "Nostalgia and Progress," for a discussion of Turner's Midwestern agrarianism.

14. Dorman argues that it was, in one sense, a "last-ditch" effort—insofar as it signified a lack of faith in the political process and a move toward voluntarism (317).

15. Peter Wild and Tom Lynch see Abbey's text as "firmly rooted in the mythology of the frontier" with its "individualistic anarchy and contempt for what are perceived to be artificial rules and a disdain for the presumed civilizing influence of women" (Wild 140; Lynch 100). If some of Abbey's works can be called "anti-pastoral," then others, including *Desert Solitaire*, seem to be pro-frontier, at least in

terms of the anarchic individualism and the "nineteenth-century brand of frontier justice" he brings to bear against the "modern atrocities he sees everywhere" (Gifford 120; Ronald 183–84).

"A Tear for the Fate of America"

This phrase comes from the website of "America Remembers," an NGO that honors "notable Americans and historic American events" by issuing "unique and handsomely designed commemorative firearms." The "Iron Eyes Cody" model, which has been discontinued, used to sell for $2,195.

1. Since Reagan was one of the least environmentally responsible presidents, and since Westerns have historically been instrumental in both eulogizing Indians and promoting stereotypes about them, the irony of these actors' partnership is noteworthy.

2. The Ad Council website claims this campaign "helped to reduce litter by as much as 88% in 300 communities, 38 states, and several countries" (www.adcouncil.org). The site also notes that the PSA won "two Clio awards and the campaign was named one of the top 100 advertising campaigns of the 20th Century by *Ad Age Magazine*." Iron Eyes Cody was honored with a star on the Hollywood Walk of Fame in 1982.

3. Krech goes on to argue that this myth of the "Ecological Indian," of which the Crying Indian is the "paramount example," does not accurately reflect how indigenous cultures have behaved historically in relation to nonhuman nature (16). See Schweninger (*Listening*) for an overview of the controversies and risks associated with Krech's project, among them "appearing to take an anti-Indian stance" (11).

4. See Angela Aleiss for an account of his ancestry.

5. Gottlieb gives one example of this when he notes how Gary Snyder, in response to events at Berkeley's People's Park, compared trees to "other exploited minorities, such as blacks, Vietnamese, and hippies" (102).

6. See Louv, "Children and Nature Movement." Louv's *Last Child in the Woods* and its catchy phrase "nature-deficit disorder" have inspired nonprofits like the Children and Nature Network as well as a slew of local and regional (and often bipartisan) campaigns to "leave no child inside." National parks have developed a "Children in Nature" initiative to show renewed commitment to inspiring young visitors, and the Forest Service began a "More Kids in the Woods" program in 2007.

4 / Remembering the Earth

1. Fixico's *Termination and Relocation* provides an informative book-length study.

2. See Fixico, *Urban Indian Experience*, especially 1–25.

3. For a comprehensive discussion of the Red Power movement and its legacies, see Alvin Josephy Jr., et al., especially 1–60. Sean Teuton's book *Red Land, Red Power* is also a good resource.

4. For more background on these gains, see "Alcatraz Is Not an Island." See also Troy R. Johnson, especially chapter 3.

5. Hal Rothman describes the 1960s in similar terms, as a decade of utopianism driven by the commonly shared sentiment "that humanity would be happier in simpler circumstances" (83–84).

6. See Peter Braunstein and Michael William Doyle for a useful overview of the counterculture. In this collection Andrew Kirk argues that "counterculture

environmentalists" provided one of the most lasting contributions of the broader
countercultural movement by seeing potential in "alternative technologies" (355). He
admits that even those who fall under this label did not share a single perspective;
there was "rarely a clear program of action or analysis" (356).

7. See, for example, "The Death of Environmentalism."

8. Gottlieb's history tracks alternates to the mainstream movement, including
Ralph Nader's citizen network, anti-nuclear movements, anti-toxics movements, and
groups like Greenpeace and Earth First!.

9. Of course, there are several ways to date this movement. One could mark its
origin with the 1982 battle in Warren County, North Carolina, over a hazardous waste
landfill, or with the United Church of Christ's study on environmental racism, published in 1987. One could also say that the movement really began to cohere in 1991,
when the First National People of Color Environmental Leadership Summit was held.
Giovanna Di Chiro provides a concise overview of this history.

10. Schweninger's "Introduction: An Ethical Regard for the Land" provides a useful overview of research and debates concerning Indians and land ethics.

11. For more discussion of these issues, see Tatonetti's book review essay in *WAL*
and Huhndorf's article in *PMLA*, which provides a helpful overview of trends, questions, debates, and directions in Native American Studies.

12. See, for instance, Christopher Douglas's reading.

13. Momaday describes Father Olguin as "alienated from the realities of his environment" by "his white arrogance and pride" (Woodard 190).

14. Douglas's article recaps the various readings of the albino, including the possibility of him representing a "traditional Jemez witch" (see note 7).

15. Angela seems well intentioned, as does Milly, the social worker who becomes
Abel's friend and lover after his prison term ends. But these women's perspectives
should be seen as on par with the ideologies behind the Relocation Program, which
Momaday is critiquing. Some scholars have critiqued Momaday from a feminist perspective. See, for instance, Kathleen M. Donovan.

16. This passage resonates with Simon Ortiz's definition of "cultural authenticity"
as the "creative responses to forced colonization" that maintain tribal identity and
resist loss (9, 12).

17. Teuton claims that Abel avoids reinforcing "popular assumptions of savage
nobility or ignobility" (52).

18. Chadwick Allen counters charges of racism by suggesting that Momaday's
formulation works against the U.S. government's attempts to quantify Indian identity in terms of blood quantum. Su reads racial memory as complicating ontological
questions about race by "challenging widespread assumptions that race is a readily
identifiable category" ("Ghosts" 369). Teuton skirts the debate but defends Momaday
from charges of essentialism (51).

19. Teuton points out that Abel's seven specific recollections occur in "places laden
with cultural meaning," and that seven is itself a "ritual number" (60).

20. The recently remade film *The Exiles* contains a similar scene.

21. Bevis argues that "coming home, staying put, contracting, even what we call
'regressing' to a place, a past where one has been before . . . is a primary mode of
knowledge and a primary good" in much Native American literature (qtd. in Toy
29).

22. Fixico (*Urban Indian Experience*) writes that as many as 70 percent of the early participants in relocation returned to their reservations, though these numbers have been controversial (20).

23. See Susan Scarberry-Garcia's *Landmarks of Healing*, as well as essays by Larry Evers ("Words and Place") and S. K. Aithal for examples of this sort of reading. For an alternate take on ritual and initiation in the novel, see Larry Landrum.

24. Paula Gunn Allen identifies Momaday as the first writer of a third wave of American Indian literature insofar as his text helped "reestablish . . . [ritual's] central place in the Native narrative," but through a "new narrative" that fused Western and tribal modes (10–11).

Patenting "The Last of Nature's Creations"

1. Information about the coalition is hard to come by, though the ad lists several high-profile organizations as members, including the Sierra Club and the Humane Society. One site, activistcash.com (supported by the Center for Consumer Freedom), claims that most of Turning Point's money during the time it ran its advertisements came from one source: Douglas Tompkins (founder of The North Face and Esprit clothing) and his Foundation for Deep Ecology.

2. The "ear" was grown from cow cartilage cells harnessed in a biodegradable structure and grafted onto the mouse's back. Since no mouse DNA was modified, the "ear mouse" was not genetically engineered. For explanations of the technology, which was first developed by Bob Langer and Joseph Vacanti in the late 1990s, see "The Bionic Body" and Karl S. Kruszelnicki, "Mouse with Human Ear."

3. Artists and intellectuals have dealt with genetic research in more nuanced ways. Maarten Vanden Eynde's website, Rebecca Elson's poem "OncoMouse, Kitchen Mouse," and Kathy High's "Embracing Animal" project are especially provocative. Thanks to Donna Haraway for bringing these to my attention.

4. My analysis focuses on the United States, but it is worth noting that the patent application stirred more controversy in Europe. The European Patent Office initially rejected the application but did ultimately grant it in 1992 (Haraway, *Modest_Witness* 98).

5. For Rifkin's view, see "Fears of a Brave New World." Leon Kass shares many of Rifkin's concerns.

6. Lynne Huffer, Janice Doane, and Devon Hodges are among those who balk at "the imaginative past of nostalgic writers, [when] men were men, women were women, and reality was real" (Huffer 3). Like Haraway, they emphasize that nostalgia can be counterproductive for feminists due to its tendency to imply totalizing origins, identities, and "essences" of women.

7. See "Fears of a Brave New World." Notably, Rifkin himself applied for a patent on chimeras so that he could set up a twenty-year "conservancy" for these animals to buy time for public debate ("Are You a Man or a Mouse?").

5 / Don DeLillo's Postmodern Homesickness

1. Linda Hutcheon accuses Jameson of his own nostalgia for a time before late capitalism robbed parody of its critical edge. She insists, "There is nothing natural about the 'real' and there never was" (*Politics* 33).

2. Interestingly, McKibben identified his "end of nature" thesis as "an idea, like the closing of the frontier," although his work is also concerned with the material implications of nature's end (67). Dana Phillips also notes echoes of frontier rhetoric in postmodern theories like Jameson's (245).

3. Stegner describes the rebellion as a "blind, greedy, and reactionary outburst from western stockmen," and he critiques the revisionist historical narrative of local control ("Legacy" 242).

4. Hollywood films of the 1980s like *Rambo* and *Die Hard* shared this agenda. See Susan Jeffords for analysis of these films.

5. Luke W. Cole and Sheila R. Foster add "where we learn" to this formulation (16).

6. See Ladino, "Local Yearnings."

7. On nostalgia for transcendence in *Underworld*, see Todd McGowan 132.

8. See Peter Knight 819.

9. David Evans notes its "deadpan ironies and post-nostalgic cool" as well as its ability to parody nostalgia (104). For a discussion of DeLillo's parodic nostalgia in relation to the 1950s, see Molly Wallace. Stephen J. Mexal mentions the "irony . . . of using nostalgia in order to critique nostalgia" (334n4)—a point that is salient to my essay.

10. Paul A. Cantor concurs with Phillips's view when he remarks, "Part of DeLillo wants to say that we have lost touch with everything that was authentic in our world and in our culture. But . . . part of DeLillo wants to say that nothing has really changed; things have always been this way" (59). Gifford's fourth quality of the post-pastoral is precisely this: that the literary work "convey[s] an awareness of both nature as culture and of culture as nature" (162).

11. Heise offers a helpful list of the elements of the "risk society" (Ulrich Beck's phrase) the Gladneys confront on a daily basis ("Toxins" 750–51).

12. Phillips uses the mall as an example of the postmodern pastoral in the text.

13. Heise's reading of the "Dylarama" section as "simply the narrative inversion of the risk scenario" in the airborne toxic event section is compelling ("Toxins" 753).

Nature Survives

1. The concept for the show was developed by a British television producer, Charlie Parsons, and it first aired in Sweden in 1997 as "Expedition Robinson." Versions have been created in several countries since, but American audiences seem to be its biggest fans. Nielsen ratings have consistently been high for *Survivor*, ever since over 50 million viewers tuned in to the first season's finale and made *Survivor* the second most-watched show for that season (behind the Super Bowl).

2. Interestingly, Steven G. Kellman compares the show to academia in his humorous *Chronicle of Higher Education* piece: like Survivors, academia's "contestants" learn to master social politicking, endure a degree of public surveillance, and, ultimately, face similar penalties for failure.

3. Burnett has published several books explaining these connections, including *Survivor: The Ultimate Game* (2000), *Survivor II: The Field Guide* (2001), and *The Survivor Manual: Based on U.S. Armed Forces Survival Techniques* (2001).

4. The link between *South Pacific* and *Survivor Vanuatu* is far from arbitrary: both romanticize racial difference as ahistorical pluralism while simultaneously facilitating American imperialism along the Pacific Rim.

5. The "rites" (which are described in detail on the CBS site) split the tribes by gender, and they remain divided along those lines until episode 5. Although my analysis does not focus on gender, there is plenty of fruitful ground for exploration here.

6. Another website titles the episode "They Came at Us with Spears," thereby highlighting the "fierce battle cry" of the "spear-wielding" Natives. See John Fisher's "Hawaii Travel Guide," which includes an "episode guide" to *Survivor*. That this show is being used as part of a travel guide to a region it exploits suggests the extent to which media representations often precede, and shape, our encounters with the world.

7. I am not the first to make this observation. See Raymond Williams, "Ideas of Nature." Neil Smith explains this tension as "the 'ideology' of nature": "The hostility of external nature justifie[s] its domination and the spiritual morality of universal nature provide[s] a model for social behavior" (*Uneven Development* 15).

8. Rory's nemesis in the all-male tribe is "Sarge," the ex-military man who deems Rory "a bad seed" in episode 5. Another teammate calls Rory "different" in the first episode, and Rory receives votes in every tribal council, which indicates his unpopularity.

9. See episode 4, in which "the services of an authentic Vanuatu tribesman named Dah" are the prize for the tribe that wins a particular physical challenge.

6 / Nostalgia and Nature at the Millennium

1. Linda Martín Alcoff and Satya P. Mohanty explain: "For those on the Right, these movements appear to be threatening individual freedom, while for those on the Left, they are seen as threatening the progressive coalition and wallowing in victimization" (2).

2. More than just economic policy, Brown explains, neoliberalism constitutes human subjectivity within the economic order of global capitalism by "*extending and disseminating market value to all institutions and social action*" (7, original emphasis).

3. Greg Garrard describes postmodern ecology as a shift in ecological discourse away from "balance and harmony" (which he notes, interestingly, are "versions of pastoral") and toward a conception of nature as "a process rather than an object" (178).

4. See Mohanty, Heise, and Jeffrey Myers, respectively. Sean Teuton's notion of "tribal realism" is also influenced by postpositivist realism. We might also add David Palumbo-Lui's "progressive humanism" to this list ("Multiculturalism Now").

5. Buell admits American domination is only, ever, "partial" (554). Similarly, Duggan reminds us that global neoliberalism is "based in but not reducible to U.S. corporate dominance" (xv).

6. These include, briefly: "awe" of the natural world; a cyclical "creative-destructive universe"; a recognition of "inner human nature . . . in relation to external nature"; "an awareness of both nature as culture and . . . culture as nature"; a recognition that "with consciousness comes conscience"; and an ecofeminist awareness that "the exploitation of the planet is of the same mindset as the exploitation of women and minorities" (150–65).

7. Barbara Kingsolver calls the book "Edward Abbey's *The Monkey Wrench Gang* updated by thirty years, with modern environmental challenges on the map and women in the front seat, driving the story" (qtd. on book jacket).

8. Julie Sze offers one reading of *My Year of Meats* as an environmental justice text. My essay ("New Frontiers") situates it as a socialist ecofeminist novel with an environmental justice agenda.

9. See Michael Bennett ("Wide Open Spaces") for a lucid discussion of the tensions and the common ground between deep and social ecology. Garrard points out social ecology's "clear affinity with environmental justice movements," which makes it an attractive framework for addressing multicultural literature (*Ecocriticism* 29, 55).

10. Like many scholars, Chuh disowns nostalgia, citing Toni Morrison's observation that critical race studies should avoid "pathetic yearning and futile desire" especially for "an irretrievable and probably nonexistent Eden" (124).

11. The phrase was first coined by the late Pope John Paul II, and George W. Bush picked up on its use to justify his administration's policies concerning abortion, euthanasia, and stem cell research (see Michael A. Fletcher).

12. This fictional group was apparently inspired by a direct-action coalition that destroyed a crop of GM corn plants at the University of Maine. See McHugh (51n28).

13. McHugh makes the connection to Haraway in her essay. I allude to species interconnections in *All Over Creation* in "Unlikely Alliances."

14. Ozeki downplays her own political agenda: "I don't think of my novels as didactic or polemical. I certainly don't write them in order to 'teach' or to 'convert'" ("Conversation").

15. Ozeki describes him as "not good or bad," but "just amoral" (Clyne, "Interview").

16. I'm thinking here of moves toward recognizing history as contingent narrative—not entirely unlike fiction—made by key postmodern thinkers such as Foucault and Hayden White.

17. Mitchell's lyrics to this song, "Big Yellow Taxi," are included in McKibben's recent collection of nature writing, *American Earth: Environmental Writing since Thoreau* (2008).

18. See Rachel Stein for a thoughtful analysis of Lilith's site. Stein argues that the novel exposes how "neocolonial, patriarchal controls on women's sexuality and reproduction are still problematically justified through ideologies of nature, the natural, environmental need, and agriculture" (178).

19. See Emily Cheng for a provocative reading of *My Year of Meats* that counters Chiu's—I think, convincingly.

20. Neoliberalism is frequently likened to religious faith. See Duggan (xiii), Noam Chomsky (32), and Robert W. McChesney (8).

21. I examine intersections between religious and environmental groups in more detail in "Unlikely Alliances."

22. Of course, abortion is itself a complex social issue. Indeed, many argue that it's "a sign that society has failed to meet the needs of women" and that dealing with broader problems, such as poverty and inadequate educational systems, are the best ways to reduce abortions (Vincent Gragnani 16–17).

23. Ozeki notes geographic scales from the book's opening page: Fuller Farms is "vast, by human scale," and the earth's crust becomes "small . . . by global or geologic measure" (3). For a geographer's perspective on the importance of attending to these various scales, see Matthew W. Klingle.

Conclusion

1. Since animals do not respect human-created boundaries, bison roam in and out of Yellowstone's borders and pose a threat to ranchers, who fear the bison will transmit diseases like brucellosis—which causes cows to abort fetuses—to their cattle. Each year, then, wildlife managers "haze" bison to return them to park lands. In previous years, many bison would simply be killed. The Buffalo Field Campaign, a nonprofit group that documents and protests this treatment, keeps a running tally of animals who have been "eliminated from the last wild population in the U.S." ("Weekly Update from the Field"). There has never been a documented case of bison transmitting brucellosis to cattle in the wild, though it has occurred in controlled conditions ("Bison and Brucellosis").

2. For example, many parks have turned over campground management to private companies, who can better finance and repair them than the underfunded NPS. But the park and its visitors suffer from the lack of a strong ranger presence in the campgrounds, with the educational benefits and personal contact that provides.

3. Michael Shellenberger and Ted Nordhaus suggest it is time for a new environmental vision that articulates "a set of core beliefs, principles, or values" (32).

4. Andrew Ross, for example, accuses ecological movements of serving up a "dog's breakfast of self-denial, self-restraint, guilt, and disavowal" (*Chicago Gangster* 269). Kate Soper, too, calls for a sexier environmental rhetoric that emphasizes "the pleasure to be realized by breaking with current market-defined and capitalist promoted conceptions of the good life" (*What Is Nature?* 271).

5. In her often-anthologized essay "Black Women and the Wilderness," Evelyn White explains how her "genetic memory of ancestors hunted down and preyed" inspires her fear of wilderness but also how these same ancestors' experiences as "herders, gatherers, and fishers" inspire her to overcome that fear (318, 320). Camille T. Dungy's essay in *The Colors of Nature* raises similar issues.

Bibliography

Abbey, Edward. *Desert Solitaire: A Season in the Wilderness*. New York: Ballantine, 1968.

Adams, Ansel. *Born Free and Equal: The Story of Loyal Japanese-Americans at Manzanar Relocation Center, Inyo County, California*. New York: U.S. Camera, 1944. 18 June 2010. http://memory.loc.gov/ammem/collections/anseladams /aamborn.html.

Adamson, Joni, and Scott Slovic. "The Shoulders We Stand On: An Introduction to Ethnicity and Ecocriticism." *MELUS* 34.2 (2009): 5–24.

Aithal, S. K. "The Redemptive Return: Momaday's *House Made of Dawn*." *North Dakota Quarterly* 53.2 (1985): 160–72.

"Alcatraz Is Not an Island." *PBS*. 18 June 2010. http://www.pbs.org/itvs/alcatraz isnotanisland/activism.html.

Alcoff, Linda Martín, and Satya P. Mohanty. "Reconsidering Identity Politics: An Introduction." *Identity Politics Reconsidered*. Ed. Linda Martín Alcoff, Michael Hames-García, Satya P. Mohanty, and Paula M. L. Moya. New York: Palgrave Macmillan, 2006. 1–9.

Aleiss, Angela. "Iron Eyes Cody: Wannabe Indian." *Cineaste* 25 (1999): 30.

Allen, Chadwick. "Blood (and) Memory." *American Literature* 71.1 (March 1999): 93–116.

Allen, Paula Gunn, ed. *Song of the Turtle: American Indian Literature, 1974–1994*. New York: Ballantine, 1996.

Anderson, Benedict. *Imagined Communities: Reflections on the Origin and Spread of Nationalism*. New York: Verso, 1983.

Andrejevic, Mark. *Reality TV: The Work of Being Watched*. Lanham: Rowman and Littlefield, 2004.

Appadurai, Arjun. *Modernity at Large: Cultural Dimensions of Globalization.* Minneapolis: University of Minnesota Press, 1996.

Aronowitz, Stanley. "Seeds of a Movement: From Seattle to Washington and Beyond." *The Battle of Seattle: The New Challenge to Capitalist Globalization.* Ed. Eddie Yuen, Daniel Burton Rose, and George Katsiaficas. New York: Soft Skull Press, 2001. 195–200.

Austin, Linda M. *Nostalgia in Transition, 1780–1917.* Charlottesville: University of Virginia Press, 2007.

"'Back by Popular Neglect' PSA." KAB Multimedia. *Keep America Beautiful.* 18 June 2010. http://www.kab.org/site/PageServer?pagename=media_multimedia.

Baker, Houston A., Jr. "Modernism and the Harlem Renaissance." *Modernist Culture in America.* Ed. Daniel Joseph Singal. New York: Wadsworth, 1991. 107–25.

Banerjee, Subhankar. *Arctic National Wildlife Refuge: Seasons of Life and Land.* Seattle: Mountaineers, 2003.

Barillas, William. *The Midwestern Pastoral: Place and Landscape in Literature of the American Heartland.* Athens: Ohio University Press, 2006.

Barrett, Laura. "'How the Dead Speak to the Living': Intertextuality and the Postmodern Sublime in *White Noise.*" *Journal of Modern Literature* 25.2 (2001–2): 97–113.

Baudrillard, Jean. *America.* Trans. Chris Turner. New York: Verso, 1988.

———. "Precession of Simulacra." Trans. Paul Foss and Paul Patton. *Art after Modernism: Rethinking Representation.* Ed. Brian Wallis. New York: New Museum of Contemporary Art, 1984.

Bederman, Gail. *Manliness and Civilization: A Cultural History of Gender and Race in the United States, 1880–1917.* Chicago: University of Chicago Press, 1995.

Beidler, Philip D. "*South Pacific* and American Remembering: or, 'Josh, We're Going to Buy This Son of a Bitch!'" *Journal of American Studies* 27 (1993): 207–22.

Bennett, Michael. "Anti-pastoralism, Frederick Douglass, and the Nature of Slavery." *Beyond Nature Writing: Expanding the Boundaries of Ecocriticism.* Ed. Karla Armbruster and Kathleen R. Wallace. Charlottesville: University of Virginia Press, 2001. 195–210.

———. "From Wide Open Spaces to Metropolitan Places: The Urban Challenge to Ecocriticism." *ISLE* 8.1 (2001): 31–51.

———, and David W. Teague, eds. *The Nature of Cities: Ecocriticism and Urban Environments.* Tucson: University of Arizona Press, 1999.

Bent, Stephen. "Issues and Prospects in the USA." *Animal Patents: The Legal, Economic and Social Issues.* Ed. William H. Lesser. New York: Palgrave Macmillan, 1989. 5–15.

Bernadin, Susan. "The Lessons of a Sentimental Education: Zitkala-Ša's Autobiographical Narratives." *Western American Literature* 32.3 (1997): 212–38.

Berry, Wendell. *The Art of the Commonplace: The Agrarian Essays of Wendell Berry.* Ed. Norman Wirzba. Washington, D.C.: Counterpoint, 2002.

Bhabha, Homi K. *The Location of Culture*. New York: Routledge, 1994.

Bibby, Brian. "Native American Art of the Yosemite Region." *Yosemite: Art of an American Icon*. Ed. Amy Scott. Berkeley: University of California Press, 2006.

"The Bionic Body." *PBS*. 15 May 2010. http://www.pbs.org/saf/1107/features/body.htm.

Birth of a Nation. Dir. D.W. Griffith. Perf. Lillian Gish, Mae Marsh, Henry Walthall, Miriam Cooper, Ralph Lewis, Wallace Reed, Robert Harron. Republic Pictures, 1915.

"Bison and Brucellosis." *Montana Fish, Wildlife and Parks*. 18 June 2010. http://fwp.mt.gov/hunting/brucellosis.html.

Bol, Marsha C., ed. *Stars Above, Earth Below: American Indians and Nature*. Niwot: Roberts Rinehart for Carnegie Museum of Natural History, 1998. Distributed by Publishers Group West.

Boym, Svetlana. *The Future of Nostalgia*. New York: Basic Books, 2001.

Braun, Bruce, and Noel Castree, eds. *Remaking Reality: Nature at the Millennium*. New York: Routledge, 1998.

Braunstein, Peter, and Michael William Doyle. "Introduction: Historicizing the American Counterculture of the 1960s and '70s." *Imagine Nation: The American Counterculture of the 1960s and '70s*. Ed. Peter Braunstein and Michael William Doyle. New York: Routledge, 2002. 5–14.

Brody, Baruch. "Evaluation of the Ethical Arguments Commonly Raised against the Patenting of Transgenic Animals." *Animal Patents: The Legal, Economic and Social Issues*. Ed. William H. Lesser. New York: Palgrave Macmillan, 1989. 141–56.

Brown, Wendy. *States of Injury: Power and Freedom in Late Modernity*. Princeton: Princeton University Press, 1995.

Buell, Frederick. "Nationalist Postnationalism: Globalist Discourse in Contemporary American Culture." *American Quarterly* 50.3 (1998): 548–91.

Buell, Lawrence. "Ecoglobalist Affects: The Emergence of U.S. Environmental Imagination on a Planetary Scale." *Shades of the Planet: American Literature as World Literature*. Ed. Wai-chee Dimock and Lawrence Buell. Princeton: Princeton University Press, 2007. 227–48.

———. *The Environmental Imagination: Thoreau, Nature Writing, and the Formation of American Culture*. Cambridge: Belknap Press of Harvard University Press, 1995.

———. *The Future of Environmental Criticism: Environmental Crisis and Literary Imagination*. Malden: Blackwell, 2005.

———. *Writing for an Endangered World: Literature, Culture and Environment in the U.S. and Beyond*. Cambridge: Harvard University Press, 2001.

Callicott, J. Baird. "The Conceptual Foundations of the Land Ethic." *Companion to* A Sand County Almanac: *Interpretive and Critical Essays*. Ed. J. Baird Callicott. Madison: University of Wisconsin Press, 1987. 186–214.

———. "The Land Aesthetic." *Companion to* A Sand County Almanac: *Interpretive and Critical Essays.* Ed. J. Baird Callicott. Madison: University of Wisconsin Press, 1987. 157–71.

———. "Traditional American Indian and Western European Attitudes toward Nature: An Overview." *In Defense of the Land Ethic: Essays in Environmental Philosophy.* New York: SUNY Press, 1989. 177–202.

Campbell, Neil. *The Cultures of the American New West.* Chicago: Fitzroy Dearborn, 2000.

———. *The Rhizomatic West: Representing the West in a Transnational, Global, Media Age.* Lincoln: University of Nebraska Press, 2008.

Cantor, Paul A. "Adolf, We Hardly Knew You." *New Essays on* White Noise. Ed. Frank Lentricchia. New York: Cambridge University Press, 1991. 39–62.

Carson, Rachel. *Silent Spring.* New York: Fawcett Crest, 1964.

Cather, Willa. *Not Under Forty.* New York: Knopf, 1936.

———. *The Professor's House.* New York: Random House, 1990.

Chase, Malcolm, and Christopher Shaw, eds. *The Imagined Past: History and Nostalgia.* Manchester: Manchester University Press, 1989.

Cheng, Emily. "Meat and the Millennium: Transnational Politics of Race and Gender in Ruth Ozeki's *My Year of Meats.*" *Journal of Asian American Studies* 12.2 (2009): 191–220.

Chomsky, Noam. *Profit over People: Neoliberalism and Global Order.* New York: Seven Stories, 1999.

Chiu, Monica. "Postnational Globalization and (En)Gendered Meat Production in Ruth L. Ozeki's *My Year of Meats.*" *Lit: Literature Interpretation Theory* 12.1 (2001): 99–128.

Chuh, Kandice. *Imagine Otherwise: On Asian Americanist Critique.* Durham: Duke University Press, 2003.

Claborn, John. Review of Paul Outka, *Race and Nature from Transcendentalism to the Harlem Renaissance. Journal of Ecocriticism* 2.1 (2010): 87–88.

Clifford, James. *Routes: Travel and Translation in the Late Twentieth Century.* Cambridge: Harvard University Press, 1997.

Clyne, Catherine. Interview with Ruth Ozeki. *Satya Magazine.* March 2003. http://www.ruthozeki.com/about/profiles-reviews/satya-magazine-interview.

Coats, Lauren, and Nihad M. Farooq. "Regionalism in the Era of the New Deal." *A Companion to the Regional Literatures of America.* Ed. Charles. L. Crow. Oxford: Blackwell, 2003. 74–91.

Cole, Luke W., and Sheila R. Foster. *From the Ground Up: Environmental Racism and the Rise of the Environmental Justice Movement.* New York: New York University Press, 2001.

Coltelli, Laura. *Winged Words: American Indian Writers Speak.* Lincoln: University of Nebraska Press, 1990.

Committee on the Judiciary (1988). *Transgenic Animal Patent Reform Act. Animal Patents: The Legal, Economic and Social Issues.* Ed. William H. Lesser. New York: Palgrave Macmillan, 1989.

Coontz, Stephanie. *The Way We Never Were: American Families and the Nostalgia Trap.* New York: Basic Books, 1992.

———. *The Way We Really Are: Coming to Terms with America's Changing Families.* New York: Basic Books, 1998.

Cooper, Michael. *Remembering Manzanar: Life in a Japanese Relocation Camp.* New York: Houghton Mifflin Harcourt, 2002.

Cooper, Wayne F. *Claude McKay: Rebel Sojourner in the Harlem Renaissance.* Baton Rouge: Louisiana State University Press, 1987.

Cothran, Boyd. "Working the Indian Field Days: The Economy of Authenticity and the Question of Agency in Yosemite Valley." *American Indian Quarterly* 34.2 (Spring 2010): 194–223.

Cronon, William. "A Place for Stories: Nature, History, and Narrative." *Journal of American History* 78.4 (1992): 1347–76.

———. Foreword. *Uncommon Ground: Rethinking the Human Place in Nature.* Ed. William Cronon. New York: Norton, 1996. 19–22.

———. "The Trouble with Wilderness; or, Getting Back to the Wrong Nature." *Uncommon Ground: Rethinking the Human Place in Nature.* Ed. William Cronon. New York: Norton, 1996. 69–90.

Crow, Charles. L. *A Companion to the Regional Literatures of America.* Oxford: Blackwell, 2003.

Cutter, Martha J. "Zitkala-Ša's Autobiographical Writings: The Problems of a Canonical Search for Language and Identity." *MELUS: Journal of the Society of Multi-Ethnic Literature* 19.1 (1994). 31-44.

Dash, J. Michael. *Haiti and the United States: National Stereotypes and the Literary Imagination.* New York: St. Martin's, 1997.

Davidov, Judith Fryer. "'The Color of My Skin, the Shape of My Eyes': Photographs of the Japanese-American Internment by Dorothea Lange, Ansel Adams, and Toyo Miyatake." *Yale Journal of Criticism* 9.2 (1996): 223–44.

Davis, Fred. *Yearning for Yesterday: A Sociology of Nostalgia.* New York: Free Press, 1979.

Deitering, Cynthia. "The Postnatural Novel: Toxic Consciousness in Fiction of the 1980s." *The Ecocriticism Reader: Landmarks in Literary Ecology.* Ed. Cheryl Glotfelty and Harold Fromm. Athens: University of Georgia Press, 1996. 196–203.

DeLillo, Don. "The Power of History." *New York Times Book Review* 7 September 1997. http://www.nytimes.com/library/books/090797article3.html.

———. *Underworld.* New York: Scribner's, 1997.

———. *White Noise.* New York: Penguin, 1984.

Delisle, Jennifer. "'For King and Country': Nostalgia, War, and Canada's Tomb of the Unknown Soldier." *Dalhousie Review* 85.1 (2005): 15–32.

Deloria, Philip J. *Playing Indian*. New Haven: Yale University Press, 1998.

Deming, Alison H., and Lauret E. Savoy. "Widening the Frame." *The Colors of Nature: Culture, Identity, and the Natural World*. Ed. Alison H. Deming and Lauret E. Savoy. Minneapolis: Milkweed, 2011. 3–12.

Derrida, Jacques. "And Say the Animal Responded?" Trans. David Willis. *Zoontologies: The Question of the Animal*. Ed. Cary Wolfe. Minneapolis: University of Minnesota Press, 2003. 121–46.

Di Chiro, Giovanna. "Nature as Community: The Convergence of Environment and Social Justice." *Uncommon Ground: Rethinking the Human Place in Nature*. Ed. William Cronon. New York: Norton, 1996. 298–320.

Diana, Vanessa Holford. "'Hanging in the Heart of Chaos': Bi-cultural Limbo, Self-(Re)Presentation, and the White Audience in Zitkala-Ša's *American Indian Stories*." *Cimarron Review* 121 (1997): 154–72.

Dixon, Melvin. *Ride Out the Wilderness: Geography and Identity in Afro-American Literature*. Urbana: University of Illinois Press, 1987.

Dixon, Thomas, Jr. *The Clansman: An Historical Romance of the Ku Klux Klan*. New York: Doubleday, Page, 1905.

Doane, Janice, and Devon Hodges. *Nostalgia and Sexual Difference: The Resistance to Contemporary Feminism*. New York: Methuen, 1987.

Donovan, Kathleen M. *Feminist Readings of Native American Literature: Coming to Voice*. Tucson: University of Arizona Press, 1998.

Dorman, Robert. *Revolt of the Provinces: The Regionalist Movement in America, 1920–1945*. Chapel Hill: University of North Carolina Press, 1993.

Douglas, Christopher. "The Flawed Design: American Imperialism in N. Scott Momaday's *House Made of Dawn* and Cormac McCarthy's *Blood Meridian*." *Critique: Studies in Contemporary Fiction* 45.1 (2003): 3–24.

Douglass, Ann. *Terrible Honesty: Mongrel Manhattan in the 1920s*. New York: Farrar, 1995.

Du Bois, W. E. B. *The Souls of Black Folk*. New York: Penguin, 1989.

Duggan, Lisa. *The Twilight of Equality: Neoliberalism, Cultural Politics, and the Attack on Democracy*. Boston: Beacon, 2003.

Dungy, Camille T. "Tales from a Black Girl on Fire, or Why I Hate to Walk Outside and See Things Burning." *The Colors of Nature: Culture, Identity, and the Natural World*. Ed. Alison H. Deming and Lauret E. Savoy. Minneapolis: Milkweed, 2011. 28–32.

Duvall, John. "From Valparaiso to Jerusalem: DeLillo and the Moment of Canonization." *MFS: Modern Fiction Studies* 45 (1999): 559–68.

———. "Regionalism in American Modernism." *The Cambridge Companion to American Modernism*. Ed. Walter Kalaidjian. Cambridge: Cambridge University Press, 2005. 242–60.

Enoch, Jessica. "Resisting the Script of Indian Education: Zitkala Ša and the Carlisle Indian School." *College English* 65.2 (2002): 117–41.

Evans, David. "Taking Out the Trash: Don DeLillo's *Underworld*, Liquid Modernity, and the End of Garbage." *Cambridge Quarterly* 35.2 (2006): 103–32.

Evers, Larry, and Ofelia Zepeda, eds. *Home Places: Contemporary Native American Writing from Sun Tracks*. Tucson: University of Arizona Press, 1995.

———. "Words and Place: A Reading of *House Made of Dawn*." *Western American Literature* 11 (1977): 297–320.

The Exiles. Dir. Kent Mackenzie. Perf. Yvonne Williams, Homer Nish, Tom Reynolds. 1961. Milestone, 2008.

Eynde, Maarten Vanden. "Genetologic Research: The Science of First Things." 15 May 2010. http://www.genetologisch-onderzoek.nl.

Fabre, Genevieve, and Michel Feith, eds. *Temples for Tomorrow: Looking Back at the Harlem Renaissance*. Bloomington: Indiana University Press, 2001.

Fetterley, Judith, and Marjorie Pryse. *Writing Out of Place: Regionalism, Women, and American Literary Culture*. Champaign: University of Illinois Press, 2005.

Fischer, John. "Survivor Vanuatu - Episode Guide." *Hawaii Travel Guide*. 15 June 2010. http://gohawaii.about.com/od/survivor_vanuatu/a/survivor_vanu _a.htm.

Fisher, Dexter. "Foreword: Zitkala-Ša: The Evolution of a Writer." *American Indian Stories*. University of Nebraska Press, 1985. v-xx.

Fixico, Donald. *Termination and Relocation: Federal Indian Policy, 1945–1960*. Albuquerque: University of New Mexico Press, 1990.

———. *The Urban Indian Experience in America*. Albuquerque: University of New Mexico Press, 2000.

Fletcher, Michael A. "Bush Hails Progress toward 'Culture of Life.'" *Washington Post* 25 January 2005. A03.

Floyd, Myron F. "Managing National Parks in a Multicultural Society: Searching for Common Ground." *George Wright Forum* 18.3 (2001): 41–51.

Foote, Bonnie. "The Narrative Interactions of *Silent Spring*: Bridging Literary Criticism and Ecocriticism." *New Literary History* 38.4 (2007): 739–53.

Foreman, Dave. "Around the Campfire." *Wild Earth* (1996–97): 1–4.

Foucault, Michel. *Discipline and Punish: The Birth of the Prison*. Trans. Alan Sheridan. New York: Pantheon, 1977.

———. "Nietzsche, Genealogy, History." *Language, Counter-Memory, Practice: Selected Essays and Interviews*. Ed. Donald F. Bouchard. Trans. Donald F. Bouchard and Sherry Simon. Ithaca: Cornell University Press, 1980. 139–64.

Franklin, Sarah. *Dolly Mixtures: The Remaking of Genealogy*. Durham: Duke University Press, 2007.

Frawley, Oona. *Irish Pastoral: Nostalgia and Twentieth-Century Irish Literature*. Dublin: Irish Academic Press, 2005.

Fritzell, Peter A. "The Conflicts of Ecological Conscience." *Companion to* A Sand County Almanac: *Interpretive and Critical Essays*. Ed. J. Baird Callicott. Madison: University of Wisconsin Press, 1987. 128–56.

Fromm, Harold. "Aldo Leopold: Aesthetic 'Anthropocentrist.'" *The ISLE Reader: Ecocriticism, 1993–2003*. Athens: University of Georgia Press, 2003. 3–9.

Frow, John. "The Last Things before the Last: Notes on *White Noise*." *Introducing Don DeLillo*. Ed. Frank Lentricchia. Durham: Duke University Press, 1991. 175–91.

Garrard, Greg. *Ecocriticism*. London: Routledge, 2004.

———. "Radical Pastoral?" *Studies in Romanticism* 35.3 (1996): 449–65.

Gifford, Terry. Introduction. *John Muir: The Eight Wilderness-Discovery Books*. London: Diadem, 1992. 13–20.

———. "Post-pastoral." *Pastoral*. London: Routledge, 1999. 146-74.

Glotfelty, Cheryl, and Harold Fromm, eds. *The Ecocriticism Reader: Landmarks in Literary Ecology*. Athens: University of Georgia Press, 1996.

———. "Cold War, *Silent Spring*: The Trope of War in Modern Environmentalism." *And No Birds Sing: Rhetorical Analyses of Rachel Carson's* Silent Spring. Ed. Craig Waddell. Carbondale: Southern Illinois University Press, 2000. 157–73.

Gone with the Wind. Dir. Victor Fleming. Perf. Vivien Leigh, Clark Gable, Barbara O'Neill, Thomas Mitchell, Evelyn Keyes. David O'Selznick, 1939.

Gottlieb, Robert. *Forcing the Spring: The Transformation of the American Environmental Movement*. Washington, D.C.: Island Press, 1993.

Gragnani, Vincent. "A Little Less Confrontation, A Little More Action." *U.S. Catholic* (September 2006): 12–17.

Grand Teton Association. 18 June 2010. http://www.grandtetonpark.org/video_rivers_s/71.htm.

Graulich, Melody. "'Cameras and Photographs Were Not Permitted in the Camps': Photographic Documentation and Distortion in Japanese American Internment Narratives." *True West: Authenticity and the American West*. Ed. William R. Handley and Nathanial Lewis. Lincoln: University of Nebraska Press, 2004. 222–56.

Grossberg, Lawrence, Cary Nelson, and Paula Treichler, eds. *Cultural Studies*. New York: Routledge, 1991.

Grossman, James R. "Black Labor Is the Best Labor: Southern White Reactions to the Great Migration." *Black Exodus: The Great Migration from the American South*. Ed. Alferdteen Harrison. Jackson: University Press of Mississippi, 1991. 51–71.

———, ed. *The Frontier in American Culture*. Berkeley: University of California Press, 1994.

———. *Land of Hope: Chicago, Black Southerners, and the Great Migration*. Chicago: University of Chicago Press, 1989.

Hamming, Jeanne. "Wallowing in the 'Great Dark Lake of Male Rage': The Masculine Ecology of Don DeLillo's *White Noise*." *Journal of Ecocriticism* 1.1 (2009): 26–42.

Haraway, Donna. *The Companion Species Manifesto: Dogs, People, and Significant Otherness*. Chicago: Prickly Paradigm, 2003.

———. "A Manifesto for Cyborgs: Science, Technology, and Socialist Feminism in the 1980s." *Coming to Terms: Feminism, Theory, Politics*. Ed. Elizabeth Weed. London: Routledge, 1989. 173–204.

——. *Modest_Witness@Second_Millennium.FemaleMan©_Meets_Onco-Mouse™*. New York: Routledge, 1997.

Harris, Eddy L. *Mississippi Solo: A River Quest*. New York: Henry Holt, 1998.

Hayles, Katherine. *How We Became Posthuman: Virtual Bodies in Cybernetics, Literature and Informatics*. Chicago: University of Chicago Press, 1999.

Haytock, Jennifer. "Looking at Agony: World War I in *The Professor's House*." *Cather Studies* 6 (2006). 29 June 2011. http://cather.unl.edu/cs006_haytock.html.

Heise, Ursula K. "Ecocriticism and the Transnational Turn in American Studies." *American Literary History* 20 (2008): 381–404.

——. "The Hitchhiker's Guide to Ecocriticism." *PMLA* 121 (2006): 503–16.

——. *Sense of Place and Sense of Planet: The Environmental Imagination of the Global*. New York: Oxford University Press, 2008.

——. "Toxins, Drugs, and Global Systems: Risk and Narrative in the Contemporary Novel." *American Literature* 74.4 (2002): 747–78.

High, Kathy. "Embracing Animal." 15 May 2010. http://www.embracinganimal.com.

Hitt, Christopher. "Toward an Ecological Sublime." *New Literary History* 30 (1999): 603–23.

Hobbs, Michael. "'An Orgy of Acquisition': Intellectual and Commercial Ownership in *The Professor's House*." *Teaching Cather* 3.2 (2003): 4–7.

Hochman, Jhan. *Green Cultural Studies: Nature in Film, Novel, and Theory*. Moscow: University of Idaho Press, 1998.

Hogan, Linda. *Dwellings: A Spiritual History of the Living World*. New York: Simon and Schuster, 1995.

hooks, bell. "Touching the Earth." *Literature and the Environment: A Reader on Nature and Culture*. Ed. Lorraine Anderson, Scott Slovic, and John P. O'Grady. New York: Addison-Wesley, 1999. 169–73.

Houston, Jeanne Wakatsuki. "Crossing Boundaries." *The Colors of Nature: Culture, Identity, and the Natural World*. Ed. Alison H. Deming and Lauret E. Savoy. Minneapolis: Milkweed, 2011. 33–40.

——, and James D. Houston. *Farewell to Manzanar: A True Story of Japanese American Experience during and after the World War II Internment*. New York: Houghton Mifflin Harcourt, 2002.

Huffer, Lynne. *Maternal Pasts, Feminist Futures: Nostalgia, Ethics, and the Question of Difference*. Stanford: Stanford University Press, 1998.

Huhndorf, Shari. *Going Native: Indians in the American Cultural Imagination*. Ithaca: Cornell University Press, 2001.

——. "Literature and the Politics of Native American Studies." *PMLA* 120.5 (2005): 1618–27.

Hutcheon, Linda. "Irony, Nostalgia, and the Postmodern." *Methods for the Study of Literature as Cultural Memory*. Ed. Raymond Vervliet and Annemarie Estor. Atlanta: Rodopi, 2000. 189–207.

———. *The Politics of Postmodernism*. New York: Routledge, 1989.

Hutchinson, George. *The Harlem Renaissance in Black and White*. Cambridge: Harvard University Press, 1995.

———. Introduction. *The Cambridge Companion to the Harlem Renaissance*. Ed. George Hutchinson. Cambridge: Cambridge University Press, 2007. 1–10.

I'll Take My Stand: The South and the Agrarian Tradition, by Twelve Southerners. New York: Harper, 1930.

"Iron Eyes Cody 'People Start Litter, People Can Stop It' PSA." KAB Multimedia. *Keep America Beautiful*. 18 June 2010. http://www.kab.org/site/PageServer?pagename=media_multimedia.

"Iron Eyes Cody: The 'Crying Indian.'" *America Remembers*. http://www.americaremembers.com/Products/IECTRI/IECTRI_info.htm.

Isernhagen, Hartwig. *Momaday, Vizenor, Armstrong: Conversations on American Indian Writing*. Norman: University of Oklahoma Press, 1999.

Jameson, Fredric. *Postmodernism, or, the Cultural Logic of Late Capitalism*. Durham: Duke University Press, 1991.

Jeffords, Susan. *Hard Bodies: Hollywood Masculinity in the Reagan Era*. Piscataway: Rutgers University Press, 1993.

Johnson, James Weldon. *The Autobiography of an Ex-Colored Man*. New York: Penguin, 1990.

———. "The Truth about Haiti." *The Crisis* 20 (1920): 217–24.

Johnson, Kirk. "Deal Puts Yellowstone Bison on Ted Turner's Range." *New York Times* 21 May 2010. 18 June 2010. http://www.nytimes.com/2010/05/22/us/22bison.html.

Johnson, Troy R. *The American Indian Occupation of Alcatraz Island: Red Power and Self-Determination*. Lincoln: University of Nebraska Press, 2008.

Josephy Jr., Alvin, Troy R. Johnson, and Joane Nagel, eds. *Red Power: The American Indians' Fight for Freedom*. 2nd ed. Lincoln: Bison Books, 1999.

Judis, John B. *Grand Illusion: Critics and Champions of the American Century*. New York: Farrar Straus and Giroux, 1992.

Kass, Leon. *Toward a More Natural Science: Biology and Human Affairs*. New York: Free Press, 1985.

Keller, Robert H., and Michael F. Turek. *American Indians and National Parks*. Tucson: University of Arizona Press, 1999.

Kellman, Steven G. "In Academe and 'Survivor,' Sociability Trumps Talent." *Chronicle of Higher Education* 47.3 (2000): B16–18. http://chronicle.com/article/In-AcademeSurvivor/21419.

Kim, Elaine. Preface. *Charlie Chan Is Dead: An Anthology of Contemporary Asian American Fiction*. Ed. Jessica Hagedorn. New York: Penguin, 1993. vii-xiv.

Kirk, Andrew. "'Machines of Loving Grace': Alternative Technology, Environment, and the Counterculture." *Imagine Nation: The American Counterculture of the 1960s and '70s*. Ed. Peter Braunstein and Michael William Doyle. New York: Routledge, 2002. 353–78.

Klingle, Matthew W. "Spaces of Consumption in Environmental History." *History and Theory* 42 (2003): 94–110.

Knight, Peter. "Everything Is Connected: *Underworld*'s Secret History of Paranoia." *Modern Fiction Studies* 45 (1999): 811–35.

Kowalewski, Michael. "Contemporary Regionalism." *A Companion to the Regional Literatures of America*. Ed. Charles L. Crow. Oxford: Blackwell, 2003. 7–24.

Krech, Shepard, III. *The Ecological Indian: Myth and History.* New York: W.W. Norton, 1999.

Kruszelnicki, Karl S. "Mouse with Human Ear." *ABC Science.* 15 May 2010. http://www.abc.net.au/science/articles/2006/06/02/1644154.htm.

Ladino, Jennifer. "'Local Yearnings': Re-Placing Nostalgia in Don DeLillo's *Underworld.*" *Journal of Ecocriticism* 2.1 (January 2010): 1-18.

———. "Longing for Wonderland: Nostalgia for Nature in Post-Frontier America." *Iowa Journal of Cultural Studies* 5 (2004): 88–109.

———. "New Frontiers for Ecofeminism: Women, Nature, and Globalization in Ruth L. Ozeki's *My Year of Meats.*" *New Directions in Ecofeminist Literary Criticism.* Ed. Andrea Campbell. Newcastle upon Tyne: Cambridge Scholars, 2008. 124–47.

———. "Unlikely Alliances: Notes on a Green Culture of Life." *Journal of Religion and Society, Supplement Series 3.* Ed. Ronald A. Simkins. Omaha: Kripke Center, 2008. http://moses.creighton.edu/jrs/toc/SS03.html.

———. "Rewriting Nature Tourism in 'an Age of Violence': Tactical Collage in Marianne Moore's 'An Octopus.'" *Twentieth-Century Literature* 51.3 (2005): 285–315.

Landrum, Larry. "The Shattered Modernism of Momaday's *House Made of Dawn.*" *MFS: Modern Fiction Studies* 42.4 (1996): 763–86.

Langford, Nathaniel Pitt. *Diary of the Washburn Expedition to the Yellowstone and Firehole Rivers in the Year 1870.* St. Paul, Minn., 1905. Open Library. org. http://www.archive.org/stream/diaryofwashburne00langrich#page/n5/mode/2up.

Latour, Bruno. *We Have Never Been Modern.* Trans. Catherine Porter. Cambridge: Harvard University Press, 1993.

Le Coney, Christopher, and Zoe Trodd. "Reagan's Rainbow Rodeos: Queer Challenges to the Cowboy Dreams of Eighties America." *Canadian Review of American Studies* 39.2 (2009): 163–83.

Leopold, Aldo. *A Sand County Almanac, with Essays on Conservation from Round River.* New York: Oxford University Press, 1966.

Lentricchia, Frank. Introduction and "Tales of the Electronic Tribe." *New Essays on* White Noise. Ed. Frank Lentricchia. New York: Cambridge University Press, 1991. 1–14; 87–113.

Lesser, William H., ed. *Animal Patents: The Legal, Economic and Social Issues.* New York: Palgrave Macmillan, 1989.

Limerick, Patricia. "The Adventures of the Frontier in the Twentieth Century." *The Frontier in American Culture*. Ed. James R. Grossman. Berkeley: University of California Press, 1994. 66–102.

———. *The Legacy of Conquest: The Unbroken Past of the American West*. New York: W. W. Norton, 1987.

Lionnet, Françoise, and Shu-mei Shih. "Introduction: Thinking through the Minor, Transnationally." *Minor Transnationalism*. Ed. Françoise Lionnet and Shu-mei Shih. Durham: Duke University Press, 2005. 1–23.

Löbbermann, Dorothea. "Harlem as a Memory Place: Reconstructing the Harlem Renaissance in Space." *Temples for Tomorrow: Looking Back at the Harlem Renaissance*. Ed. Genevieve Fabre and Michel Feith. Bloomington: Indiana University Press, 2001. 210–21.

Locke, Alain. *The New Negro: Voices of the Harlem Renaissance*. New York: Touchstone, 1999.

Lomawaima, K. Tsianina. "Domesticity in the Federal Indian Schools: The Power of Authority over Mind and Body." *Deviant Bodies: Critical Perspectives on Difference in Science and Popular Culture*. Ed. Jennifer Terry and Jacqueline Urla. Bloomington: Indiana University Press, 1995. 197–217.

Lopez, Barry. "American Geographies." *Orion Magazine* (Autumn 1989): 52–61.

Louv, Richard. "The Children and Nature Movement: Notes from the Field." http://richardlouv.com/last-child-movement.

———. *Last Child in the Woods: Saving Our Children from Nature-Deficit Disorder*. New York: Algonquin, 2008.

———. "Leave No Child Inside." *Orion Magazine*. http://www.orionmagazine.org/index.php/articles/article/240/.

Lowe, Lisa. *Immigrant Acts: On Asian American Cultural Politics*. Durham: Duke University Press, 1996.

———. "Canon, Institutionalization, Identity: Contradictions for Asian American Studies." *The Ethnic Canon: Histories, Institutions, and Interventions*. Ed. David Palumbo-Liu. Minneapolis: University of Minnesota Press, 1995. 48–68.

Lowenthal, David. "Nostalgia Tells It Like It Wasn't." *The Imagined Past: History and Nostalgia*. Ed. Malcolm Chase and Christopher Shaw. New York: Manchester University Press, 1989. 18–32.

Lowney, John. "Haiti and Black Transnationalism: Remapping the Migrant Geography of *Home to Harlem*." *African American Review* 34.3 (2000): 413–29.

Lynch, Tom. "Nativity, Domesticity, and Exile in Edward Abbey's 'One True Home.'" *Coyote in the Maze: Tracking Edward Abbey in a World of Words*. Salt Lake City: University of Utah Press, 1998. 88–105.

Lytle, Mark Hamilton. *The Gentle Subversive: Rachel Carson, Silent Spring, and the Rise of the Environmental Movement*. New York: Oxford University Press, 2007.

Marx, Leo. *The Machine in the Garden: Technology and the Pastoral Ideal in America*. New York: Oxford University Press, 2000.

———. "Pastoralism in America." *Ideology and Classic American Literature*. Ed. Sacvan Bercovitch and Myra Jehlen. Cambridge: Cambridge University Press, 1986. 36–69.

Maxwell, William. *New Negro, Old Left*. New York: Columbia University Press, 1999.

McChesney, Robert W. "Noam Chomsky and the Struggle against Neoliberalism." http://www.chomsky.info/onchomsky/19990401.htm.

McClure, John A. "Postmodern Romance: Don DeLillo and the Age of Conspiracy." *Introducing Don DeLillo*. Ed. Frank Lentricchia. Durham: Duke University Press, 1991. 99–115.

McGowan, Todd. "The Obsolescence of Mystery and the Accumulation of Waste in Don DeLillo's *Underworld*." *Critique* 46.2 (Winter 2005): 123–45.

McHugh, Susan. "Flora, not Fauna: GM Culture and Agriculture." *Literature and Medicine* 26.1 (2007): 25–54.

McKay, Claude. *Home to Harlem*. New York: Harper and Brothers, 1928.

McKibben, Bill. *Deep Economy: The Wealth of Communities and the Durable Future*. New York: St. Martin's Griffin, 2008.

———. *The End of Nature*. 1989. 2nd ed. New York: Random House, 2006.

———. *Enough: Staying Human in an Engineered Age*. New York: Henry Holt, 2003.

Meisenheimer, D. K., Jr. "Regionalist Bodies/Embodied Regions: Sarah Orne Jewett and Zitkala-Ša." *Breaking Boundaries: New Perspectives on Women's Regional Writing*. Ed. Sherrie A. Inness and Diana Royer. Iowa City: University of Iowa Press, 1997. 109–23.

Mexal, Stephen J. "Spectacular Spectacular! *Underworld* and the Production of Terror." *Studies in the Novel* 36.3 (2004): 318–36.

Mohanty, Satya P. *Literary Theory and the Claims of History: Postmodernism, Objectivity, Multicultural Politics*. Ithaca: Cornell University Press, 1997.

Momaday, N. Scott. *House Made of Dawn*. New York: Harper and Row, 1989.

———. *The Man Made of Words: Essays, Stories, Passages*. New York: St. Martin's, 1997.

Morrow, Lance. "Be My Neighbor." Review of Bill McKibben's *Deep Economy*. *New York Times* Sunday Book Review 22 April 2007. 15 May 2010. http://www.nytimes.com/2007/04/22/books/review/Morrow.t.html.

Moses, Michael Valdez. "Lust Removed from Nature." *New Essays on White Noise*. Ed. Frank Lentricchia. New York: Cambridge University Press, 1991. 63–86.

Moya, Paula. "Postmodernism, 'Realism,' and the Politics of Identity: Cherríe Moraga and Chicana Feminism." *Reclaiming Identity: Realist Theory and the Predicament of Postmodernism*. Ed. Paula M. L. Moya and Michael R. Hames-García. Berkeley: University of California Press, 2000. 67–101.

Mumford, Kevin. *Interzones: Black/White Sex Districts in Chicago and New York in the Early Twentieth Century*. New York: Columbia University Press, 1997.

Murray, Keat. "Surviving *Survivor*: Reading Mark Burnett's Field Guide and De-naturalizing Social Darwinism as Entertainment." *Journal of American and Comparative Cultures* 24.3–4 (2001): 43–54.

Murray, Robin L., and Joseph K. Heumann. *Ecology and Popular Film: Cinema on the Edge*. New York: State University of New York Press, 2009.

Myers, Jeffrey. *Converging Stories: Race, Ecology, and Environmental Justice in American Literature*. Athens: University of Georgia Press, 2005.

Nash, Roderick. "Aldo Leopold's Intellectual Heritage." *Companion to* A Sand County Almanac: *Interpretive and Critical Essays*. Ed. J. Baird Callicott. Madison: University of Wisconsin Press, 1987. 63–90.

Newmark, Julianne. "Writing (and Speaking) in Tongues: Zitkala-Ša's *American Indian Stories*." *Western American Literature* 37.3 (2002): 335–58.

Nichols, Martha. "Guilt Trip into the Woods: Do Kids Really Need Nature?" *Brain Child: The Magazine for Thinking Mothers*. http://www.brainchild mag.com/mamapedia/spring2010_nichols.asp.

Nye, David. *American Technological Sublime*. Boston: MIT Press, 1996.

Okada, John. *No-No Boy*. Seattle: University of Washington Press, 1978.

Omi, Michael, and Howard Winant. *Racial Formation in the United States: From the 1960s to the 1990s*. New York: Routledge, 1994.

Ortiz, Simon. "Towards a National Indian Literature: Cultural Authenticity in Nationalism." *MELUS* 8.2 (1981): 7–12.

Osofsky, Gilbert. *Harlem: The Making of a Ghetto: Negro New York, 1890–1930*. 2nd ed. New York: Harper, 1971.

Outka, Paul. *Race and Nature: From Transcendentalism to the Harlem Renaissance*. New York: Palgrave MacMillan, 2008.

Ozeki, Ruth. *All Over Creation*. New York: Penguin, 2003.

———. "Conversation with Ruth Ozeki." *Ozekiland: Ruth Ozeki's Webworld*. http://www.ruthozeki.com/books-films/all-over-creation/conversation -with-ozeki.

———. *My Year of Meats*. New York: Penguin, 1998.

Palumbo-Liu, David. *Asian / American: Historical Crossings of a Racial Frontier*. Stanford: Stanford University Press, 1999.

———. *The Ethnic Canon: Histories, Institutions, and Interventions*. Minneapolis: University of Minnesota Press, 1995.

———. "Multiculturalism Now: Civilization, National Identity, and Difference before and after September 11th." *boundary 2* 29.2 (2002): 109–27.

———. "Rational and Irrational Choices: Form, Affect, and Ethics." *Minor Transnationalism*. Ed. Françoise Lionnet and Shu-mei Shih. Durham: Duke University Press, 2005. 41–72.

Pamphile, Leon Denius. *Haitians and African Americans: A Heritage of Tragedy and Hope*. Gainesville: University Press of Florida, 2001.

Park, Robert. *Race and Culture*. Glencoe: Free Press, 1950.

Parrish, Timothy L. "From Hoover's FBI to Eisenstein's *Unterwelt*: DeLillo Directs the Postmodern Novel." *Modern Fiction Studies* 45 (1999): 696–723.

Pedersen, Carl. "The Tropics in New York: Claude McKay and the New Negro Movement." *Temples for Tomorrow: Looking Back at the Harlem Renaissance*. Ed. Genevieve Fabre and Michel Feith. Bloomington: Indiana University Press, 2001. 259–69.

Peyser, Thomas. "Globalization in America: The Case of Don DeLillo's *White Noise*." *CLIO* 25.3 (1996): 255-71.

Phillips, Dana. "Don DeLillo's Postmodern Pastoral." *Reading the Earth: New Directions in the Study of Literature and Environment*. Ed. Michael P. Branch et al. Moscow: University of Idaho Press, 1998. 235–46.

Pickering, Jean, and Suzanne Kehde, eds. *Narratives of Nostalgia, Gender, and Nationalism*. New York: New York University Press, 1997.

Pister, Edwin P. "A Pilgrim's Progress from Group A to Group B." *Companion to A Sand County Almanac: Interpretive and Critical Essays*. Ed. J. Baird Callicott. Madison: University of Wisconsin Press, 1987. 221-32.

"Pollution: Keep America Beautiful–Iron Eyes Cody (1961–1983)." *Ad Council*. http://www.adcouncil.org/Our-Work/The-Classics/Pollution-Keep-America-Beautiful-Iron-Eyes-Cody.

Porter, Joy. "Historical and Cultural Contexts to Native American Literature." *The Cambridge Companion to Native American Literature*. Ed. Joy Porter and Kenneth M. Roemer. Cambridge: Cambridge University Press, 2005. 39–68.

Pratt, Mary Louise. *Imperial Eyes: Travel Writing and Transculturation*. New York: Routledge, 1992.

Price, Jennifer. *Flight Maps: Adventures with Nature in Modern America*. New York: Basic Books, 2000.

Rabinow, Paul. "Artificiality and Enlightenment: From Sociobiology to Biosociality." *Incorporations*. Ed. Jonathan Crary and Sanford Kwinter. Boston: Urzone, 1992. 234–52.

Ransom, J. C. "Reconstructed but Unregenerate." *I'll Take My Stand: The South and the Agrarian Tradition, by Twelve Southerners*. New York: Harper, 1930. 1–27.

Regan, Tom. *All That Dwell Therein: Animal Rights and Environmental Ethics*. Berkeley: University of California Press, 1982.

Remnick, David. "Profile of Don DeLillo." *New Yorker* 15 September 1997: 42–48.

Rifkin, Jeremy. "Are You a Man or a Mouse?" 15 May 2010. http://www.guardian.co.uk/comment/story/0,3604,1437701,00.html.

———. "Fears of a Brave New World." 15 May 2010. http://www.unesco.org/courier/1998_09/uk/dires/txt1.htm.

Ritivoi, Andreea Deciu. *Yesterday's Self: Nostalgia and the Immigrant Identity*. New York: Rowman and Littlefield, 2002.

Rogers, Tim B. "Revisioning Our Views of 'Nature' through an Examination of Aldo Leopold's *A Sand County Almanac*." *ISLE: Interdisciplinary Studies in Literature and Environment* 10.2 (Summer 2003): 47–73.

Ronald, Ann. *The New West of Edward Abbey*. 2nd ed. Reno: University of Nevada Press, 2000.

Roos, Bonnie, and Alex Hunt. *Postcolonial Green: Environmental Politics and World Narratives*. Charlottesville: University of Virginia Press, 2010.

Roosevelt, Theodore. *The Strenuous Life*. New York: Review of Reviews, 1910.

Rosaldo, Renato. "Imperialist Nostalgia." *Representations* 26 (1989): 107–22.

Rose, Nikolas. "Governing 'Advanced' Liberal Democracies." *Foucault and Political Reason: Liberalism, Neo-liberalism and Rationalities of Government*. Ed. Andrew Barry, Thomas Osborne, and Nikolas Rose. Chicago: University of Chicago Press, 1996. 37–64.

Ross, Andrew. *The Chicago Gangster Theory of Life: Nature's Debt to Society*. New York: Verso, 1994.

———. "The Social Claim on Urban Ecology" (interview with Michael Bennett). *The Nature of Cities: Ecocriticism and Urban Environments*. Ed. Michael Bennett and David W. Teague. Tucson: University of Arizona Press, 1999. 15–30.

Rothman, Hal. *The Greening of a Nation? Environmentalism in the United States since 1945*. Fort Worth: Harcourt Brace, 1998.

Rubenstein, Roberta. *Home Matters: Longing and Belonging, Nostalgia and Mourning in Women's Fiction*. New York: Palgrave, 2001.

Rubin, Louis D., Jr. "Introduction: A Statement of Principles." *I'll Take My Stand: The South and the Agrarian Tradition, by Twelve Southerners*. New York: Harper, 1930. ix–xx.

Ruffin, Kimberly N. *Black on Earth: African American Ecoliterary Traditions*. Athens: University of Georgia Press, 2010.

Russ, Robert A. "'There's No Place Like Home': The Carnival of Black Life in Claude McKay's *Home to Harlem*." *Harlem Renaissance Re-examined*. Ed. Victor A. Kramer and Robert A. Russ. New York: Whitston, 1997. 355–73.

Said, Edward. *Beginnings: Intention and Method*. New York: Basic Books, 1975.

———. "Reflections on Exile." *Reflections on Exile and Other Essays*. Cambridge: Harvard University Press, 2000. 173–86.

Sayre, Robert F. "Aldo Leopold's Sentimentalism." *North Dakota Quarterly* 52.2 (1991): 112–25.

Scanlan, Sean. "Introduction: Nostalgia." *Iowa Journal of Cultural Studies* 5 (2004): 3–9.

Scarberry-Garcia, Susan. *Landmarks of Healing: A Study of* House Made of Dawn. Albuquerque: University of New Mexico Press, 1990.

Schiff, Sarah Eden. "Power Literature and the Myth of Racial Memory." *MFS: Modern Fiction Studies* 57.1 (2011): 96–122.

Schweninger, Lee. "American Indians and Environmentalism: The Problematics of the Land Ethic Stereotype." *Journal of American Studies of Turkey*

8 (1998): 3–12. 18 June 2010. http://www.bilkent.edu.tr/~jast/Number8
/Schweninger.html.

———. *Listening to the Land: Native American Literary Responses to the Land-scape.* Athens: University of Georgia Press, 2008.

Selinger, Bernard. "*House Made of Dawn*: A Positively Ambivalent Bildungsro-man." *MFS: Modern Fiction Studies* 45.1 (1999): 38–68.

Sellars, Richard West. *Preserving Nature in the National Parks.* New Haven: Yale University Press, 1997.

Shaffer, Marguerite S. "Negotiating National Identity: Western Tourism and 'See America First.'" *Reopening the American West.* Ed. Hal K. Rothman. Tucson: University of Arizona Press, 1998.

Shellenberger, Michael, and Ted Nordhaus. "The Death of Environmentalism: Global Warming Politics in a Post-Environmental World." 2004. 15 June 2010. http://www.grist.org/article/doe-reprint.

Shiva, Vandana. "The Future of Food: Countering Globalisation and Recoloni-sation of Indian Agriculture." *Futures* 36 (2004): 715–32.

Silko, Leslie Marmon. *Almanac of the Dead.* New York: Simon and Schuster, 1991.

———. "Landscape, History, and the Pueblo Imagination." *The Norton Book of Nature Writing.* Ed. Robert Finch and John Elder. New York: W.W. Norton, 2002. 1003–14.

Slotkin, Richard. *Gunfighter Nation: The Myth of the Frontier in Twentieth-Cen-tury America.* Norman: University of Oklahoma Press, 1998.

———. "Nostalgia and Progress: Theodore Roosevelt's Myth of the Frontier." *American Quarterly* 33.5 (1981): 608–37.

Slovic, Scott. "Authenticity, Occupancy, and Credibility: Rick Bass and the Rhetoric of Protecting Place." *True West: Authenticity and the American West.* Ed. William R. Handley and Nathanial Lewis. Lincoln: University of Nebraska Press, 2004. 257–74.

———. Afterword. *The New West of Edward Abbey.* By Ann Ronald. 2nd ed. Reno: University of Nevada Press, 2000. 247–68.

———. "'Be Prepared for the Worst': Love, Anticipated Loss, and Environmen-tal Valuation." *Going Away to Think: Engagement, Retreat, and Ecocritical Responsibility.* Reno: University of Nevada Press, 2008. 36-61.

———. *Seeking Awareness in American Nature Writing.* Salt Lake City: Univer-sity of Utah Press, 1998.

Smith, Neil, and Phil O'Keefe. "Geography, Marx and the Concept of Nature." *Antipode* 12 (1980): 30–39.

———. "The Production of Nature." *FutureNatural: Nature, Science, Culture.* Ed. George Robertson et al. New York: Routledge, 1996. 35–54.

———. *Uneven Development: Nature, Capital, and the Production of Space.* New York: Blackwell, 1984.

Snyder, Gary. "Nature as Seen from Kitkitdizze." *Wild Earth* 6.4 (1996–97): 8–9.

———. *The Practice of the Wild.* New York: North Point Press, 1990.

Soper, Kate. "Nature/nature." *FutureNatural: Nature, Science, Culture.* Ed. George Robertson et al. New York: Routledge, 1996. 22–34.

———. *What Is Nature? Culture, Politics, and the Non-Human.* Cambridge: Blackwell, 1995.

Soule, Michael, and Gary Lease, eds. *Reinventing Nature? Responses to Postmodern Deconstruction.* Washington, D.C.: Island Press, 1995.

Spack, Ruth. "Re-Visioning Sioux Women: Zitkala-Ša's Revolutionary *American Indian Stories.*" *Legacy: A Journal of American Women Writers* 14.1 (1997): 25–42.

Spence, Mark David. *Dispossessing the Wilderness: Indian Removal and the Making of the National Parks.* New York: Oxford University Press, 1999.

Stanfield, Rebecca, et al. "Racial Discrimination in Parks and Outdoor Recreation: An Empirical Study." Ed. John G. Peden and Rudy M. Schuster. *Proceedings of the 2005 Northeastern Recreation Research Symposium.* 10–12 April 2005. Bolton Landing, NY. Gen. Tech. Rep. NE-341. Newtown Square, PA: U.S. Forest Service, Northeastern Research Station.

Stegner, Wallace. "A Capsule History of Conservation." *Where the Bluebird Sings to the Lemonade Springs: Living and Writing in the West.* New York: Penguin, 1992. 117–34.

———. "Finding the Place: A Migrant Childhood." *Where the Bluebird Sings to the Lemonade Springs: Living and Writing in the West.* New York: Penguin, 1992. 3–21.

———. "The Legacy of Aldo Leopold." *Companion to* A Sand County Almanac: *Interpretive and Critical Essays.* Ed. J. Baird Callicott. Madison: University of Wisconsin Press, 1987. 233–45.

Stein, Rachel. "Bad Seed: Imperiled Biological and Social Diversity in Ruth Ozeki's *All Over Creation.*" *Postcolonial Green: Environmental Politics and World Narratives.* Ed. Bonnie Roos and Alex Hunt. Charlottesville: University of Virginia Press, 2010. 177–93.

Steinbeck, John. *The Grapes of Wrath.* New York: Viking, 1939.

Steinberg, Ted. "Conservation Reconsidered." *Down to Earth: Nature's Role in American History.* Oxford: Oxford University Press, 2002. 138–56.

Stephens, Michelle A. "Black Transnationalism and the Politics of National Identity: West Indian Intellectuals in Harlem in the Age of War and Revolution." *American Quarterly* 50.3 (1998): 592–608.

Stevens, Jason W. "Bear, Outlaw, and Storyteller: American Frontier Mythology and the Ethnic Subjectivity of N. Scott Momaday." *American Literature: A Journal of Literary History* 73.3 (2001): 599–631.

Stewart, Susan. *On Longing: Narratives of the Miniature, the Gigantic, the Souvenir, the Collection.* Baltimore: Johns Hopkins University Press, 1984.

Stoff, Michael B. "Claude McKay and the Cult of Primitivism." *The Harlem Renaissance Remembered.* Ed. Arna Bontemps. New York: Dodd, Mead, 1972. 126–46.

Strand, Ginger. "The Crying Indian." *Orion Magazine* November/December 2008. http://www.orionmagazine.org/index.php/articles/article/3642.

Su, John J. *Ethics and Nostalgia in the Contemporary Novel*. New York: Cambridge University Press, 2005.

———. "Ghosts of Essentialism: Racial Memory as Epistemological Claim." *American Literature* 81.2 (2009): 361–86.

Susag, Dorothea M. "Zitkala-Ša (Gertrude Simmons Bonnin): A Power(full) Literary Voice." *Studies in American Indian Literatures: The Journal of the Association for the Study of American Indian Literatures* 5.4 (1993): 3–24.

Swartz, Aaron. "Rachel Carson, Mass Murderer? The Creation of an Anti-environmental Myth." *Fair: Fairness and Accuracy in Reporting*. September/October 2007. 30 March 2010. http://www.fair.org/index.php?page=3186.

Sze, Julie. "Boundaries and Border Wars: DES, Technology, and Environmental Justice." *American Quarterly* (2006): 791–814.

Tabbi, Joseph. *Postmodern Sublime: Technology and American Writing from Mailer to Cyberpunk*. Ithaca: Cornell University Press, 1995.

Tallmadge, John. "Anatomy of a Classic." *Earthly Words: Essays on Contemporary American Nature and Environmental Writers*. Ed. John R. Cooley. Ann Arbor: University of Michigan Press, 1994. 119–34.

Tatonetti, Lisa. "The Both/And of American Indian Literary Studies." *Western American Literature* 44.3 (2009): 276–88.

Teuton, Sean. *Red Land, Red Power: Grounding Knowledge in the American Indian Novel*. Durham: Duke University Press, 2008.

Tiffin, Helen, and Graham Huggan. *Postcolonial Ecocriticism: Literature, Animals, Environment*. New York: Routledge, 2010.

Totten, Gary. "Zitkala-Ša and the Problem of Regionalism: Nations, Narratives, and Critical Traditions." *American Indian Quarterly* 29.1–2 (2005): 84–123.

Toy, Phyllis. "Racing Homeward: Myth and Ritual in House Made of Dawn." *Études Anglaises* 51.1 (1998): 27–38.

Trotter, Joe William, Jr. *The Great Migration in Historical Perspective: New Dimensions of Race, Class, and Gender*. Bloomington: Indiana University Press, 1991.

Turner, Frederick Jackson. "The Significance of the Frontier in American History." 1893. *The Early Writings of Frederick Jackson Turner; with a list of all his works compiled by Everett E. Edwards, and an introduction by Fulmer Mood*. Madison: University of Wisconsin Press, 1938. 185–229.

Turning Point Project. "Who Plays God in the 21st Century?" *New York Times* 17 October 1999.

"Vanuatu: Islands of Fire." *Survivor*. CBS. Accessed 15 April 2006. http://www.cbs.com/primetime/survivor.

"Video Rivers." *Grand Teton National Park*. 18 June 2010. http://home.nps.gov/grte/photosmultimedia/video_rivers.htm.

Vizenor, Gerald. *Fugitive Poses: Native American Indian Scenes of Absence and Presence.* Lincoln: University of Nebraska Press, 1998.

Waldman, Amy. "Torn from Moorings, Villagers Grasp for Past." *New York Times* 6 March 2005.

Wall, Drucilla. "Simulations of Authenticity: Imagined Indians and Sacred Landscape from New Age to Nature Writing." *True West: Authenticity and the American West.* Ed. William R. Handley and Nathanial Lewis. Lincoln: University of Nebraska Press, 2004. 97–116.

Wallace, Molly. "'Venerated Emblems': DeLillo's *Underworld* and the History Commodity." *Critique* 42 (2001): 367–83.

"Weekly Update from the Field." *Buffalo Field Campaign.* 3 June 2010. http://www.buffalofieldcampaign.org/media/update0910/060310.html.

Wexler, Laura. "Tender Violence: Literary Eavesdropping, Domestic Fiction, and Educational Reform." *The Culture of Sentiment: Race, Gender and Sentimentality in Nineteenth-Century America.* Ed. Shirley Samuels. New York: Oxford University Press, 1992. 9–38.

White, Evelyn. "Black Women and the Wilderness." *Literature and the Environment: A Reader on Nature and Culture.* Ed. Lorraine Anderson, Scott Slovic, and John P. O'Grady. New York: Addison-Wesley, 1999. 316–20.

White, Hayden. "The Historical Text as Literary Artifact." *The Content of the Form: Narrative Discourses and Historical Representation.* Baltimore: Johns Hopkins University Press, 1987.

White, Richard. "Frederick Jackson Turner and Buffalo Bill." *The Frontier in American Culture.* Ed. James R. Grossman. Berkeley: University of California Press, 1994. 7–65.

Wiegman, Robyn. *American Anatomies: Theorizing Race and Gender.* Durham: Duke University Press, 1995.

Wilcox, Leonard. "Baudrillard, DeLillo's *White Noise*, and the End of Heroic Narrative." *Contemporary Literature* 32 (1991): 346–65.

Wild, Peter. "Sentimentalism in the American Southwest: John C. Van Dyke, Mary Austin, and Edward Abbey." *Reading the West: New Essays on the Literature of the American West.* Ed. Michael Kowalewski. Cambridge: Cambridge University Press, 1996. 127–43.

Williams, Raymond. *The Country and the City.* New York: Oxford University Press, 1973.

———. "Ideas of Nature." *Problems in Materialism and Culture: Selected Essays.* London: Verso, 1980. 67–85.

Wills, Gary. *Reagan's America: Innocents at Home.* New York: Penguin Books, 2000.

Wirzba, Norman. "The Challenge of Berry's Agrarian Vision." *The Art of the Commonplace: The Agrarian Essays of Wendell Berry.* Ed. Norman Wirzba. Washington, D.C.: Counterpoint, 2002. vii–xx.

Woodard, Charles. L. *Ancestral Voice: Conversations with N. Scott Momaday.* Lincoln: University of Nebraska Press, 1989.

Xavier, Silvia. "Crosstown Jakes in 1920s Manhattan: Racial Formations in John Dos Passos' *Manhattan Transfer* and Claude McKay's *Home to Harlem.*" *MFS: Modern Fiction Studies* 54.4 (2008): 715–43.

Yard, Robert Sterling. *The National Parks Portfolio.* Department of the Interior, National Park Service. Washington, D.C.: Government Printing Office, 1917.

Young, Stark. "Not in Memoriam, but in Defense." *I'll Take My Stand: The South and the Agrarian Tradition, by Twelve Southerners.* New York: Harper, 1930. 328-60.

Yosemite Paiutes. "Yosemite Miwok or Paiute Baskets?" *Indian Country Today* 30 June 2009. http://www.indiancountrytoday.com/yourict/49511947.html.

Yuen, Eddie, Daniel Burton Rose, and George Katsiaficas, eds. The Battle of Seattle: The New Challenge to Capitalist Globalization. New York: Soft Skull Press, 2001.

Zitkala-Ša, *American Indian Stories.* Lincoln: University of Nebraska Press, 1985.

Index

Under the Sign of Nature
EXPLORATIONS IN ECOCRITICISM

Rachel Stein
Shifting the Ground: American Women Writers' Revisions of Nature, Gender, and Race

Ian Marshall
Story Line: Exploring the Literature of the Appalachian Trail

Patrick D. Murphy
Farther Afield in the Study of Nature-Oriented Literature

Bernard W. Quetchenbach
Back from the Far Field: American Nature Poetry in the Late Twentieth Century

Karla Armbruster and Kathleen R. Wallace, editors
Beyond Nature Writing: Expanding the Boundaries of Ecocriticism

Stephen Adams
The Best and Worst Country in the World: Perspectives on the Early Virginia Landscape

Mark Allister
Refiguring the Map of Sorrow: Nature Writing and Autobiography

Ralph H. Lutts
The Nature Fakers: Wildlife, Science, and Sentiment (reprint)

Michael A. Bryson
Visions of the Land: Science, Literature, and the American Environment from the Era of Exploration to the Age of Ecology

Robert Bernard Hass
Going by Contraries: Robert Frost's Conflict with Science

Ian Marshall
Peak Experiences: Walking Meditations on Literature, Nature, and Need

Glen A. Love
Practical Ecocriticism: Literature, Biology, and the Environment

Scott Herring
Lines on the Land: Writers, Art, and the National Parks

Heike Schaefer
Gender, Genre, and Geography: Mary Austin's Concept and Practice of Regionalism

Mark Allister, editor
Eco-Man: New Perspectives on Masculinity and Nature

Kate Rigby
Topographies of the Sacred: The Poetics of Place in European Romanticism

Alan Williamson
Westernness: A Meditation

John Elder
Pilgrimage to Vallombrosa: From Vermont to Italy in the Footsteps of George Perkins Marsh

Mary Ellen Bellanca
Daybooks of Discovery: Nature Diaries in Britain, 1770–1870

Rinda West
Out of the Shadow: Ecopsychology, Story, and Encounters with the Land

Bonnie Roos and Alex Hunt, editors
Postcolonial Green: Environmental Politics and World Narratives

Paula Willoquet-Maricondi, editor
Framing the World: Explorations in Ecocriticism and Film

Deborah Bird Rose
Wild Dog Dreaming: Love and Extinction

Axel Goodbody and Kate Rigby, editors
Ecocritical Theory: New European Approaches

Scott Hess
William Wordsworth and the Ecology of Authorship: The Roots of Environmentalism in Nineteenth-Century Culture

Dan Brayton
Shakespeare's Ocean: An Ecocritical Exploration

Jennifer Ladino
Reclaiming Nostalgia: Longing for Nature in American Literature